SEPTEMBER STREAK

SEPTEMBER STREAK

The 1935 Chicago Cubs
Chase the Pennant

by Doug Feldmann

McFarland & Company, Inc., Publishers
Jefferson, North Carolina, and London

LIBRARY OF CONGRESS CATALOGUING-IN-PUBLICATION DATA

Feldmann, Doug 1970–
    September streak : the 1935 Chicago Cubs chase the
pennant / by Doug Feldmann.
      p.   cm.
    Includes bibliographical references and index.

    ISBN 0-7864-1591-6 (softcover : 50# alkaline paper) ∞

    1. Chicago Cubs (Baseball team)   I. Title.
GV875.C6F45   2003
796.357'64'0977311—dc21   2003008124

British Library cataloguing data are available

On the cover, top: Gabby Hartnett shakes hands with Chicago
Mayor Ed Kelly before Game Three of the World Series on
October 4, 1935, at Wrigley Field. To Mayor Kelly's left is Postmaster General of the United States James Farley. *Bottom:* The
1935 Chicago Cubs. (Chicago Historical Society)

Manufactured in the United States of America

McFarland & Company, Inc., Publishers
  Box 611, Jefferson, North Carolina 28640
    www.mcfarlandpub.com

To Julie, Chuck, Amanda, Ryan, Annie—and our
very own "Jolly Charlie."

Acknowledgments

The author would like to thank the following for their assistance in the research for this book: the campus libraries of Loyola University of Chicago, DePaul University, and the University of Chicago; the Chicago Historical Society; and the National Baseball Hall of Fame and Museum in Cooperstown, New York.

Table of Contents

Prologue

The year 1935 in the world: Germany denounced the Versailles Treaty and entered all of its young men into compulsory military service. And an Englishman named Robert Watson-Watt developed a device soon to be known as "radar."

The year 1935 in the United States: Huey Long, who threatened to "soak the rich" with his plan of socialist redistribution of wealth, was assassinated in his home state of Louisiana by Dr. Carl Weiss. And George Gallup developed his famous poll, which would correctly predict the outcome of the 1936 presidential election.

The year 1935 in Chicago: Jane Addams died. "Big Ed" Kelly was elected mayor. And an enterprising 18-year-old named Sol Polk opened a full-service appliance warehouse in the north part of the city, and soon after enlisted the help of four family members. Not too long after, Polk Brothers became *the* state-of-the-art department store, offering a one-stop shop for every need and quick delivery to homes and businesses.

Also by the mid–1930s, the Chicago mob war between the north side Irish gang of Bugs Moran and Al Capone's Italian southsiders had dissipated. Capone had been sentenced to 11 years in federal prison for tax evasion in 1931, and Moran had successfully gone into hiding from the law in the open areas of Ohio for a time, but was later apprehended for a petty crime and brought to justice on other charges. Six of the power-brokers of Moran's gang had been killed in the infamous St. Valentine's Day Massacre of 1929, at a garage at 2122 North Clark Street. On the day the attack was to take place, a lookout for Capone was stationed across the street on the third floor of the building at 2133 Clark. When the lookout spotted a man who looked like Moran walking by the garage, he gave the signal for Capone's gunmen to move in. The man was not Moran,

1

however, and the boss's life was spared. But he lost six of his closest asso-
ciates, and it was the final blow that effectively gave control of the under-
world scene to Capone. The assailants had dressed as police officers, and
when they instructed Moran's men to face the wall of the garage, the victims figured it was a typical shakedown for liquor, racketeering receipts,
or some other "minor" infraction that would be of little consequence, so
little resistance appeared to be given. The assailants opened fire without
warning, and Moran's men were killed instantly.

Life in Chicago was remarkably different back then; the first 35 years
of the 1900s were quite a different time for baseball in Chicago, too. The
Chicago Cubs, by and large, were expected to be at the top of the National
League standings on a regular basis. But like the drifting away of a one-
time-close friend, the relationship evolved over many years into one that
brought ultimate, continuous disappointment. If one is a fan of the Cubs,
one has gotten used to fast starts, June swoons, and September heart-
breaks. At the very last Cubs game of the 1900s—on October 3, 1999, at
Busch Stadium in St. Louis—one group of Cardinal fans displayed a particularly stinging banner. It read: "ANYBODY CAN HAVE A BAD CENTURY"
with the familiar Cubs logo planted at the end.

There is the famous "Billy Goat Curse" in which a Greek tavern
owner, after being told he couldn't bring his pet goat into the home park
for the 1945 World Series, put a hex on the ballclub; there are the supposed draining effects that extra day games have on players, as the hot
sunshine zaps the pennant life out of the guys in the blue pinstripes; and
countless other factors, differing with almost each Cub follower with
whom one speaks. But one thing remains true—that is, while not without talent on many of their teams, the North Siders have not won a
National League pennant since a month after the Japanese surrender in
the Pacific, and are approaching a full 100 years since they won the World
Series.

All things considered, to anyone who has followed the team, the
Cubs have been a disappointment. But it could be argued that this disappointment lies only in the standings, although this is indeed the bottom line. There are certainly other areas in which the team has been at
the forefront of baseball. There is the architectural beauty of its ballpark,
Wrigley Field; there is the great early history of the team; and there is
the genuine quaintness of the neighborhood in which the club plays.

As I was completing this book, I had the pleasure of moving to
Wrigleyville, the neighborhood bordered by the streets of Southport, Irving Park, Sheffield, and Belmont. I knew that becoming a "local" would
add an irreplaceable perspective to this work, but at the time, I wasn't

sure how. As the reasons emerged, the many ways became unique. Growing up in the suburbs, I was very familiar with the drive into the neighborhood; in becoming a resident, I learned the milieu of living there. For example, I received a tidbit of information from the prior resident of my building as he was moving out. "Make sure you check the Cubs' schedule for night home games," he warned. "If you don't have your parking sticker and you get home after five o'clock, you'll be parking in Wisconsin."

So with my next-door neighbors and fellow Indiana alums, Jason and Jen, I walked down to Bernie's and we commenced a workshop on the Cubs' probable batting order for the upcoming season, our brainstorming scribbled out on a cocktail napkin.

As we gazed out the window across Clark Street, the wonderful structure lay there before us, guarded by the best car wash in the city. Wrigley Field. When my friends asked me if Patterson should bat in the lead-off spot or sixth, they caught me in a daze. Wrigley Field ... *I live by Wrigley Field! Where else would I rather live? Where else today can fans reach out and shake hands with a relief pitcher in the bullpen? Where else can you go to a game where there are no advertisements in the ballpark? And from where else can you walk from your hundred-year-old residence to a major league game?*

But it has been argued by some that Wrigley, the very salt of Cubdom, has actually been the team's albatross, its most immovable obstacle in pursuit of a pennant. Notwithstanding the fact that fewer luxury boxes reside on its premises than most major league parks, which apparently doesn't provide the sustenance needed for modern competition, the fact that the Friendly Confines continues to be filled for nearly every Cub home game—and will be for the duration of its existence—has delivered a plague of lethargy upon the North Side, a poster child for low expectations and ensuing underachievement. Like all true reforms in our lives, good or bad, it didn't happen overnight; the culture of losing evolved upon the place, beginning at an indiscernible point somewhere in the 1940-, 1950-, or 1960-somethings. But before that mysterious origin, the demand for a pennant-contending National League ballclub was as perennial as the annual huffy speeches of the local politicians, from which the great city got its adjective "windy"—not, as is popular belief, from the powerful zephyrs that howl off the lake.

Yes, Virginia, there is a Santa Claus. And yes, baseball fans, there was a time when the Cubs were expected to win. And they did.

Doug Feldmann

Overcoming the "Gang"

It has been said that affinity is the key to public success. If customers can see a relationship between themselves and a seller providing a product, a natural bond is formed—no matter what the business. This was perhaps no more true of baseball in the 1930s than anytime in American history. Since the game's inception, America has always turned to baseball for heroes. Young boys of character imitated the on- and off-field qualities of the "Christian Gentleman" and great pitcher of the early part of the century, Christy Mathewson.

Affinity, however, can also run down the wrong streets. As they grew into adulthood, those same boys would later laugh at the uncouth antics of the fun-loving, carousing Babe Ruth as reported in the morning newspapers. Before television, the images of these larger-than-life figures were painted in the minds of readers by the gifted sportswriters of the day. Ruth's activities—such as fraternizing with gangsters and lounging in speakeasies—were beyond the imagination of most people, as he "put the city to bed with great regularity," as John Lardner of the *New York Post* once wrote of him. Or, as another said of his voracious appetite for all things in life, "Babe Ruth will eat anything that doesn't eat *him*."

Yes, he stood alone. Public affinity was not with Ruth, although admiration (to a certain extent) certainly was. When he signed his landmark contract with Yankees owner Jacob Ruppert for $80,000 over two years, it was yet another example of Ruth's separation from the common public—and a foreshadowing of a larger fiscal rift to come in later decades between players and the fans.

Still, as Ruth did as he pleased, public connection with the average player continued to develop. As major league owners discovered the benefits of radio broadcasts in the 1930s (i.e., as an expansion of their fan base), the connection developed even more. Radio became another source of description of the players' personal and professional lives, in addition to the customary daily newspaper headlines. Whereas once the image of a player was formed in the mind of a fan from the *pen to the eye*, it now came from the *mouth to the ears*. As the exciting background sounds of the ballpark could be heard through the broadcaster's microphone, casual fans became more encouraged to go and see major league games for themselves. Once at the ballpark, the players—who were previously dreamt of as supernatural beings, by young and old alike—were revealed as ordinary men, complete with smiles, frowns, waves, sneers, laughs, and dirty clothes. And in trying to capitalize on this expanding fan base, Phil Wrigley's Chicago Cubs in 1935 would be the first to have all of its games broadcast on radio, as the chewing gum king wanted to bring his other product into as many homes as possible. As the Cubs' president, Wrigley didn't draw a salary for the work he did, but savored the game, and loved every minute of the job.

Going to the ballpark was indeed a special event in one's life in the 1930s—and it was even reflected in how the fans dressed. The Detroit Tigers' second baseman Charlie Gehringer told the *Detroit Free Press* in later years, "It was a little different than it is today. Everybody dressed like they were going to the theater or maybe church. We played in the afternoons and the lawyers would come out from their offices. They would be all spiffed up. The women in the box seats looked just beautiful. You'd think they were there for a garden party."

Attendance suffered since the stock market crash, seen plainly in the attendance figures in the National League since 1929:

> 1930—5,446,532
> 1931—4,583,815
> 1932—3,841,334
> 1933—3,162,821
> 1934—3,200,105

Save Ruth, Lou Gehrig, and a few other well-paid stars, it *was* the worldly concept of money that brought ballplayers and the public together as much as any other entity during the Great Depression. No special exceptions were made for major leaguers, as almost all of them endured salary cuts during the 1930s—some to the tune of 40 percent or more. With as much as a quarter of the American workforce unemployed at various points in the decade, those who could afford to enjoy a baseball game knew that the men on the field commiserated with their financial predicaments. There were waiting lines in this business as well, as many young men—not even skilled in the game—sought tryouts at all levels of professional baseball in hope of finding some form of work. In an attempt to promote the stability of good-paying jobs, the National Labor Relations Board was established in 1935 and designed to foster cooperation between employers and employees. This also helped in the development of unions, which also hastened the closure of the infamous Chicago Union Stockyards where unsuccessful strikes were launched by butchers in 1894 and 1904. With improved working conditions for employees, coupled with stockyards moving out from urban areas in general, Wilson's became the first major company to leave Chicago in 1955 and, ultimately, the carnal center that made Chicago "Hog Butcher for the World" shut its doors in 1971. Until that time, workers in the stockyards—just like ballplayers on the field—gave their best efforts until there was no more blood, sweat, and tears left in their bodies, for there was always a hungry man waiting outside to take his place.

Times were indeed no easier in 1935 than the year before, as the Great Depression was at the peak of its wrath. People were starting to question the very tenets of economic and social existence, and Europe seemed to be on the brink of war after being in a six year depression herself. In Germany, citizens yearning for any kind of hope listened to the politic-centric words of Adolf Hitler; by 1935, he had risen from chancellor of Germany to dictator. In America, Sinclair Lewis released his novel *It Can't Happen Here*, a hypothetical account of a candidate using the 1936 Presidential election to elevate himself to dictatorial status by promising great things for a downtrodden people—the same strategy used by Hitler. Lewis became the first American to win the Nobel Prize for Literature, and it perhaps served as a reminder of dispelling fascist regimes despite the candidate carrying an encouraging message during tough times. Fortunately, Americans did not cave to new-fangled ideas in a time of crisis. Rather, they stuck to things such as democracy, capitalistic competition, and baseball—things that had helped make the country strong in the past.

The year 1935 also saw the development of a formidable political force in China. Chinese Communists, led by Mao Tse-Tung, had been engaged in a civil war against the Kuomintang, or Nationalist party. Trapped in the southeastern part of the country by the Kuomintang in 1934, the Communists were able to break through the besiegement, but were followed fervently by the enemy troops. The prolonged escape simply became known as "The Long March," and Mao's army trudged more than 6,000 miles through all kinds of terrain in search of safety. After a year's time, and reaching the Shensi province in the north, Mao and his followers were finally able to rest, re-organize, and defeat the Kuomintang. The Communists had originally been aligned with the Kuomintang and their leader, Sun Yat-Sen. But upon Sun's death in 1925, a new leader by the name of Chiang Kai-Shek assumed power of the Nationalists and a gulf of mistrust grew between the two groups, ultimately leading to war. The two factions formed a loose alliance when Japan launched an all-out assault on China in 1937, but resumed their own hostilities in 1945 with the end of World War II. By October 1949, the Kuomintang had been driven to the island of Formosa (now known as Taiwan), and Mao's Communists had gained complete control of China.

Also in 1935, President Franklin Roosevelt signed into law the Banking Act, which not only centralized the control of the Federal Reserve but also introduced the concept of deposit insurance, as it fully put into effect the Federal Deposit Insurance Corporation (FDIC), founded two years earlier, to guarantee deposit accounts up to $15,000. It was designed to restore a sense of greater public faith in the banking system, which plummeted with the stock market in 1929. The power in the Reserve was now entrusted to a Board of Governors, who were given 14-year terms. These were moves in a series of programs to lift the nation out of its doldrums, symbolized by Roosevelt himself lifting his own body out of his wheelchair. Perhaps the low point had been seen two years earlier in 1933, when more than 15 million Americans—25 percent of the nation's labor force—were without work. By the time Hitler had promised a better future to Germans as he ascended to the role of chancellor in January 1933, across the world, in the United States, nearly half of the country's 25,000 banks had failed. Supply from the product-happy Industrial Age had finally overcome demand, which had seemed impossible in the free-spirited 1920s. Falling prices had also hurt U.S. farmers in the 1920s; they represented one-fourth of the American economy, but had seen a demand for their goods reduce after World War I had ended in Europe. Roosevelt responded in 1933 with the Agricultural Adjustment Act, in which farmers received direct governmental subsidies in return for not growing surplus crops—which, the government and many others believed, had accelerated the downward spiral of the prices of farm goods.

Much of the farm crisis was due to the Dust Bowl that plagued the Midwest, driving people off their dried-up land, blinding their eyes, and in some cases, causing deaths. In early April 1935, the storm ravaged much of Oklahoma, as some church congregations held prayer vigils three times a day in hope of rain. Gravel carried by the wind was doing tremendous damage, and shards of glass from broken windows were everywhere. The editor of the local paper in Buffalo, Oklahoma, called a state politician from his ravaged office, and informed that representative that, with the onslaught of dust, he could not see the person sitting in the next chair.

Therefore, if the poorly-paying Thirties provided anything for baseball, it at least ensured a highly competitive product for fans. If a veteran player allowed his skills or effort to diminish, there was not only the thought of a young player taking his job, but also the concern of what he would do for a living. To further illustrate this point, one need look only at the rough play in the 1934 World Series between the Tigers and the St. Louis Cardinals. The winner's share in the series was $5,941—more than what many players were making for an entire season. The players didn't think of this windfall as a bonus; like everyone else, they were in the throes of the Depression, and they fought for this extra money to help their families survive. Thinking of the contemporary game, with the average major league salary over $2 million, it is difficult to imagine today's stars thinking much about the extra World Series check.

With this caste-like connection, the blue-collar Cardinals quickly became everyone's heroes. They represented a cross-section of America in almost every regard. The players came from all corners of the country, the sons of immigrants, sharecroppers, businessmen, and coal miners. They wore the same clothes for weeks. In a time when most people were underpaid (if employed), the Cardinals held one of the lowest payrolls in the league. Shortstop Leo Durocher once said of Cardinals general manager Branch Rickey, "If you went into his office to talk salary, and left four hours later taking a nickel less than what you wanted, he would consider that a victory." In fact, most of the Cardinals, like many other players, had to assume second jobs in the off season; for a while, even the great pitcher Jay "Dizzy" Dean himself ran a gas station in Florida. In addition, it did not hurt that St. Louis was the furthest major league outpost south and west at the time. For anyone coming from the "West," which at the time included Oklahoma or even other areas of Missouri, St. Louis was the first town to have a big league team. When the Cardinals appeared in a World Series, it was a special pilgrimage to get to their home field of Sportsman's Park for followers from Mississippi, Alabama, Arkansas, and other places, for fans did not know when the next opportunity would arise.

The National League pennant fight wound up a two-team race in 1934, as the Cardinals caught the New York Giants in September after the latter blew a seven game lead with three weeks left in the season.

Entering the 1935 season, the Cardinals—led by fiery player-manager Frankie Frisch—seemed to have every piece in place from their victorious '34 club. The only exception was an anticipated improvement in centerfield with the arrival of Terry Moore, a dashing young outfielder from Vernon, Alabama, with a rocket arm and solid bat. Moore was expected to be an everyday replacement for the platoon of Ernie Orsatti and Chick Fullis, who had provided decent but not spectacular coverage at the position the previous year. Dean and his brother Paul, a rookie pitcher in '34, sought even higher heights in 1935 than their combined 49 wins the year before (in addition to all four wins in the World Series). One of the few weak points for the Cardinals in '34 had been the bullpen; "Diz" would often be called on to close a game even after he had gone nine innings the day before. That being the case, the club acquired Bud Tinning from the Cubs, who had proven himself a dependable reliever in Chicago. This gave the club the flexibility to release veterans Dazzy Vance and Burleigh Grimes (Grimes actually went on the voluntarily retired list) shortly before the beginning of the 1935 season. Grimes was given the assignment of managing the Cardinals' farm team at Bloomington, Illinois, while Vance quickly signed with the Brooklyn Dodgers—the same team with which he logged more strikeouts than any other pitcher of the 1920s. He had made $184,000 with the Dodgers throughout the '20s, and logged 182 wins for an ending price of more than $1,000 per triumph (compared with the $50,000 that Alex Rodriguez would roughly receive per *at-bat* for ten years, starting in 2002). Back in 1924, Vance had beaten out Rogers Hornsby for the first-ever National League Most Valuable Player Award— the same year that Hornsby hit .424, still the highest figure since 1900 (going into the 1935 season, Hornsby had the highest career average among active players at .359).

Brimming with his usual confidence, Dean began the off-season asking for $40,000 from the Cardinals. If they did not come through, he warned, there was a job waiting for him in East St. Louis, Illinois, to sell furniture. On February 5, he lowered his demand all the way down to $25,000, and signed the next day for $19,500 after "negotiations" with the clever Rickey (as mentioned earlier, Rickey and frugality invariably went hand-in-hand. When he was in college in Ohio, the story goes, his mother sent him a dollar a month to help with his expenses and every month, he sent the dollar back to her). Although Dean ruffled feathers from time to time, most of his playfulness was shrugged off. Ford Frick, the newly-chosen president of the National League, was as big a fan of the brash pitcher as anyone. "I'm looking forward to Dizzy Dean's next chapter," Frick said in anticipation of the 1935 season. "You never know what Diz is going to do next." Frick, a former English teacher in Colorado Springs by way of DePauw University (then DePauw College) and Noble County, Indiana, looked for great things for baseball in the coming season.

But sometimes, Frick and others in positions of authority did have to deal with Dean getting a little carried away. Dick Slack was the owner of the aforementioned East St. Louis furniture store, and it was soon discovered that Slack was more of a benefactor to Diz than had been realized. Dean and Bobo Newsom (a pitcher for the St. Louis Browns of the American League) were called into the office of Kenesaw Mountain Landis, the commissioner of baseball, on April 10 as spring training was winding down towards the 1935 season. When probed by Landis, it was discovered that the pair had apparently signed a deal for promotional work for Slack's store; Dean was to get $5,000 for three radio spots a week, and appearances at the store on various Saturdays. Newsom had cut a similar deal, although he didn't reveal to Landis the amount he was getting. Newsom sat there quietly, and later left as Landis requested a private audience with Dean. The two then began trading barbs about the propriety of accepting money outside of baseball.

"I got a contract with Slack for $5,000 this season for radio work and personal appearances at his store. That's all," Diz reportedly said, wide-eyed as a lamb. "He's a pretty nice guy, Judge. And he's got lots of dough."

"Just answer my question, Dizzy," Landis reportedly shot back. "Does it interest you to know where 'lots of dough' comes from?"

"Say, listen, Judge," Diz retorted, thinking (just like in his unsuccessful salary debate with Rickey) that he was taking a shrewd upper hand in the debate, "Supposin' a guy comes up and hands you $3,000 or $4,000. What about it?"

After Landis explained in two words that such things don't normally happen, he instructed the young man, "If anybody offers you that amount of money 'just for doing nothing,' you kick his teeth in, or promise me that you'll grab a baseball bat and hit him on the head."

"Yes sir," Dean replied, as he replaced his hat and left the office.

Despite Dean and star outfielder Joe Medwick staging minor holdouts, they arrived at spring training exercises in 1935 in time to get the Cardinals ready for the start of the National League season. "I want three more good years under my belt," Dizzy said, giving the first indications of a modest threat to retire after the 1937 season. Dean received a lot of grief from the press about his very controlling wife, Pat (at one point leading to a fight with columnists Mike Miley and Irv Kupcinet), but

Mrs. Dean kept the family books in good order—and always looked for possibilities for Diz to leave the game when he was financially able to do so.

In the midst of the worldwide turmoil, baseball continued to be one of the few things that made sense to Americans. And as usual, the Giants were chomping at the bit for a crack at their chief thorn, the Cardinals. The Cardinals had been in first place for only 11 days in 1934, while New York led the league for 127 morning editions of the newspaper. Two of the Cardinals' days on top, however, were the last two of the season when the Dodgers beat the Giants. Giants' player-manager Bill Terry had created ominous storm clouds in the spring of 1934 when quizzed about the fortitude of the cross-town rival Dodgers. When asked by the writers if Brooklyn would be a factor in the National League race, he scratched his head and said, "Brooklyn? Are they still in the league?" Fittingly, the Dodgers later teamed with the Cardinals in knocking New York out of the pennant fight. Casey Stengel's men marched into the Giants' home of the Polo Grounds, which sat below Coogan's Bluff on the outskirts of Harlem, and swept New York on the season's final two days. Meanwhile, the Cardinals clinched the flag back in St. Louis against the Cincinnati Reds.

Like the Cardinals, the Giants looked to upgrade their bullpen for 1935, acquiring Allyn Stout from the Reds and Leon Chagnon from the Pittsburgh Pirates, in addition to returning Hi Bell and Adolfo Luque, the latter a hard-drinking 43-year-old, Cuban with a hot temper and a switchblade always in his pocket—even when he was on the field. The heart and soul of the Giants remained their "Big Four" starting pitchers, which included Carl Hubbell, Hal Schumacher, Freddie Fitzsimmons, and Roy Parmelee. Hubbell, rivaling Dean as the most dominant National League pitcher of the decade, had a masterful performance in the '34 All-Star Game, in which he struck out Ruth, Gehrig, Jimmie Foxx, Al Simmons, and Joe Cronin in succession (in the off-season before the 1935 campaign, Cronin became the player-manager of the Boston Red Sox, being bought by Red Sox owner Tom Yawkey for $250,000). The Giants were also returning all of their key position players, with the exception of Blondy Ryan and Johnny Vergez at third base. That position would now be manned by Travis Jackson, the All-Star moving over from shortstop to make room for the flashy Dick Bartell. Bartell had arrived from the Phillies for Vergez, where he had batted .310 and scored 102 runs for Philly the previous summer. Terry knew that the Giants didn't need a major overhaul; some fine tuning, he figured, would get them past St. Louis. The euphoria over the Deans' success had lasted throughout the winter, as the Cardinals seemed indomitable to some with the brothers back on the mound in '35. But when the sportswriters settled in at their typewriters after a few months of thought, the Giants returned as the consensus favorites in the National League—primarily because of the promising Bartell being inserted into the lineup. In addition, the Giants also picked up second baseman Mark Koenig from the Reds, a member of the Yankees' "Murderers' Row" lineup from 1927. Now, with his fifth major league team, Koenig would split time at the keystone position with fellow veteran Hughie Critz.

Terry had sent the club on a 3,000-mile odyssey in March 1935, playing exhibition games all over the country. Despite being forced to eat his words about Brooklyn in 1934, Terry's confidence had not wavered. At the conclusion of the voyage, he said frankly, "I honestly believe that this is the best Giant team I have ever played on, and therefore see no reason why I should hesitate in predicting that we will bring the pennant back to New York this year ... if the club comes along as I think it should, we'll be so far out in front at the end of the season that there won't be any race to it." Yet Terry, perhaps somewhat wiser with experience, decided to direct his specific confidence at a team beyond the boundaries of Gotham. "The Cardinals will give us plenty of opposition," he granted, "but I do not expect the Dean brothers to have the success against us they did last year." Terry—who hit .401 in 1930, still the last National Leaguer to break the .400 mark—also hinted that 1936 might be his final season as a player.

The Reds were looking for a run at the first division, as manager Charley Dressen shook things up in Cincinnati by injecting more discipline into the ranks. Dressen had taken over in late July 1934, when Bob O'Farrell was let go with the club mired in last place. Just before the 1935 season began, the club made what it figured to be a major cost-cutting move. It received $55,000 from the Cardinals for the return of first baseman Johnny Mize to St. Louis, claiming that Mize was "damaged goods" from examination of an injury that hadn't quite healed. Doctors had told Dressen that Mize's leg problem would get better only with surgery, which would put him on the shelf for a long time. The deal had been contingent on Mize passing the physical, so the Cardinals couldn't object much to paying the money; many thought that Mize's career was over at that point. Mize had been the highest-priced rookie to ever enter camp with the Reds, and despite sending him on his way, Dressen called him "the greatest rookie first baseman I ever saw." The deal did not become news to Cardinals president and owner Sam Breadon until Mize had already arrived back in St. Louis. Former Cardinals star "Sunny Jim" Bottomley would remain the centerpiece for the Reds, as he and catcher Ernie Lombardi tried to work with gifted pitcher Paul Derringer and outfielder Chick Hafey (also former Cardinal) to give Dressen's club some leadership. Hafey was looking to return to stardom, as the 32-year-old was seeking to overcome some aches and pains from a rough 1934 season. "I haven't felt this good in years. I'm right in the pink," he said.

After the Mize deal fell through, Bottomley knew he had Cincinnati in a corner and held out for $10,000. He and the Reds found a compromise, however, as Bottomley was promised that figure if the ballclub drew 230,000 or more fans to Crosley Field on the year; if the gate amount was not reached, the agreement noted, Bottomley's salary would be paid in proportion to the actual attendance.

In Pittsburgh, the locals looked to some proven veterans to bring the Pirates back to the top. New to the club was former Cubs pitcher Jim Weaver, coming to a team that desperately needed arms to complement the strong hitting of Lloyd, Paul Waner, Arky Vaughan, and Gus Suhr. Weaver, listed at six-foot-six, was claimed by the *Brooklyn Eagle* to be the "tallest hurler in baseball." The disappointing Pirates slipped under .500 and into fifth place at the end of the '34 season, one which had started with promise. "Well, we've got Weaver and Bush and [rookie Cy] Blanton and [Waite] Hoyt," player-manager Pie Traynor told the press about his starting staff. Traynor was in his sixteenth major league season, and second as Pittsburgh's skipper. "Yeah, they can throw that ball through there. You couldn't call 'em softball pitchers. This is the best pitching we've had in a long time. We could use a good right-handed hitter, but outside of that our club's all right as soon as we get set." In 1934, the Pirates were caught in the season's last week by the Boston Braves, who rode the power hitting of Wally Berger (34 home runs) to a 78–73 record and fourth place behind the Cardinals, Giants, and Cubs. Only one major change would appear on the Braves' roster in 1935, and that move would rattle the baseball world.

Stengel still had some good athletes at his disposal in Brooklyn. Outfielders Buzz Boyle and Len Koenecke could run well, as could second-year shortstop Lonnie Frey. First baseman Sam Leslie finished fifth in the 1934 National League batting race at .332, and Van Lingle Mungo's 184 strikeouts off the mound were second only to Dean's 195 in all of baseball. While Al Lopez was a first-rate catcher, the team was plagued by poor defense and a thin pitching staff. It was hoped that Vance, at age 44, could recapture his magic of years gone by. "Stengel will someday be recognized as one of the great managers," predicted Chester Smith of the *Pittsburgh Press*. "Underneath his clowning is a keen perception of what it takes to win, and an ability to lead that is found in few men."

The Phillies were another team looking to keep the opponent from scoring more, as their third-best .284 team batting average couldn't offset a staff earned run average of 4.76. Former Cardinals catcher Jimmie Wilson was running the club, and was optimistic about the '35 campaign despite the loss of Bartell.

While a lot of the sportswriters were agreeing with Terry's predicted return to the top, a semblance of the same line of thinking held true with most American League writers. "Among the experts there is a chronic tendency to predict that the pennant winner of the previous year will repeat," explained Irving Vaughan, who covered the Chicago White Sox and the Junior Circuit for the *Chicago Tribune*. "This year is an exception. Detroit's Tigers, who took it on the chin in the last World Series after a brilliant dash through the competition in their own league, are not regarded as anything more than a possible threat. The majority of the dopesters lean toward Cleveland's Indians. Those who advise a small wager on the New York Yankees are limited, but they may prove to be correct." The belief about the Tigers was due to a lack of perceived bench strength, and too much reliance on the success of pitcher Lynwood "Schoolboy" Rowe in 1934, as he and Tommy Bridges both posted 20-win seasons for catcher-manager Mickey Cochrane's club.

With their home field across the Harlem River from the Giants' Polo Grounds, the Yankees were also looking to return to championship form after being beaten out by the Tigers in '34. Almost unthinkable, the club would take the field without Ruth, as the home run beast had received his release from Ruppert on February 26. Perhaps a result of the tough economic times, or perhaps a result of his welcome wearing with Ruppert, Ruth had seen his salary fall from a high of $80,000 down to $35,000. He was quickly picked up by the Braves of the National League for a price of $20,000 in a role as player-coach, with the possibility of becoming the full-time manager in 1936. All in New York, however, were not in tears about the dismissal of the icon. "For the first time in fifteen years the big fellow who used to tear ball games apart almost single handedly and who overshadowed everybody, including the Yanks, will be out of the cast," wrote John Drebinger of the *New York Times*. "The Yanks, of course, will always miss the Babe. But it will be the Babe of four or five years ago. Not the aging monarch of 1934 who, in the opinion of many, proved more of a liability than an asset except for his continued phenomenal drawing power at the turnstiles." Always good for a story, Ruth had recently told writers that he believed he would have hit 100 homers back in 1927 if the Yankees had still played at the Polo Grounds (which was the club's original home until Yankee Stadium opened across the river in 1923). And stories for Drebinger's paper had recently come under new leadership, as Arthur Sulzberger took over as publisher of the *Times*, ending the reign of Adolph Ochs who had overseen production since 1896.

Before the end of spring workouts, the veteran firstbaseman Gehrig was named captain of the club—the first such leader of the Bronx Bombers in ten years, when the title was removed from Ruth as a disciplinary measure by manager Miller Huggins. "I feel we would have beaten the Tigers last year but for the tough breaks we had," Gehrig opined, referring to the numerous injuries the club sustained. "This year it will be different.... From an all-around viewpoint, we have the best team in the American League." Secondbaseman Tony Lazzeri, also of Murderers' Row fame, had lost ten pounds in the off-season and reported that he felt quicker than ever before. "I know that a lot of people thought I was through as far back as five or six years ago," Lazzeri told the press. "But I've got five years more of good baseball in me yet." The Yankees also believed they had bolstered their pitching staff by purchasing Pat Malone from the Cardinals on March 26. Despite his departure from St. Louis, Malone was reputed by the writers to be Dizzy Dean's best friend in baseball—outside of brother Paul. No one around the league would dare mess with Malone, who already had logged 51 professional fights under his boxing name of "Kid Williams."

Going into the 1935 season, Gehrig had run his consecutive games streak to 1,504—which, as noted that spring by James Dawson of the *Times*, "does not include the countless exhibitions and World Series games in which he has participated since becoming a regular under the Ruppert banner." Gehrig had been staying fit over the winter by working out at the gym of boxer Jack Dempsey, and had inked his contract with Ruppert for 1935 back on February 18, one week before Ruth was released. The deal would pay Gehrig $30,000—the most in baseball upon that time. Ironically, he would have one of his worst springs ever, batting .069 as the preseason neared its end.

The Indians had become the favorite in the American League because of their powerful hitting. In addition, they had a strong pitching staff, who, "with ten men over six feet," impressed *Chicago Tribune* sports editor Arch Ward with their imposing size. The club would lose their secondbaseman Billy Knickerbocker, however, for the first month of the season as he recovered from surgery for an infection. The Yankees stock outside New York had dropped for several reasons, but the main causes were the departure of Ruth and the doubted comeback of star centerfielder Earle Combs. Combs was the only Yankee left from the nine on the field when Gehrig started his consecutive games streak in 1925. He had fractured his skull pursuing a fly ball in July 1934, colliding with the concrete wall in Sportsman's Park while groggy from the searing St. Louis heat.

In Philadelphia, Connie Mack was beginning his 36th year at the helm of the A's. He was drawing much criticism for his decision to put the slugger Foxx at catcher, as the position seemed inherently dangerous. Foxx had been a firstbaseman, thirdbaseman, and outfielder in his career to that point. "Let one foul tip crash against Foxx's fingers," warned one local writer, "and you'll probably hear him yelling for his return to the less hazardous position." Mack's mainstay on the mound for many years, Robert Moses "Lefty" Grove, was in Boston trying to regain his old form—and a pain-free arm—with the Red Sox.

The 72-year-old Mack predicted a wide-open American League pennant fight for 1935: "I think the race this year is a free-for-all. Everybody has a chance except our club and St. Louis. Personally, I like Cleveland. You know, there's such a thing in baseball as a 'team's year.' Last season it seemed to me it was Detroit's year. This season, I think it's Cleveland's." He still had confidence in his former star catcher Cochrane, however. "A lot depends on Mickey," he added about the Tigers' chance to repeat. "He pulled his club through last year and he may do it again. He has a great competitive spirit. There's nobody quite like him." Nicknamed "Black Mike" for his growling demeanor on the ballfield, Cochrane had sustained numerous injuries in the rough World Series against the Cardinals in '34, including a large gash in his leg which caused him to spend a night in the hospital before the seventh game. The city of Detroit had bestowed all sorts of gifts upon him, and the respected baseball man was adored by fans and admired by competitors. "Cochrane should finish his career as the greatest of all backstops," wrote famed New York writer Grantland Rice, "when you check in all the details that make a great catcher—including batting, base running, smartness, and hustle."

The 1935 season would also be the first for Mack's "Spite Fence" in right field at Shibe Park in Philadelphia. In prior years, local residents who lived behind the 12-foot high wall could watch the games free of charge, something of which the stingy Mack had grown weary. When he lost a suit against the city to prevent the view that was "on the house," he instead constructed a higher blockade that obstructed the locals' view. The A's would eventually share the park—the first in the majors constructed with concrete and steel—with the Phillies beginning in 1938, and the National League club would outlast the A's tenure at the location until their move into Veterans' Stadium in 1971. Echoes of this move were heard in 2002, as the Chicago Tribune Company—owner of the Cubs since 1981—decided to erect wind screens above the bleachers to obstruct the view of residents from rooftops along Waveland and Sheffield Avenues. A feud erupted. The Cubs claimed that the neighbors were charging exorbitant prices for the cultural delicacy of viewing a Cubs game from the perch; the neighbors claimed that they were simply part of the neighborhood and should be respected. The battle rages on.

So with the geo-political world still in disarray in 1935, the only place where the status quo ruled appeared to be the American and National Leagues, and especially in the latter. The usual cast of characters from New York and St. Louis were set to battle it out, with the Cubs making moves that had them believing a pennant was within reach as well. *Tribune* writer Edward Burns thought that the third-place prediction by most for the Cubs was appropriate. "Chicagoans who picked the Cubs in recent campaigns did it sometimes on a civic pride basis ... it takes a lot of civic pride to install the Cubs in first place this year, and it takes confidence to guess them as high as second; fair judgment to rate them third."

Gabby, Jolly Cholly, and the Grimm Reapers

It was finally on October 23, 1934, that chewing gum heir Phillip K. Wrigley purchased the controlling shares in the Chicago Cubs Baseball Club, and succeeded William Walker as president of the organization. Wrigley's longtime love of the team was apparent, and he wanted to make their stadium the best in the major leagues.

The ballpark at Clark and Addison Streets was constructed in 1914, just two years after its contemporary, Fenway Park in Boston. The opening of Fenway the first week of April 1912 didn't get the headlines, however ... a seemingly-indestructible ship by the name of *Titanic* sank the same week after hitting an iceberg from the British Isles en route to the United States. When the Chicago team started to do battle, a live bear cub was in attendance at the first game at their new home park, and the Cubs beat the Reds 7–6 in extra innings. A few years after "Cubs Park" opened, the site was privy to perhaps the greatest pitching duel of all time in 1917. Hippo Vaughn of the Cubs and Fred Toney of Cincinnati matched no-hitters for nine innings, after which the Reds won in the tenth on a base knock by the legendary all-around athlete Jim Thorpe.

The property was originally purchased by Charles Weeghman, and a seminary had previously stood on it. Weeghman quickly constructed a ballpark for the price tag of a quarter of a million dollars, and soon named it after himself. The field was home to the maverick Federal League in 1914 and 1915, after which Weeghman bought the Cubs. It was then that he moved the team to the ballpark at the corner of Addison and Clark. Before the team had played at the old West Side Grounds. In 1920,

Weeghman sold the team and the park to William Wrigley, Jr. Six years later, the stadium bore *his* name, as young Phillip was groomed for ultimate control. And in 1930, the largest crowd ever to watch a Cubs game at Wrigley Field appeared on June 27, as over 51,000 showed up to see the North Siders take on the Dodgers. It was not a money day for Mr. Wrigley, however, as nearly 40 percent of the spectators had been admitted free as part of a "Ladies' Day" promotion.

Much of Wrigley Field as it is known today did not appear until 1937. It was then that the Wrigley family constructed the famous bleachers and manual scoreboard. For the 1935 season, the old scoreboard would again be operated by Charles Tallman, who claimed he was starting his "fiftieth year as a baseball fan" and his thirty-sixth at operating the board, going back to the Cubs' days at West Side Grounds (Tallman also operated the scoreboard at Comiskey Park when the White Sox were home). The famous ivy was planted on the outfield wall at Wrigley in 1937 as well—and the gardener was none other than the great showman-to-be, Bill Veeck. Although no batted ball has ever hit the massive scoreboard, two hitters have come close—Bill Nicholson in 1948 and Roberto Clemente in 1959, the former sending a ball past the mammoth display to the right and the latter to the left. The stadium would not get another major renovation until the 1980s when the Tribune Company bought the team.

In 1970, by which time the bleacherites had been getting a little too rowdy for the liking of the Cubs' brass, a basket was installed to hang over the top of the wall (which unfortunately, did not prevent other kinds of hangovers generated at the park). The move was designed to keep fans from dropping beer bottles and cans and other sorts of things on the heads of enemy outfielders, but over the years it has also caught many home runs that would have otherwise landed in play.

And, of course, the inevitable occurred on August 8, 1988, when the Cubs played the Phillies in the first night game ever at Wrigley Field (easily remembered as 8-8-88). The date, however, would not go into the baseball books—the contest was rained out after 3½ innings (begging the question: Did the Good Lord want lights at Wrigley in the first place?). The Cubs beat the Mets the next night, 6-4, to officially usher in nocturnal play at the Friendly Confines. But while the majority of Cubs games still finish before the workday is through, the club maintains a way of informing the locals of the team's success. The elevated train, which carries thousands of yuppies to their downtown jobs daily, runs parallel to the park along the rightfield wall adjacent to Sheffield Avenue. Moving along as they pass center field, riders on the train notice either a white or blue flag hoisted atop the scoreboard—white signifying a Cubs victory, blue a defeat. This banner of the outcome is flanked by the numbers "14" (Ernie Banks) and "26" (Billy Williams) perched on the left- and right-field foul poles respectively.

It is undeniable that, for better *and* worse, Wrigley Field has had a history of being slow to change, for many years forestalling the fruition of lights, internal improvements, and other amenities so common to the twenty-first century stadium. Even back in 1935, the Cubs' manager forbid the playing of music over the stadium loudspeaker during pre-game batting practice, for fear that it would distract his players from work on which they needed to concentrate. For the most part, however, the manager was a laid-back, easygoing guy whose two favorite things were to relax on his farm back in Missouri, and pick at his banjo—preferably, he said, done at the same time. He was in such a permanently good mood, and got along so well with everyone, that it changed the very pronunciation of his first name. He was Charlie Grimm, better known to his charges as "Jolly Cholly."

The son of a German immigrant who settled in St. Louis, Grimm broke into the major leagues as a firstbaseman with the Philadelphia A's in 1916, but did not see regular action until 1920 at which time he found himself with the Pittsburgh Pirates. After putting up a 25-game hitting streak in 1923 (stopped by Braves coach Dick Rudolph, who activated himself to alleviate the shortage of pitchers the club was experiencing), Grimm became the Cubs' firstsacker in 1925 at the age of 29, ready to establish himself among the game's elite at the position. Grimm was forced to miss much of the Cubs' pennant run in 1929, as he severely injured his hand on August 21; however, he was able to recover in time to bat .389 in the series with the Cubs' lone home run as they lost in five games to the A's.

After several seasons of displaying his leadership qualities, Grimm was a natural choice to replace Hornsby as manager; he did so on August 2, 1932. Grimm finished out the season impressively, logging a 37–18 mark down the stretch and leading the Cubs into the World Series against the New York Yankees. His light-hearted personality was a stark contrast to the rigorous, business-like approach of Hornsby. Grimm could be assertive when he felt he had to be, as in the case of the outlawed pregame music (not too long afterwards in 1944, however, Wrigley Field would be the first stadium in the majors with organ music piped throughout the ballpark). An intelligent and progressive-thinking man, Grimm did authorize the installation of a canvas screen behind the left field section in the early 1930s, because he felt that the hitting background was poorest there, and thus attempted to give lefthanded batters a bit more of a break. Grimm was a firm believer in the routine of good habit; for nearly every day of his adult life, he went to bed promptly at ten o'clock and arose at five.

The Chicago newspapers, in recognition of the official title bestowed upon Grimm by Wrigley, began calling him "Vice President Grimm," a term of endearment that the players picked up on as well.

There was little doubt that the Cubs were the third-best team in the National League in 1934. While playing a side role in the Cardinals-Giants duel for a while, they resigned themselves to a solid third place finish, ten games ahead of the fourth-place Braves but a full eight behind St. Louis and six behind New York. The Cubs had their individual stars, such as outfielder Hazen "Kiki" Cuyler, who finished first in the league in doubles (42), second in stolen bases (15), and third in batting average (.338). Catcher Gabby Hartnett, secondbaseman Billy Herman, and shortstop Billy Jurges were becoming recognized as among the finest defensively in baseball at their positions. And starting pitchers Lon Warneke, Guy Bush, Pat Malone, Bill Lee, and Jim Weaver combined for 78 of the club's 86 wins, but a mediocre bullpen let the team down in the rest of the work. Grimm, however, knew that the talent was there, and only a bit of tweaking was necessary for a pennant run in '35. A stronger bullpen and a stronger bench was sought, but the Cubs were assuredly unrivaled at the spot where championship teams are made: defensively up the middle. In Hartnett, Herman, Jurges, and Cuyler, Chicago could outpace any team in the center of the diamond, either individually or collectively. And with the great leadership of each, Grimm essentially had four more player-managers on the field.

Hartnett was born in 1900 in Woonsocket, Rhode Island, his given name Charles Leo, the oldest of 14 children. His father, Fred, was a notable semi-pro player in the Massachusetts area, and taught all of his children—the boys *and* the girls—how to play ball (the Hartnett daughters would go on to distinguished careers with traveling softball teams). When Gabby once broke his arm as a child, his parents didn't coddle him; rather, they made him carry a bucket of stones everywhere he went to accelerate the healing process. Hartnett appreciated the discipline that his parents gave him, and the hard-working background from which he came.

"I was living in Millville and working in the American Steel and Wire Mill in Worcester, 26 miles from my home," Hartnett recalled of his teenage years. "I had to arise at 5:30 in the morning to get to my job, and I never got home for supper until 7:30 in the evening. One morning, it was twenty degrees below zero when I set out for the scene of my employment. When I got into the warmth of the plant I discovered that both my ears had been frozen, causing me the greatest pain I've ever known. I was sure that both of them were going to explode or drop off.

"The situation startled and angered me. Right then and there, I denounced work in all its branches and vowed I'd never work again. And I never have."

Meaning, that he began his pursuit as a professional baseball player.

Gabby signed a contract to play for Worcester in the Eastern League in 1921 at the age of 21, and he may never have had a career in baseball if his father had not worked for the local rail line that served the team. Hartnett spent just one season in Worcester before debuting with the Cubs, who bought him for a price of $2,500. He received his nickname at spring training his rookie year, as a reporter covering the Cubs at Catalina Island wanted to know the identity of the talkative young newcomer. Soon after, the young Gabby would catch the great Grover Alexander in his first big league game in 1922 and set himself as the Cubs' permanent man behind the plate.

On the last day of the 1925 season, Hartnett dropped a foul pop up that led to the Cubs loss—a loss that would put them in last place at 68–86, a half game behind both Philadelphia and Brooklyn. Unwittingly, the error and subsequent basement standing for the Cubs allowed them to have the number one pick in the minor draft, and a portly outfielder by the name of Hack Wilson was theirs for $5,000. Ultimately, Wilson would post an incredible 190 runs batted in for 1930, along with 56 home runs and a .356 average. Hartnett would lead the league in errors for three of his first four seasons, but the Cubs' management knew that his talent would eventually allow him to improve.

He was continuing to post solid numbers heading into the 1929 season when it all nearly came to an end. While in spring training that year, Hartnett began to develop a mysterious pain in his arm. It was most painful to throw, and no matter what he tried, no treatment could cure it. He was frustrated to the point of nearly quitting the game altogether when he got word from his mother on another home remedy for his arm (he was hoping that she wouldn't suggest carrying a bucket of stones again). Hartnett had his new bride Martha with him, who was expecting their first child. Hartnett's mother told him that, as soon as Martha gave birth, his arm would feel better. Gabby missed almost the entire 1929 season with the sore wing (he would catch in only one game that year, and appear as pinch-hitter only in the World Series, going hitless in three at-bats). But come December 1929, the child was born—and the pain in Gabby's arm left just as mysteriously as it came, and he resumed his work behind the plate.

During 1933 and 1934, Hartnett set the major league record for catchers for consecutive chances without an error (452). For 1935, he would be backed up by rookie Ken O'Dea, fresh from the minors and hailing from Lima, New York. The Cubs were excited about him, and envisioned O'Dea as a full-time replacement for Hartnett one day.

Herman was from New Albany, Indiana, just across the Ohio River from Louisville. He broke in with one of the greatest rookie seasons in Cubs history in 1932, after spending the majority of four campaigns in the minors. That year, he amassed 206 hits and batted .314 as part of another Cubs run to the National League pennant. After Ruth allegedly called his shot in the '32 series, Herman maintained for the rest of his life that he believed the big man was pointing at the Cubs' dugout exclusively, not the center field stands as legend likes to tell. "I got a mental picture of the ball going out of the ballpark," Herman said, remembering the scene. "This particular time at bat, he took the first strike and then he took the second strike right down the middle. He holds up his two fingers as if to say, 'That's only two strikes.'" The homer itself was not debatable, however. As the *New York Times* described it, "It was a tremendous smash that tore straight down the center of the field in an enormous arc, came down alongside the flagpole and disappeared behind the corner formed by the scoreboard and the end of the right-field bleachers." It would be the last World Series for Ruth, who had played in the most championship finals ever (10), and also had hit the most home runs (13) and driven in the most runs (33) in World Series play.

In considering his nearly-flawless bat control, Grimm had come to the opinion that Herman was his ideal number-two hitter in the lineup, and he was rarely not in that place.

Jurges and Herman rose through the system together, and honed their double-play skills while playing side-by-side at Louisville in the shadows of Herman's home. Jurges' game was his glove, and like his counterpart Durocher in St. Louis, any hitting that the club received from him was a bonus. His fielding was good enough, in fact, to cause the Cubs to ignore the .201 average he posted in his rookie year in 1931 at the age of 23—for his greatest asset lay in the ground he covered at short. They were so confident in his talent that they moved all-league shortstop Woody English over to third to make room for the youngster. He did have his moments with the stick, though; in 1934 he stroked nine consecutive hits. Like Hartnett, the Brooklyn native at one point was ready to quit baseball, and he asked a local friend to find him a job as a truck driver. Instead, he kept pursuing his dream of being a ballplayer and made the varsity team at Richmond Hill High School in Flatbush, the same secondary program that would later produce the Yankees' star shortstop Phil Rizzuto. However, it was an incident a year after joining the Cubs that would truly change Jurges' life forever.

On July 6, 1932, Jurges received a phone call at his hotel room in Chicago. On the other end of the line was a woman named Violet Valli, who had taken an extra-special liking to Billy and kept track of him wherever the club went. When she discovered that her love was unrequited, she showed up at Jurges' room with a pistol, intent on killing herself. When Jurges tried to talk her out of it, she became more unstable and pulled the trigger. Jurges physically intervened, and the bullet—which Valli had intended for herself—struck the Cub player in his hand. Another shot was fired that hit him in the ribs and caromed up to his shoulder. Fans and fellow players were startled when Jurges—thought of as lucky just to survive, let alone play baseball again—was back at shortstop for the Cubs just over two weeks later. Not only did Jurges decide not to press charges against her, but in a prelude to the tabloid era, Valli even went on to capitalize on her "fame" by singing in nightclubs around Chicago, and actually enjoyed her reputation as "the most talked about girl in Chicago." Even though Jurges returned quickly to the lineup, Koenig was brought over from the Yankees to assist. When the loser's share from the series was divided up among the Cubs later that year, Koenig was voted to receive only a half-share, which angered many of the New York players, including Ruth.

With a firm hold on third base for the Cubs entering the 1935 season was Stan Hack, a man who would become one of the more popular Chicago players of all time. In his first year of professional baseball (1931), he batted .352 in the Pacific Coast League, and didn't remain in the West long as the Cubs quickly offered him a contract.

Hack was the ploy in one of the first stunts pulled by Veeck at the ballpark. In a promotion that was announced as "Smile with Stan Hack," Veeck toured the bleachers at Wrigley and handed out small mirrors with a picture of the Cubs' thirdbaseman on the back. Fans soon got the idea: the mirrors weren't for shaving or a quick makeup check, but rather for directing the glare of the sun into opposing batters' eyes. When other teams began to complain, the keepsakes were forbidden in the stands.

The Cubs' management thought the addition of outfielder Chuck Klein before the 1934 season was the final piece to their pennant puzzle. He had just won the Triple Crown in 1933 with the Phillies (.368 batting average, 28 home runs and 120 RBIs), which was preceded by a National League Most Valuable Player Award in 1932, during which he led the league in hits and home runs. And back in 1930, Klein set the

National League record for runs scored with 158—still the most in the NL for the last century—and his 107 extra base hits were the most in National League history until he was tied by Barry Bonds in 2001. Some critics felt that the Baker Bowl in Philadelphia catered too much to his swing, with the right field wall a mere 280 feet from home plate and its tin often rattled by blows off of Klein's bat. Most National League managers felt that Klein wouldn't be the same power factor in Chicago that he was in Philly, and they were correct—his home run numbers slipped from 28 in 1933 to 20 in 1934 (although he played in 37 fewer games in the latter year). But he was still feared by opposing pitchers, and the Indianapolis native—who had broken in with the Phillies in 1928—quickly became one of the preeminent power hitters in the game. No less evidence of this was his National League record of 43 home runs that he struck in 1929 (Wilson would break the record with his 56 a year later, however). When he came to Chicago, the Cubs felt Klein had many good years left to come. In addition to his offensive skills, he permitted no one to take extra bases on balls hit into the outfield. Also in 1930, he set the modern major league record for assists by an outfielder with 44, as he gunned down baserunners with uncanny ease (this while also providing a sterling .386 mark at the plate that season). Not too many players in the game had a better offensive stretch from 1929 to 1933 than Klein, and he led the NL in homers for four out of the five seasons, bowing only to Mel Ott of the New York Giants in '32 (which would be the first of six home run titles for Ott).

Klein was the fixture in right field, but some juggling would be taking place on the other side of the pasture. Babe Herman, a strong-hitting but horrendous-fielding outfielder, had been dealt to the Pirates along with pitchers Bush and Weaver. He had been the last Cub to hit for the cycle on September 30, 1933, against none other than Dizzy Dean. Two months earlier, Babe had been the last Cub to hit three home runs in a game. While being (self-admittedly) terrible on defense, Herman's departure was thought to be leaving a gaping hole in the Cubs' batting order.

Grimm was considering several possibilities for the left field position. The off-season between 1934 and 1935 saw the release of veteran Cub outfielder Riggs Stephenson, which added to the confusion. The most likely candidate for regular duty looked to be Freddie Lindstrom, acquired the past winter from Pittsburgh along with pitcher Larry French. Lindstrom, a Chicago native who had batted .290 for the Pirates the previous season in 92 games, was a former infielder who Grimm planned to use to give Hack a rest from time to time as well. Lindstrom had led the

National League in hits in 1928 with 231, and finished fourth with the same amount in the bat-happy season of 1930. When he came up with the Giants in 1924, John McGraw stuck him at third base. His fielding woes at the position would soon draw the ire of Johnny Mac, and McGraw finally moved him to the outfield in 1931 where he would remain though his stint with Pittsburgh in 1933 and 1934 (Lindstrom had requested a trade in 1932, when Terry received the Giants' managerial position after McGraw's retirement, a decision that made Lindstrom very bitter. The players and the media had been clandestinely informed of McGraw's resignation and Terry's elevation by a typed message affixed to the clubhouse door). Despite his defense that was becoming erratic, Lindstrom's bat always kept him in the lineup, and his defense at third was never as bad as McGraw made it out to be. As a result, Lindstrom's spats with McGraw became legendary among the other New York players.

When Lindstrom was a rookie with the Giants in 1924, McGraw snarled at him after one particular game in which Lindstrom made a couple of errors at third.

"You—what a punk you are," Mac started in on him. "A fresh young busher who is riding along on a reputation from last year. What a great play you made today, you [bleeping bleep]."

Flustered and unable to respond with something more soothing, Lindstrom—still two months shy of his nineteenth birthday—shot back. "Listen, you gray-bearded old mossback, another word out of you and I'll let you have one. Who in the [bleep] do you think you're talking to, huh? Trying to bully someone? If you want a fight, step up and take one, you silly old man. Shut up and stay shut."

The usually-revered McGraw was stunned, and he turned and went out the door of the locker room. Lindstrom capitalized on his momentum by turning to twelve-year veteran Frank Snyder, who was shaking from fear of what McGraw might come back and do, and said, "And that goes for you too, you has-been. Anything else?"

Just then, McGraw stormed back in the room and stomped over to Lindstrom, quivering with rage. "No, I take it back," the Giants' boss started up again. "You're not a [bleeping bleep]. You're a jackass." Unable to contain themselves any longer, Frisch, Terry, and the other players in the room fell off their seats in laughter.

Later that season, Lindstrom would become the youngest player to ever appear in a World Series. He knocked four hits off Walter Johnson in Game Five, but later saw a ball "hit a pebble," as he put it, and bound over his head into left field in Game Seven. The Senators won the championship on the single by Earl McNeely.

Incidents like the one above were common between Lindstrom and McGraw, and continued through all his seasons with the Giants. Years later, while in Chicago to play the Cubs in 1931, Lindstrom and catcher Bob O'Farrell asked permission of McGraw to stay at their own residences instead of the team hotel. McGraw granted the request, which was unusual for him. But after the Cubs won the first two games of the series McGraw's mood had changed, and he stormed over to O'Farrell's locker.

"You plant your big pants in the hotel tonight, you hear?"

O'Farrell nodded and said, "Yes, sir."

It didn't help, and the Cubs made it three in a row the next day for a clean sweep. Looking for someone to unload on, McGraw then turned to Lindstrom.

"Why weren't you in the hotel last night?" he snapped. Lindstrom responded that *he* specifically had not been forbidden to stay at *his* residence.

"Didn't you hear me tell O'Farrell to be in?" McGraw screamed back.

"Well, I'm not O'Farrell," Lindstrom told him. "I don't care what he does."

"Oh you don't, huh?" McGraw retorted. "Well, that just cost you $50."

"*Cost me $50?* Why, you stupid-looking gazebo. I hope you break your leg."

Ten minutes later after leaving the stadium, McGraw, while crossing a street with Giants' scout Dick Kinsella, was hit by a cab and, in fact, broke his leg. After getting his leg cast, McGraw's first order of business was to hobble over to Lindstrom's house and tell him that the $50 fine still stuck.

One day, Lindstrom stumbled upon the ultimate ace to hide up his sleeve. He found a box score from an old newspaper that reported McGraw having eight errors in one game at third base. Lindstrom taped the box score up in his locker for all to see, and sometimes even carried it around in his pocket for quick use.

Nobody was beyond reproach as far as Lindstrom was concerned. When Hornsby arrived in New York in 1927, McGraw's dream had finally been realized; he had sought Hornsby's services all along, although he had to deal his beloved Frisch to the Cardinals in return. McGraw immediately appointed Hornsby the team captain, and the newcomer began organizing the workouts himself in spring training, freeing up McGraw to attend to other matters. In an interview given to *The Sporting News* in 1929, Giants infielder Travis Jackson described the scene as the 31-year-old captain Hornsby admonished the 21-year-old Lindstrom for throwing too hard on the first day of practice, in fear of the youngster hurting his arm.

"Who do you think you are?" Lindstrom answered Hornsby, in no way in awe of the legendary player. "You're no more than a rookie on this ball club as far as we're concerned. We're playing for McGraw, and he's sittin' over there on the bench. And what's more, how the hell can you tell anybody about fielding? Listen, if you lost that bat tonight you'd be in the bushes tomorrow."

Despite having the personality of a boiled lobster on the field, Lindstrom was one of the more avid church-goers in the major leagues. He made it a point on Saturday nights—even when on the road—to gather up other players interested in attending mass the next morning, and make careful plans to go.

New to the Cubs in 1934 like Klein, and now vying for the left field job in 1935, was a fleet-footed youngster named Augie Galan. Galan grew up in the Berkeley, California, area, the son of a laundry owner, and signed professionally with the San Francisco Seals in 1931. "If something happened to take me out of baseball, I could make a living in the laundry business," Galan said. "I started working for my father after school hours when I was 12 years old and know every branch of the business." When a big league barnstorming team came through in 1932, they got permission from the Seals to acquire Galan to play shortstop for the remainder of the trip. Taking his place at shortstop for the Seals' final three games of the season was a 17-year-old local boy named Joe DiMaggio, who the following year would hit in 61 straight games and bat .340 while arousing the interest of major league clubs throughout the land. Galan would return to the Seals to play alongside DiMaggio in 1933, and he outdid Joltin' Joe by batting .356 with an incredible 265 hits for the year. The Cubs were first in line to sign Galan, and they sent seven players, along with $25,000, to the Seals to acquire him.

Due to a childhood accident that shattered his right elbow, Galan had made it through professional baseball with a deformed throwing arm, but it affected his play. While hitting a serviceable .260 in 192 at-bats in 1934, Galan couldn't adjust defensively in the 43 games he played at second base. After the season was over, Grimm thought that Galan might be better suited to the outfield, where he could utilize his great speed. He was then instructed to arrive at spring training for 1935 as such.

Yet another candidate to take the left field job was Frank Demaree. After hitting .272 as a replacement for the injured Cuyler in 1933, Demaree was surprisingly sent to Los Angeles of the Pacific Coast League in 1934, and he was named the league's Most Valuable Player. He batted a blistering .383 with 45 home runs and 173 runs batted in, although he played in 186 games to accomplish the feat (that alone being an accomplishment). He felt he had nothing more to prove in the minors, and arrived at spring workouts ready to claim any of the outfield jobs that were presented. Also competing for a slot was the young, athletic George "Tuck" Stainback, who Burns described as "a great kid and a great ballplayer if they can get him going." Interestingly, Stainback's wife had been a stand-in for Joan Crawford in the 1930s movie *Chained*.

When the discussion is of sports—and baseball in particular—one of the topics most debated is the adaptability of a player from one era to another. In the 1920s, before the advent of radar guns, filmmakers attempted to calculate the speed of Walter Johnson's fastball through the use of movies. Students of the game love to compare the physical traits of yesteryear's warrior to the bionic creatures of today. If there was one position player from the 1920s and '30s that would have transferred successfully to the modern game, a strong case could have made for Cuyler. While Klein had the immense power that became fashionable in the game in later years, Cuyler had mastered all facets of baseball, in both a physical and cerebral sense. He was one of the fastest players of the first half-century, leading the National League in stolen bases four times. He coupled his speed in the outfield with one of the best throwing arms in the game—equal to or even surpassing that of Klein's—as he displayed bodily attributes generations ahead of his time (he received his nickname Kiki—pronounced "Kye-Kye"—in the minor leagues, as several of his fellow fielders chasing fly balls would simultaneously utter the first syllable of his *last* name, calling him for help to make the catch). He arrived in the big leagues in 1921 with the Pirates, and by 1925 was one of the game's true stars with 26 triples, 144 runs scored, and a .357 batting average. Also during that year, he became a World Series hero for the Bucs. In Game Seven against Johnson and the Washington Senators, Cuyler slammed an eighth-inning double that scored three runners and proved to be the difference in the series. Cuyler, along with everyone in the park, thought that he had hit an inside-the-park home run, but was ordered back to second base when the umpire called a ground-rule double instead. He soon proved that he could hit for power *and* average, posting a career-high 134 RBIs for the Cubs in 1930.

Cuyler was from Harrisville, Michigan, and played for the Chevrolet Company baseball team while helping his family make a living by working at the plant. He soon signed with the Pirates after attending West Point, and broke into the big leagues slowly. From 1921 to 1923, his first three years in the majors, Cuyler appeared in only 13 games (only one each in his first two seasons). In 1924, however, he let his ability take over, and swatted the ball for a .354 average that was good for fourth in the National League, as was his 16 triples. But he was also a free-swinger, and his 62 strikeouts that year—while almost a desirable total in modern times—were the second most in the league, and became a cause of concern for Pirates officials. He was acquired by the Cubs from Pittsburgh before the 1928 season, after he and Pittsburgh manager Donie Bush had differences that could not be resolved (Cuyler had been mysteriously benched for the 1927 World Series against the formidable Yankees, despite enjoying a torrid August and September as Bush decided to go with Clyde Barnhart in the outfield instead). To hasten his exit out of the Steel City, Cuyler continued to be at odds with Pirates owner Barney Dreyfuss over salary issues, becoming one of the first modern-era superstars to challenger his employer. Cubs manager Joe McCarthy, always impressed with Cuyler's off-the-charts athleticism, gladly welcomed him aboard in Chicago. Pittsburgh got utilityman Sparky Adams and minor league outfielder Pete Scott, and the Cubbies made off with one of their best trades of all time. After his arrival in Chicago, Cuyler—along with fellow Cubs Hartnett, Wilson, and Cliff Heathcote—even tried his hand at a theatrical bit which seemed destined for a vaudeville set before the group disbanded.

The Cubs' first base position, manned by Grimm for so many years, had been in a year-long state of transition. In 1934, the team thought they had found an able sub and heir for the tiring Grimm when they acquired Don Hurst from Philadelphia. Hurst, however, turned out to be a disappointment. After arriving from the Phillies he hit just .199 in 151 at-bats, a surprising downturn in a career that saw him bat .298 lifetime with Philadelphia since 1926. Hurst would be out of baseball by 1935, as the Cubs' first-sacker job was thrown wide open for the taking.

So at spring training that year, an 18-year-old Chicago schoolboy named Phil Cavarretta was making a run for the starting position. Cavarretta had the thrill of hitting his initial home run in his first big league start on September 25, 1934—the lone Cubs run in a 1–0 victory over Whitey Wistert and the Cincinnati Reds (Wistert, a Chicago native, would pitch in just one other major league game despite his own tremendous performance that day). Grimm was actually making Cavarretta's case easy for him; Jolly Cholly had been hitting not-so-jolly, going 0-for-43 in spring training, upon which he felt compelled to permanently write "Cavy's" name on the lineup card instead of his own. Cavarretta had just finished playing at Lane Tech High School in Chicago—which happens to be located on Addison Street, the same drag on which Wrigley Field sits and a mere 14 blocks to the west. Before getting his diploma at Lane, Cavarretta had been sent to the Peoria club in the Central League for the summer of '34 before getting his big league call-up that September. Cub fans were wary of a high-schooler holding down the first base job, but the impressive athletic ability he displayed in training camp allayed any significant fears that Grimm had.

The Cubs felt extremely positive about their starting pitching staff entering the 1935 season, and with good reason. Although gone were Bush and Weaver to the Pirates and their 29 wins, as well as the hard-throwing and hard-drinking Malone to the Yankees and his fourteen wins, many arms were present to create a deep group. And to take the place of the three departed veterans, two new ones arrived.

French had been with the Pirates since 1929, and he was 28 years old entering the '35 season with the Cubs. He had arrived with Lindstrom in the trade with the Pirates for Bush, Weaver, and Babe Herman on November 22, 1934 (by going to Pittsburgh, Bush, the "Mississippi Mudcat" [hailing from Aberdeen of the Magnolia State], would begin his 13th season in the big leagues, which commenced with a September

The 1935 Chicago Cubs. *Top Row* (L-R): Ken O'Dea, Phil Cavarretta, Chuck Klein, Charlie Root, Fred Lindstrom, Fabian Kowalik, Roy Henshaw, Clyde Shoun. *Middle Row* (L-R): Team Physician Dr. Davis, Coach Roy Johnson, Tuck Stainback, Bill Jurges, Tex Carleton, Larry French, Bill Lee, Wally Stephenson, Hugh Casey, Trainer Andy Lotshaw. *Bottom Row* (L-R): Traveling Secretary Bob Lewis, Billy Herman, Augie Galan, Coach Red Corriden, Gabby Hartnett, Charlie Grimm, Woody English, Stan Hack, Lon Warneke, Frank Demaree. *Sitting*: Batboy Gilly Hasbrook. (Chicago Historical Society)

audition with the Cubs in 1923. He was one of the more animated pitchers in baseball, often falling to his knees on the mound after an especially hard pitch).

French had lost 18 games for the heavy-hitting Pirates in 1934—he gave up 299 hits to the opposition in only 264 innings. The Cubs had seen promise in the southpaw, however. He tossed a screwball that was not nearly as good as Carl Hubbell's, the Giants' ace who perfected the trick, but it was effective nonetheless. An oddity about French was that he always pitched with a ring on his left hand, but it was not by choice— since he had worn the ring as a young adult, he had never been able to slip it off.

James Otto "Tex" Carleton was the "other" pitcher on the Cardinals' 1934 championship club. Dizzy and Paul Dean were permanently on the marquee, and Carleton resented it. He also resented how Paul had gotten the superstar treatment before the junior Dean had even arrived in the big leagues. It was a constant—albeit underlying—source of dissension for Frisch to deal with during the season. The club had many other outward bursts of dissension, however, which usually took the headlines instead. Carleton was not alone in his feelings; many of the Cardinals were not fond of Dizzy's antics in 1934, including he and Paul missing a train to Detroit in the middle of the season, where the Cardinals were going to meet the Tigers in one of Rickey's exhibition games that few wanted to play. Carleton was dedicated to his craft of pitching, and always looked for ways in which he could improve. For instance, in every game he had ever lost, he claimed, he could trace the defeat back to a solitary moment when a batter got the deciding hit on a poor pitch that he made. Carleton had proven himself a model of consistency, once having won 13 games in a row in the minor leagues.

To be sure, one of the more colorful players on the Cubs was Warneke, the "Arkansas Hummingbird." He seemed to be on his way to complete dominance in 1934, as he opened the season with consecutive one-hitters against the Pirates and Cardinals. Warneke worked down in the strike zone, down in the zone, and then down in the zone some more, frustrating hitters by inducing repeated groundballs off their bats. Warneke's fingers were said to be so strong that he was able to slightly twist the cover of a baseball before pitching it, thus giving the ball a "high spot" that caused more break. This theory was never proven, but no one doubted Lon's forearm strength when shaking hands. This was the product of his farm work, to which he looked forward every off-season. "Lon Warneke was born a hillbilly," wrote Burns. "He is a hillbilly now. And he plans to be a hillbilly until his dying day." Burns meant the title as an honor, not a pejorative, as Warneke took great pride in his ability to hunt, fish, and stroke the banjo as efficiently as Grimm. He frequently passed the time in the winter months in Arkansas by reaching under frozen ponds and catching muskrats with his bare hands, but anyone wandering around his territory had better watch out.

"All the folks in the community I come from are open-minded and generous as long as they've got anything to give," Warneke revealed about his hometown of Mount Ida, Arkansas. "Around Mount Ida we ain't so suspicious of strangers as they are down around Greasy Cove. Greasy Cove is south of us. They're hard-working farmers, mostly poor, too. Most any nester down there will let you hunt on his place if he knows where you're from and if you ask in the right way. But they don't hanker to be bothered much, and any stranger that goes feelin' around much for somethin' that's none of his business more than likely will get his damned head blown off." Switching to a more congenial tone, he expressed gratitude to his manager for advancing his procurement of musical skill. "I sure do love mountain music, and I own a guitar that Charlie Grimm gave to me, and a musical saw and bow to go with it. Write-ups have exaggerated my ability to play, though I did show some progress last winter." Lon had also developed his more formal side, too. When he joined the Cubs, he owned one suit; at the present time, he possessed fifteen. Still, he assured folks that he wasn't getting too hifalutin. "I never had a suit I didn't buy off the shelf," he quickly pointed out.

Charlie Root was the veteran of the Cubs' pitching staff. After making $2.50 a week as a clerk in Lawson's Grocery in Middletown, Ohio, he decided to pursue professional baseball full force in 1917. Root finally received an audition with the St. Louis Browns of the American League in 1923, only to go 0–4 in 27 games and soon be banished to the minors. He resurfaced with the Cubs in 1926, and permanently stuck to the major league roster. He exploded the following season with 26 victories—twice as many as any other Chicago pitcher—as the Cubs finished in fourth place, 8 games behind the Pirates. When the Cubs ascended to the pennant two years later in 1929, Root had a remarkable 19–6 record which gave him a league-leading winning percentage of .760. What Root is perhaps best known for, however, is allowing Ruth's "called shot" home run.

Like Billy Herman, Root insisted to his dying day that Ruth never pointed to the center field bleachers. He made a strong case for it, as he affirmed that Ruth would have been dusted by his next if pitch Root thought he had pointed. Nobody in baseball in that day in age, including the great Ruth, was above getting a pitch near the head if the pitcher was shown up. Ruth himself, years later, admitted this point. "I'm going to point to the center field bleachers with a barracuda like Root out there? On the next pitch, they'd be picking it out of my ear with a pair of tweezers." And unlike today's game, the umpires let the players "govern" that aspect of the game themselves—and they did so effectively.

A pleasant surprise on the staff in 1934 was rookie righthander William Crutcher Lee, also known as "General" or simply "Big Bill," who was acquired from the St. Louis Cardinals for $40,000. His only problem coming up in the Cardinals organization was that management had to choose between him and Paul Dean for the big club's roster in '34, and Lee was sent packing to Chicago despite his 71–31 record in the minor leagues. The Cubs did not waste any time in getting the Plauqmine, Louisiana, native's feet wet, as he threw 214 innings in his first year. He made as big a splash on the '34 schedule as Warneke. Lee pitched two shutouts in his first two big-league starts.

The bullpen house from '34 was cleaned, as gone were Tinning, Dick Ward, Lynn Nelson, and Charlie Wiedemeyer, and in were Hugh Casey, Fabian Kowalik, Clay Bryant, and Roy Henshaw. None of the eight had reached the age of 30, so Grimm wasn't concerned with experience; he needed outs. Grimm knew that improvement in this area was critical to make a run at the Cardinals, and he kept Root and Roy Joiner as the lone holdovers from the relief corps. Casey and Bryant were making their maiden major-league voyages in 1935; Henshaw, Joiner, and Kowalik may just as well have been, as all three had only one season of big-league ball behind them. Because of the inexperience in the bullpen, Grimm planned from the outset to burn his seasoned, capable, innings-eating starters to the limit when the National League race began.

"I've got some pretty good pitchers," Grimm claimed as he assessed his staff. "They don't come any better than Warneke. French has been pitching in tough luck. He's a good man. So is Carleton. And I'll bet a hat that some of these youngsters of ours are going to be good, Casey and Henshaw and Kowalik. You wait and see.

"We're going to give our young people a chance this year," he added. "That's why I'll put Phil Cavarretta out on first. He last played on a Chicago American Legion team, by golly. He'll soon make them forget Charlie Grimm, this old broken-down banjo player."

The Great One
Takes a Final Bow

A financial rebound was expected for the game in 1935. "The National League launches its sixtieth season tomorrow, aiming to keep the turnstiles clicking this summer with as colorful a lot of baseball talent as ever roamed its parks," the Associated Press announced on April 15. "The league's revolutionary experiment with night baseball, scheduled for later in the summer, also should contribute to possibly the most prosperous season in years, whatever the competitive effect." Frick added his own enthusiasm. "I expect baseball, the industry, to have its most prosperous year since 1929," he predicted.

"Fan interest is at its height," suggested American League boss Will Harridge. "which, yes, does promise a prosperous season."

The Cubs came north from training camp to Chicago on April 12 to conclude their exhibition schedule with a three-game series against the White Sox. The Cubs came by way of chilly Chattanooga, Tennessee, where they had defeated the Lookouts of the Southern Association in two straight. The only player not to participate in the set was Billy Herman, who was nursing a sore leg. (Phil Wrigley, however, was on the trip. He was greeted upon arrival at the Lookouts' park by a six-man orchestra, all of whom had chewing gum wrappers as lapel pins). After sweeping Chattanooga, the Cubs had an exhibition record of 16–7 going into the White Sox series. The two clubs had actually met twice already back in March, as they played two games in Los Angeles (both won by the Sox, 9–1 and 5–0).

Warneke was scheduled to go up against Les Tietje in the first "city series" game at Wrigley Field. The games were to be a benefit for numerous area charities, which included the American Red Cross, Catholic Charities of Chicago, the Salvation Army, and others. Due to cold and rain, however, the game was nixed and the clubs prepared to meet at Comiskey Park the following day. The canceled contest caused Grimm to shuffle the pitching rotation, and French was given the ball to face John Whitehead of the Sox (Grimm wanted to save Warneke for the season opener with the Cardinals three days later).

That same night, a 21-year-old boxer named Joe Louis recorded his 14th knockout in Chicago, as he stopped Roy Lazer in the third round of a heavyweight bout at Chicago Stadium in front of over 17,000 spectators. Louis had pummeled Lazer in the first two rounds, and after Lazer was quickly floored twice at the start of the third, referee Davy Miller stopped the fight. Louis, though a native of Detroit, had been a Golden Gloves champion in Chicago and was climbing the ranks toward a shot at the title (in a tribute to his former teammates, in fact, Louis wore the blue robe from his Chicagoland Golden Gloves championship club from the previous year). His success had followed an impressive amateur record of 50–4, including 43 knockouts. Louis was originally from Lexington, Alabama, the fourth son of a cotton picker who died when Joe was two years old. When he was six, his mother moved the family to Detroit. It was while working at the Ford plant in River Rouge, outside of Detroit, that Louis decided he wanted to become a boxer. After his triumph at the Stadium, he was described by French Lane of the *Tribune* as "the greatest colored challenger for the world's highest pugilistic honors since the days of Jack Johnson." Many of the fans were late to the fight because Madison Street in front of the Stadium was jammed with people trying unsuccessfully to get tickets. Next up for Louis would be former champ Primo Carnera.

Chicago Stadium, known to city residents as "The Madhouse on Madison" or "The Big Barn," was six years old in 1935. It was the brainchild of Paddy Harmon, a Chicago businessman who envisioned a world-class arena for the city that would out-pace the highly-regarded Madison Square Garden in New York. At the time of its opening and for many years after, Chicago Stadium was the largest indoor arena in the world. Costing over $7,000,000 to build (and constructed in only six months time), the stadium played host to a variety of significant events, including the Republican and Democratic National Conventions in 1932, the first indoor National Football League game in 1933, the funeral of Chicago mayor Anton Cermak later that year (who was killed during an assassination attempt on President Roosevelt while in Miami), and the final

Presidential campaign stop of John F. Kennedy in 1960, among countless other performances of athletes, teams, musicians, and entertainers of
the widest fame. Perhaps its most distinguishable feature was the massive pipe organ, which originally had to be brought down in 24 railroad
cars from its assembly plant in Oshkosh, Wisconsin at a cost of $120,000.
It remains the largest pipe organ in the world, with volume equivalent to
25 100-piece brass bands playing simultaneously. When all of the 3,675
pipes were in use, the decibels made the massive structure vibrate noticeably.

When the modern United Center took the Stadium's place in 1994,
it looked like the end of the organ, too. William Wirtz, owner of both
the National Hockey League's Blackhawks and the Stadium itself, was
not interested in taking the organ across the street when the new arena
was built. According to some critics, Wirtz claimed that the insurance
costs for moving the organ would be too high, something that organ
experts privately refuted. Wirtz implied that if no buyer was found for
the organ by the time of the Stadium's destruction, the organ would
remain inside and be destroyed too. At the last moment, a purchasing
group was found, and the great music box was (and still is) retired to a
private home in Nevada.

The Cubs and Sox finally got to play their first Chicago exhibition
game on April 13, as the teams went to the South Side to do battle at
Comiskey. The Sox jumped on French for four runs in the first three
innings and they won again, 5–2, for three in a row over the Cubs.
English, Lindstrom, Cuyler, and Jurges all had two hits for the Cubs. The
White Sox made it four in a row the next day with another 5–2 score at
Wrigley, in front of the largest crowd of the series at 17,000.

After the first exhibition game, two Cubs were released infielder
Eddie Cihocki, who according to Burns "was drafted largely because it
was reported that he was a great piano player," and pitcher Frank Cole-
man. The Cubs enjoyed much fun with Cihocki throughout his stint in
spring training, for as the team stopped at various hotels and restaurants
on their travels, they relied on Cihocki for entertainment.

And as Opening Day for the major leagues on April 16 approached,
it looked as if nasty weather across the eastern seaboard and the Midwest
would postpone the festivities.

Mungo, the pitcher with the wonderful name and the fastball to
match, would face Curt Davis in Philadelphia as the Dodgers took on
the Phillies. In addition to finishing second to Dean for the National
League lead in strikeouts in 1934, Mungo had also finished off the Giants
in the season's final days. It was his bat that would make the most noise,

however, in the '35 inaugural. He drove in five Dodger runs as Brooklyn bashed the hometown Phillies 12–3 before only 4,000 fans. Bad weather would be a factor in almost all the openers, as a steady snowstorm that began three hours before gametime nearly blanketed the Baker Bowl. The Dodgers were also powered by a home run off the bat of Frey, and the young shortstop was hailed as the next superstar in Flatbush. The turnout would be the lowest among the National League contests, only "outdone" in the AL by the 3,500 that showed up in St. Louis for the game between the Browns and the Indians, which Cleveland won in fourteen innings, 2–1. The Brownies got their lone run in the very first inning, as Hornsby— the living legend—singled home Sammy West after West had led off with a triple.

"His right arm in fine fishing shape after a Southern fishing expedition," the Associated Press reported as President Roosevelt threw out the first ball in the opener at Washington between the Senators and Mack's Athletics. The President had an extra day to rest his throwing arm because the inclement weather in the capital forced the opener for the Senators and A's to be moved to the following day. The Washington players all spread out along the first base line, not so much in expectation of an errant throw from the President, but more so to collect a souvenir; the lucky recipient turned out to be Senators pitcher Bob Burke. A total of 20,000 fans sat in the cold with Roosevelt, and he and the rest stayed to the end to see the home team triumph over Philadelphia, 4–2. The A's' runs came off a Foxx homer in the eighth, and Roosevelt even cheered the long blast of the enemy player. Was the chief pleased with the ball-game? "Well, I've never seen them lose," Roosevelt said of his Senators.

Mack and his A's were facing a unique physical challenge, one of their own making through their own humanitarian efforts. Back in spring training, Mack had acquired a dog as a team mascot, hoping the canine would bring his club some extra luck. As it turned out, the pooch bit the hand that fed him—literally. Philadelphia infielder Dib Williams got chomped, and had to sit out the first part of the season. Williams was subsequently sold to the Red Sox, and Mack put the dog on waivers as well. "Now the Boston fans are wondering," proposed John Kieran of the *New York Times*. "Connie sold Lefty Grove to the Red Sox, and Lefty came up with a sore arm. This time Boston has received a player who was bitten by a dog. Maybe Connie thinks that Fenway Park is a clinic."

In Detroit, the upstart White Sox surprised Rowe and the defending American League champion Tigers by a score of 7–6. The start of the season for these clubs was delayed as well, with Michigan not exempt from the poor weather punishing the nation. The Tigers had used the

same ball for pre-game infield practice before every game during their
1934 pennant-winning season, and had started the 1935 campaign using
the same ball once again. However, after the Opening Day loss, the pre-
viously-lucky ball was tossed into the river.

In New York, Yankee fans welcomed back Combs with thunderous
applause, as the centerfielder returned to play after his disastrous collision with the outfield wall in St. Louis. The next loudest ovation came
for the new captain Gehrig as he emerged from the dugout, a scene as
reliable as the 5:15 train. Just under 30,000 fans were in attendance, and
the weather was no better in the Bronx than anywhere else on Opening
Day. "In fact, there was such a disagreeable sting in the air," reported
Drebinger, "that as the early arrivals bundled themselves in overcoats and
blinked out on the newly cropped lawn, it doubtless would not have surprised them at all had some two dozen helmeted huskies scampered out."
The shivering faithful would ultimately watch Wes Ferrell of the Red
Sox out-duel Vernon "Lefty" Gomez to a 1–0 score. The game began in
Yankee tradition, as the managers of the respective clubs—Cronin for the
Red Sox and Joe McCarthy for the Yankees—marched out to the cen-
terfield flag pole to raise Old Glory while an on-field band proudly performed "The Star-Spangled Banner."

The feature presentation was most certainly in Boston, as a record
Opening Day crowd of 25,000 greeted the Braves and Giants. That figure
was a little more than half what the Braves' executives were hoping for,
but the poor weather again scared many away. There was so much to celebrate: the first day of the season, the legendary Hubbell twirling for the
Giants, and the arrival of the "Great One." "Babe Ruth has never worked
harder," Braves manager Bill McKechnie stated before the first pitch was
thrown. "He is in better shape than he has been for several seasons, and
he will be used to the best advantage." In its rich baseball history, the city
of Boston had never seen anything like the gala spectacle that was presented. "Cannons boomed, airplanes overhead roared, martial strains filled
the air and the tread of military feet furrowed the grass," the scene was
described in anticipation of the day. Ruth, who had first arrived in Boston
21 years earlier as a pitcher and outfielder with the Red Sox, had played
his last game in a Yankee uniform the previous September against the
Red Sox. Before the game, a plaque was presented to Judge Emil Fuchs,
the president of the Braves, for his years of service to the organization.
The fans were anxious to see Ruth get to work, and they groaned when
Massachusetts Governor James Curley gave perhaps a bit-too-long speech
in the presentation to Fuchs. Curley gained no further admirers in his
next act either—he had to throw out the first pitch several times before

the numerous cameramen that surrounded the scene were satisfied with the quality.

In addition to Curley, governors from the states of Maine, Rhode Island, New Hampshire, Connecticut, and Vermont witnessed the celebration. "National, local and state figures representing every walk of life were in the throng," wrote James Dawson, "but over all shone the glamorous figure of Ruth ... and he was able to deliver when he knew every eye was upon him." Cronin had originally designated Ruth for first base, but at the last minute put him in left field.

About his duties for the opener, Ruth told the press that he "plans to bat three times and hopes to hit at least one home run."

Batting in the third spot in the order, Ruth gave Boston a 1–0 advantage in the first when he rocketed a single past the frightened Terry at first, scoring Bill Urbanski. "The ball came at me so fast I just couldn't see it," admitted Terry after the game. The Braves were ahead 2–0 in the fifth when Ruth made his third trip to the plate. He was facing the indomitable Hubbell, whom Ruth had robbed defensively in the top half of the inning. To the surprise of most who thought Ruth could not move at all, he charged in from a deep position in left field to make a diving catch of a flare off Hubbell's bat. Hubbell now peered in towards the plate from the pitcher's mound, with his pants rolled down low (as a personal preference in wearing his uniform—long before George Hendrick of the Cardinals made the style popular in the early 1980s).

But despite heroics with the glove, the fans came to see what happened next. "Gidge" caught hold of a screwball that didn't screw, and subsequently launched the 724th home run of his career—a blast that skidded down a runway between the center and right field bleachers at Braves Field, and "traveled about 430 feet, one of the longest he ever struck," according to Dawson. The crowd was delirious with glee as Ruth galloped around the bases.

A double by Terry plated the two Giant runs in the sixth, which was one of only five safeties for New York off Boston starter Ed Brandt. In that inning the snowflakes began to fall, and the bandleader humorously led the ensemble with a rendition of "In The Good Ol' Summertime," which was followed by "Jingle Bells." The Braves had rapped Hubbell for nine hits, five of which came in the first inning.

"If he's going to continue hitting like that," Terry announced after the game, "you can just take my word for it that Ruth will get many a base on balls from Giant pitchers. You can't afford to take chances with that fellow."

Despite the auspicious start, Ruth had not convinced everyone that more heroics were on the way—especially Cleveland manager Walter Johnson, who in 1927 had retired as one of the greatest pitchers ever. "Yes, I'm afraid my old friend Babe Ruth is through as a player and doesn't know it," Johnson told the press after the slugger's National League entrée. "That he can be of value to the Braves on the playing field is almost too hard to believe."

One writer was a bit more confident, claiming that April showers (rainouts) would bring Ruth flowers (better performance down the road). "The Babe is determined to play to the limit of his ability for the Braves this year, but even he realizes he is not as spry as he once was. Every hour of rest that comes his way now means just so much more effort for the Braves later."

Things were buzzing in Chicago, as the Cubs prepared to open the season with their rivals, the Cardinals. John Carmichael of the *Chicago Daily News* caught up with Cuyler before the first game, while he was on his way to the dentist for a checkup. "It's going to be a fight, but I think the Cubs have as good a chance as any," Cuyler said, hurriedly. "At least I'm counting on winning. We have the best catcher, in Gabby Hartnett, in the league—in either league, for that matter. We have the best double play combination in Jurges and Herman. I see no reason why Lindstrom shouldn't continue to be a great player. Our pitching will measure up to most any club's, and our outfield ought to do."

It was a classic pitching matchup in the opener at Wrigley. Warneke looked to repeat his start of the '34 season, when he fired the two straight one-hitters. In the first gem, Adam Comorsky of the Reds singled in the ninth to deprive Warneke of a no-hitter. Warneke's following start was against Dean and the Cardinals, which Chicago won 15–2 in St. Louis. In that game, the Cubs chased Diz from the mound in the third inning, scoring six runs and subsequently taking aim at brother Paul. Chicago ended the day with 22 hits—four of which came off the bat of Klein, who pounded one of the longest home runs in the history of Sportsman's Park which cleared the right field pavilion. The overpowering victory was the Cubs' fifth straight win to open the season. They would march on to 7–0 before being beaten by the Reds—sending a message to the rest of the National League that Grimm's boys were a top-tier club.

Who else but the elder Dean would be Frisch's choice to start for the Cardinals in the first game of '35? Yes, it was none other than the man coming off a 30-win season plus two more in the World Series. "The celebrated Dizzy is due for the opening assignment against Warneke not only because he rates it, but because he probably demands it," claimed John Key of the *Tribune*. "And it is a matter of record that he customarily gets what he demands." Dean, however, had less success against the Cubs than any other team in his career; Chicago had beaten him a total of three times in '34 (nearly half of his total losses on the year), as well as in seven of the last eight contests. During the 1934 matchups, the Cubs had batted .336 as a team against Dizzy, while managing only a .252 mark against brother Paul.

So, in expectation of a light-hitting affair, the April 16 headline of the *Tribune* sports page read: "NOTE TO BATTERS: JUST SWING AND HOPE."

Early pilgrims to the park found that snow had accumulated in the first few rows of the upper deck. But even though the winter had come and gone, the Gas House Gang was still a national sensation. Thus it was the Cardinals, and not the home team, that drew the pre-game attention from the onlookers at Wrigley. "Of the 5,000 or so fans who were on the grounds at 1:30 P.M.," reported Carmichael, "most of them were collected about the Cardinal dugout. The Cubs, up at the batting cage, were unattended by any citizenry. It was the world champions who were getting the public accolade today—with a double touch for the Dean brothers." Since their rocket-like ascension the previous fall, Dizzy and Paul were fawned upon wherever they went. "Farmers come out of the distant Ozarks, and Midwest traveling salesmen arrange their itineraries to catch them," Jimmy Powers from the *New York Daily News* noted of the pair. Just as interested as the fans, the Chicago press had followed the Cardinals since they arrived at the Knickerbocker Hotel the night before. To open the season, the odds-makers had St. Louis as the favorite to win the National League flag at 7–5, with the Giants and Cubs close behind at a 5–2 wager.

As game time of three o'clock approached, the temperature reached its predicted high in the low forties (which was actually an improvement from the previous day's top mark of 26 degrees). Mayor Kelly loosened his arm to throw out the first ball, and Hartnett cleanly caught the toss. Gabby then promptly gave it to his wife, who was sitting adjacent to the mayor and Mrs. Kelly. Commissioner Landis was also present, and Ward reported that "the iron rail in front of his box was too cold to rest his chin on," in reference to the judge's usual pensive pose at a ballgame. Meanwhile, Jack Bramhall's orchestra was firing away outside the ballpark. It was the 43rd Cubs' opener for the famous conductor, as his charges tooted away in the chilly conditions. The frigid crowd of 15,500—about half the number of advance tickets that had been sold—snuggled in for a game of April baseball in the North.

Even if Dean had not been pitching, there was still concern about

Larry French (left) and Phil Cavarretta do their best to brave the lakefront weather at Wrigley Field. (Chicago Historical Society)

the Chicago offense. Nonetheless, conventional wisdom suggested it was ready to arrive. "Ballplayers subscribe to the theory that there's always a feast after a famine," Burns informed about the Cubs' recent batting woes as spring training drew to a close. "And on this basis a lot of Cubs are due to slay Dean this afternoon—Galan, Herman, Klein, and Grimm not having hit the size of their hats for days and days." Lindstrom was the only Cub regular to get a hit in both games against the White Sox in Chicago, and he would indeed be Dean's chief nemesis on this day.

As planned, the only change in the St. Louis lineup was Moore in center, the rookie who was coming off a sensational campaign at Columbus the previous summer. At a meeting held in the clubhouse the previous day, Grimm announced to the team that he was going to place himself in the lineup instead of Cavarretta, as the teenager was suffering from a sore shoulder. Therefore, Galan in left and Lindstrom at third were the only differences in the Cubs' starting slate from the end of the '34 season; ironically, the two newcomers would play the primary roles in a first-inning incident that would terrify the Cardinals.

As the teams took the field, the airwaves crackled once again with WGN's broadcast of Cubs baseball. All of the games were to follow for the season, as Phil Wrigley had promised, with the typical three o'clock games sandwiched between the shows "Palmer House Ensembles" at two and "Armchair Melodies" at five. WGN was born on June 1, 1924, when there were 100,000 operating radios in the Chicago area. Its call letters stood for "World's Greatest Newspaper," as the *Tribune* had purchased its broadcasting rights from a recently-defunct station, WDAP. Almost all of the clubs had banned broadcasting, mostly for fear of losing attendance; in Brooklyn, the sportswriters single-handedly convinced the Dodgers not to put games on the radio because they wanted no one intruding on their supposed manifest-destiny of reporting the results. Wrigley proudly provided the games through the broadcasts, and his supporters pointed out that his club in the Pacific Coast League, based in Los Angeles, annually led the loop in attendance despite transmitting all of its contests. In 1934, the Walgreens company had paid WGN $45,000 for the right to sponsor the Cubs broadcasts; the figure would rise significantly in 1935.

The wooden seats squeaked in the cold as the crowd hollered for the home team when they ran from the dugout. Warneke showed he was not affected by the elements, easily retiring the Cardinals in the top half to start the game, save a single by Frisch. When he returned to the dugout, Warneke put on a thick sheepskin jacket that was being kept warm by Cavarretta. The Cubs then went to work on Dean, against whom they were the only team in baseball with a winning record in his major league career. They didn't waste any time, as Galan led off with a single. Next up was Herman, and he laid down a beautiful bunt towards third. Pepper Martin, the strong-armed but errant-throwing third baseman for the Cardinals, pounced on it but threw wildly past Rip Collins at first as Galan went to third. Dean induced Cuyler to pop out, and next was Lindstrom. Dean was keeping one eye on Galan dancing off third when Lindstrom, seeking a chance to make an immediate impression on the Chicago faithful, jumped on a hanging curveball. He waited until the precise moment, and smacked a liner that caught Diz on his left ankle as it planted on the front end of the pitching mound. The ball rolled down the first base line as Dean hobbled to retrieve it. On his last step, before grabbing the ball, his leg gave out, and he collapsed in pain as Galan darted across home with the game's first run and Lindstrom beat Dean's pain-filled throw to first. Time was called and Dean was carried from the field by Cardinals coaches Mike Gonzales and Buzzy Wares. The Chicago fans were sorry to see Diz go, for the injury occurred "just as the Cubs were setting work on him with their usual disregard for his mastery," John Keys mourned. On quite a distasteful note, Bramhall— now inside the park with his ensemble—struck up the notes for "Happy Days Are Here Again" while Diz was flat on his back.

Less than one-half inning into the season, it looked as if the Cardinals' hopes of defending their championship had been smashed.

As Dizzy was being examined in the St. Louis locker room, his tone was apologetic. "I'm sorry I fell down," he told Wares. When clubhouse boys would appear from time to time to bring him ice, Dean would constantly ask, "How we doin'?"

Lindstrom's bat wasn't done with its carnal damage for the day. At bat in the seventh inning, a ball he hit deflected into the stands along the first base line and sent yet another person in the park out for medical care.

Tinning, the man who was a true force in the Cubs' bullpen just a year earlier, was now called by Frisch into an emergency relief role. In the second, he was greeted by Hartnett with a home run to left. Galan plated by a Herman single scored his second run in as many innings. Cub fans were being introduced to the speed that Galan brought to the basepaths, for after he was hit by a Tinning pitch, he had stolen second and bolted for third after catcher Bill DeLancey's throw sailed into center field. The Cardinals got their first run of the season in the fourth, when Jack Rothrock scored from third on dropped third strike by Hartnett with Collins batting. Hartnett complained to home plate umpire Ernest Quigley that Collins had foul-tipped the ball, but the run stood.

Tinning's initial appearance as a Cardinal ended in the third, when he was replaced by a little-known rookie named Ray Harrell. Harrell finished strongly for St. Louis, pitching the last six innings of the game, but wound up the loser as Hartnett nailed him for a two-out double in the eighth that scored Lindstrom for a 4–3 final. The two-bagger struck the top of the centerfield wall, and was actually a longer drive than his homer in the second inning. And when Grimm grounded out to Frisch in the bottom of the eighth—just before Harnett's game-winner—it was the 39th consecutive plate appearance (including spring training) in which Jolly Cholly had made an out. Warneke was hardly the pitcher that dominated the Cardinals at this time the previous year, as the Cardinals socked him for twelve hits.

"Makes me mad to lose a game like that," Frisch told the *Chicago Daily News* afterwards. "There's no point to losing them now and having to struggle all September to make up the deficit." Frisch was an interesting combination of sophistication and grit; the gardener and former Fordham chemistry major had been the rough-and-tumble secondbaseman for McGraw's great Giant teams of the '20s, and they didn't come any tougher than him.

After the game, Dean had an appointment to make a personal appearance. He was supposed to give a sales talk at a Chicago department store, but Frisch and the rest of the Cardinals' staff wouldn't let him go. Instead, he stayed at the Knickerbocker and played cards with Martin and some others. To the relief of the Cardinals, an X-Ray at Edgewater Hospital in Chicago showed no break in the ankle, but a bone bruise. Upon being told there was no fracture, Dean left the hospital without looking at the X-Ray, mentioned that he was feeling much better, and requested to Frisch that he pitch the final game of the series on Thursday. "Ol' Diz [as he often called himself] has got to do something about this," Dean brashly told the papers. "When they start hitting live drives back at me, I've got to get some revenge. Yes, sir, I'll pitch Thursday and I'll beat them. And I'll win one game against Pittsburgh, too, before I get back to St. Louis." But the team doctor warned him that the ankle would hurt even more in the coming days than it did now, and that he should rest it for at least a week.

The game between the Pirates and Reds at Crosley Field in Cincinnati was actually the high draw in the National League on Opening Day—not the expected Ruth show in Boston—as it attracted 27,400 for the event. The fine attendance occurred despite the fact it was the coldest April 16 in Cincinnati in 60 years. They saw Pittsburgh win behind veteran pitcher Waite Hoyt, 12–6.

The bad weather in Chicago was too much to overcome the following day and the next contest was pushed back to Thursday, April 18. Bad weather in Boston canceled play there as well; Ruth enjoyed the postponement, as it was his sixth wedding anniversary. He spent a quiet afternoon with his wife, opening a batch of "atta-boy" telegrams from his old Yankee teammates for his smashing performance in the inaugural. Ruth proved that not all was quiet in his social life, however, as he was seen leading songs at a piano bar the same evening.

Waiting for the Cubs in the second game of the season were "biscuits from the same damn table," as Stengel liked to refer to Paul Dean. Some claimed that Paul had even better stuff than Dizzy. They both threw more sidearm than over-the-top or even three-quarters, with Paul perhaps having only slightly less velocity but the same effective curve as his older brother. He had two nicknames, "Harpo" and "Daffy"—neither of which he appreciated very much. The former referred to the Marx brother who never spoke (just as Diz took care of all the talking to the newspapers for both Dean men) and the latter to suggest that he was from the same unpredictable stock as his brother. The press pushed both misnomers on him, which he mostly ignored. In any event, the brothers were steadfastly loyal to one another, on the field and off.

Dizzy had predicted a *minimum* total of 45 wins for the pair during the season. He had also forecasted 45 the season before, and counting the World Series, the brothers ended up with a grand total of 53. With Dizzy on the shelf, it was Paul's job to get the march started towards the goal. Nonetheless, Dizzy again announced to the press that he would be able to pitch the next day in Pittsburgh if requested by Frisch.

French was making his first start as a Cub and only 3,200 ventured into the ballpark on a day that was no warmer than the opener. Both Grimm and Frisch thought that the game should have been postponed, but Cubs officials decided an hour before game time that the contest should go on. French was looking to rebound after two rough outings against the White Sox in the preseason. As the game got underway, it looked as if Paul might receive as quick a departure as his sibling—Galan led off the Cubs' half of the first with a double. Paul, however—now a seasoned pro after his rapid growth in '34—coolly struck out Herman and got Cuyler and Lindstrom to pop out to end the threat. Paul would dance with the devil all day, allowing a total of seven hits through five innings when Medwick stepped to the plate in the top of the sixth. French had been equal to the task, permitting no Cardinals to score to that point. Jersey Joe caught hold of a low fastball, a pitch out of the strike zone (his favorite kind to hit) and shot a screamer into the left field stands for a 1–0 St. Louis lead.

The Cubs other major threat came in the eighth, when Galan was again able to get to second base with nobody out. He beat out an infield hit and then raced to second on another wild throw by Martin. But once again, his teammates failed to push him across the plate. Paul finished the game by striking out Grimm and Hartnett, the former "out for a world record for non-hitting," according to the *Tribune* after Grimm's 43rd trip to the plate without reaching base. The Cubs left seven men on base, as the game finished in just over an hour and a half. French allowed only five hits and two walks in going the distance.

The Reds arrived next at Wrigley as Dressen was still seeking to implant a new vigor in the downtrodden club. They had finished dead last in the National League in 1934, and while Dressen had ignited some spark in the players by taking over the last half of the season, his winning percentage (.379) was not much better than his predecessor's, Bob O'Farrell (.310). The club found itself 42 games behind the Cardinals after St. Louis beat them on the season's last day, as they produced two 20-game *losers* in Derringer and Si Johnson. Both pitchers had great talent, however, and Dressen knew they could be the core of a comeback for the organization.

It was Johnson's turn against the Cubs in the first game, and Grimm put himself and Klein on the bench after miserable performances in the Cubs' first two contests. It was Ladies' Day at the ballpark—5,500 women of all ages enjoyed a free ticket to the game and joined 4,100 paying customers. Johnson scattered eight hits, sending Chicago to its second straight shutout, 4–0. Only one man reached third for the Cubs, and starter Bill Lee got tagged with the loss.

Carleton won in his Cubs debut the following day, 4–3, as Demaree singled home Herman in the tenth off Bennie Frey for the victory. Chick Hafey made a costly mistake in center field, bobbling a ball off Herman's bat which allowed him to get into scoring position. Earlier, it looked as if Carleton's great effort would be spoiled, as he allowed only three singles through eight innings of work. Cincinnati suddenly fought back to tie in the ninth, capped by a two-run homer off the bat of Lew Riggs. But Warneke came to the rescue to hold the opponents in check, gaining his second win of the season. Hartnett also knocked his second homer, a seventh-inning shot, which gave Chicago a 3–0 lead. When Lindstrom doubled home Herman in the third for a 1–0 Cubs lead, it broke a string of 20 scoreless innings for Grimm's men.

The Reds took the series in grand style the next day, winning 8–4 in twelve innings as they thwarted a Cub assault in the eleventh by turning the first triple play in the majors for the year. Jurges and relief pitcher Clay Bryant had walked to start the frame, bringing Galan to the plate. Augie hit one "on the screws," but it zoomed right into Bottomley's glove at first. Bottomley tagged the bag to get Bryant and completed the coup by throwing to Alex Kampouris—who claimed to be the only Greek in the major leagues—at second to triple-off Jurges. Ready to bring home a Chicago victory with Galan's hit, Jurges had almost rounded third when he looked back in shock to see Kampouris with the ball. The Cubs had displayed gallantry earlier by scoring two runs in the ninth to tie the game at four. Derringer went the entire twelve innings for the Reds, while Roy Henshaw—pitching instead of Warneke, due to the latter's relief appearance in the previous game—started and threw 18 strikes in 33 pitches. Bryant was saddled with the loss, and Klein and Grimm were still without hits.

Meanwhile, in Pittsburgh, another injury struck the defending-champion Cardinals. Frisch, trying to tag Gus Suhr at second base in the ninth inning, opened a gash on his throwing hand when Suhr's heel spike made contact and required three stitches. It was surmised that Frisch would have to miss at least a week, and St. Louis super-sub Burgess Whitehead would have to fill the void. Frisch normally used Whitehead as a defensive replacement for Martin at third base in the late innings.

The good news for St. Louis was that Dizzy Dean returned to the mound the next day, on Easter Sunday, and Diz, yearning to truly get his campaign underway, looked like a bull in a china closet as he dominated the Pirates 6–1 in getting his first win of the year. The lone Pittsburgh run came in the second, as Arky Vaughan launched a home run over the right field wall. The crowd of 28,000—there to see the return of the great hurler—was the largest at Forbes Field in six years.

In Boston, Ruth hit his second homer in the first inning against Brooklyn, but it was the only Braves run as the Dodgers rolled 8–1. In what sounds strangely familiar to what today's fans often come to see (Barry Bonds or Sammy Sosa smacking a long one), writer Roscoe McGowen suggested that the Ruth blast was satisfying enough for the Boston faithful. "George Herman Ruth hit a home run in the first inning today and gave 20,000 fans the big thrill they came to get, giving the big fellow a grand ovation as he moved around the bases in that old familiar trot," he wrote of the Bambino's Easter present to the spectators. "With that detail happily taken care of, Casey Stengel's Dodgers went about the business of winning the contest.... That, from a Brooklyn point of view, was a fair division of the honors." With the win, the usually-hapless Dodgers continued their fine start with a 4–2 record, tied with the Reds atop the standings.

Also on that Sunday, records were tied and set. Cleveland set an American League mark by playing 41 innings in three days—a combination of a 14-inning game against the Browns, and then 14- and 13-inning contests against the Tigers. And Blondy Ryan of Philadelphia, late of the Giants, got back at his former teammates by turning five double plays, which equaled the National League mark. The Phillies also tied the league record by twisting six twin-killings in all for the day. Unfortunately, the game had to end in a 4–4 tie in the top of the eleventh inning, with the Giants threatening to take the lead. It was not rain or some other atmospheric phenomenon—the clock had struck six o'clock, and under the Pennsylvania Sabbath Law, no baseball was permitted after six on Sundays. Before the previous November, baseball was not allowed on Sundays at all, but a public referendum permitted it during the afternoon window. "In the first referendum on the Sabbath Observance law," the *Philadelphia Evening Bulletin* reported back on November 8, 1934, "which has stood since 1794, Sunday sports advocates carried this city by an overwhelming majority, 370,858 to 57,740. Voters in Pittsburgh and other populous centers throughout the state also authorized local officials to license Sunday games." John Heydler, then the president of the National League, extolled the result and said that it would "assure an equalized schedule for the first time in the 59-year history of the league."

A crowd of 50,000 was expected at the Polo Grounds two days later on April 23, when Ruth made his return to New York as the Braves played the Giants. On their way to Harlem, the Braves stopped in upstate New York to play an exhibition game against the Albany Senators. With Ruth playing first base, former Cubs slugger Hack Wilson—now in a virtually anonymous role with the Albany club—grounded a ball to the shortstop.

Lunging for the bag, Wilson clipped the back leg of Ruth and both went tumbling to the earth. The aging superstars limped off the field laughing while supporting each other, but both later returned to the game under the lax re-entry rules for the exhibition.

The actual attendance figure at Coogan's Bluff turned out to be only 47,009, but it was still the largest crowd to watch a New York opener in the National League. It had been a long time since the Babe had set foot in the Polo Grounds. "The Babe will remember the park, and probably recognize some familiar faces or voices among the rooters," predicted Kieran. "There is some academic discussion going on as to just how much help Mr. Ruth will be to the Braves in their 1935 campaign ... he was hired to hit. He has been hitting. So the big fellow is doing all right so far." The jury in the stands was split on their support of the old slugger. Interestingly, the turnstiles were not hurting across the river with the Babe's absence; the Yankees had just set a first-week attendance record of 108,664.

As the Braves took the field it was Ruth who led them, and he was met with a standing ovation. He received the same honor when he left the premises, after Mel Ott won the game with a single in the eleventh inning. Ruth was 0-for-3 on the day against the Giant's portly knuckle-baller, "Fat Freddie" Fitzsimmons. Across town in Flatbush, the lively Dodgers made their home debut in a 12–5 win against the Phillies in front of over 25,000 Brooklynites.

The Cubs had a travel day on the 22nd in preparation for a series in St. Louis. That evening, they attended a dinner that honored the Dean boys, although most of the Chicago players preferred not to be there. "Some of the Cubs attended just because they heard the food was going to be good," revealed Burns. "Few Cubs felt in the mood to pay homage to the Deans, much as they deserve it." With the day off, Grimm had considered putting the team on a later train from Chicago and skip the dinner, but decided it would be a good gesture to attend. Frisch was present, hand bandaged, and he made the main congratulatory speech to the brothers. Also in the crowd were governors Horner of Illinois, Park of Missouri, Futrell of Arkansas, and St. Louis mayor Bernard Dickmann. If not the celebrities, the Cubs at least appreciated the warmer weather—temperatures in St. Louis for the week would be in the mid-70s.

Frisch was also part of the pre-game festivities the next day, when the Cardinals' world championship banner was raised on the flag pole in centerfield while the fans welcomed their heroes home. The pole was a unique hazard for the centerfielder, because it actually rested inside the outfield wall. The crowd of 10,000—small for a home opener, but large for a weekday gathering during the Depression, even in a baseball town like St. Louis—saw Paul Dean take the hill for the Redbirds. Dean's opponent would once again be French, and the two engaged in a rematch of the chilly game in Chicago from the previous week.

The home cookin' was good for the Cards, and they jumped on French early. They scored six runs in the first three innings, which couldn't be offset by homers from the bats of Hartnett and Demaree. St. Louis fought its way to a 9–5 win and Paul's second triumph over French. Medwick was the star of the day, as he drove in four runs and made an equal number of outstanding plays in the outfield—two of which included leaping grabs to rob Klein and Jurges of hits that seemed destined for extra bases.

In a familiar pattern, the Cubs won the following day behind Warneke, 7–6 in ten innings, for Warneke's and the team's third triumph of the year. The winning run crossed the dish when Galan—on his fourth hit of the day—drove home the youngster Cavarretta, who had singled and was sacrificed to second by Hartnett. "To make an exciting game quite delicious," Burns reported, "the Cubs' winning run was scored off their favorite chump, Dizzy Dean." Indeed, Dean's streak of bad luck against Chicago continued. He was the third Cardinal pitcher of the day, and Klein rounded into form with a three-hit performance. Paul Dean was the victim the next day; like his brother, he entered unsuccessfully in relief to the tune of a 7–5 Cubs win. Paul came in for Nub Kleinke, a rookie from Fond du Lac, Wisconsin, making his major league debut after winning twenty games for Rochester (a Cardinals' farm club) in 1934. Lee was to open the game for the Cubs, but a lingering back ailment caused Grimm to go with Root at the last minute. The attendance had dipped to 2,500 and they saw Chicago take the lead in the fifth on a three-run homer by Klein, his first of the year. After a St. Louis comeback, Chicago regained the lead in the eighth when Cavarretta was driven home by a Hartnett double. The Cubs added a gift run in the ninth when Klein singled and was replaced by Cuyler as a pinch-runner, who was balked to second by pitcher Ed Heusser. Cuyler then waltzed home when a throw from Durocher at shortstop sailed into the fifth row. The win evened the Cubs' record at 4–4 as they headed for Cincinnati.

The average attendance for the second round of home openers (which occurred for seven teams over the Easter weekend) was 22,000, much better than the first group of openers the previous week. This was due, obviously, to the improved weather conditions and the boost given by the Giants-Braves/Ruth attraction in the cavernous Polo Grounds. The total for all 16 home openers was 313,430, and Landis, Frick, Harridge and the other executives were highly encouraged with the figures. They predicted that interest would continue to rise with economic conditions that were apparently improving and the approach of the first night game in Cincinnati, scheduled for May 23. It had been five years since Lee Keyser, owner of the Des Moines team in the Western League, hosted what was believed to be the first professional night game against Wichita on May 2, 1930 (two weeks earlier, the Independence, Missouri, team of the Western Association played an exhibition game at night against the House of David club). Thereafter, Keyser was so enthusiastic about night baseball that he offered to install lights in the parks of his colleagues around the league.

From his days in St. Louis, Tex Carleton had built a reputation as a fighter. He scrapped several times with Medwick, a known pugilistic commodity. He also challenged Dizzy Dean—not so much that Dean was a fighter, but because Carleton was somewhat envious of the attention given to the brothers. The consensus around the league, in any event, was that Carleton had a short fuse. As was customary in the game in that era (and to a lesser degree today), the Reds felt they could rattle such a pitcher with verbal assaults from the dugout. In Cincy, the main antagonists for Carleton actually turned out to be Reds coach George Kelly and manager Dressen. By the sixth inning with the Reds leading 2–1, the two had had enough of Carleton's mouth towards their bench, as Tex was returning the taunts sent his way. Kelly raced out to the mound and tried to tackle Carleton and both benches and bullpens emptied. Just as peace seemed to be restored, Dressen cut loose, dodged both Cub and Red players trying to impede his progress, and tackled Carleton on the mound to start the fracas all over again. As the pair—a couple of former football players (Dressen professional and Carleton collegiate)—went at it, the decision went to the Reds' manager. He landed two rights and a left on the pitcher. For his troubles, Dressen was ejected and Carleton was allowed to continue. The game marked the initial Ladies' Day in Cincinnati for the season and the 8,401 women of the 13,000 in attendance watched with mouths agape at the melee occurring on the field.

Regaining the momentum, the Cubs tied the score in the seventh when Cavarretta tripled to the right field corner and subsequently scored on a long fly ball by Hartnett. Another sacrifice fly by Lindstrom in the eighth gave them the lead, one which Carleton held for a rousing 3–2 victory. He struck out eight and allowed the same number of hits in going the distance. Umpire Bill Klem, dean of the men in blue and in charge of this game, filed a report to Ford Frick about Dressen and Carleton; the *Tribune* summarized Klem's report of the incident as a "boys will be boys" episode.

Carleton's scrap in Cincinnati wasn't the only fight making news back in the Windy City. Golden Gloves boxing was scheduled to be held in Chicago Stadium on May 22, and one of the attendants was supposed to be Benito Mussolini, the Italian dictator. It was announced on April 27 that Mussolini would have to send his regrets, but would also send eight of Italy's finest boxers to take on the Chicago Golden Gloves team. Premium tickets topped out at $3.30, and general admission was available for fifty cents.

In the second game of the series, Derringer beat the Cubs for the second time that season as he squeezed home the winning run in a 2–1 triumph over French. It was the second tough defeat for the Chicago left-hander, as he had been on the short end of the 1–0 game with Paul Dean at Wrigley Field the past week. Derringer finished with a flourish, striking out the last four batters he faced. The final game of the series was won by Lee 4–1, as Phil Wrigley and his staff drove down to Cincinnati and made it just in time for the final contest. The crowd of 29,500 at Crosley Field was actually 2,000 larger than the home opener for the Reds, and players and fans alike enjoyed the sunny warm weather. Cincinnati had named the closing act "Gene Schott Day" in honor of the Reds' rookie pitcher from Batavia, Ohio. Schott, in addition to having a namesake called Marge, would become more famous for a stunt he pulled. When Crosley Field's playing surface became submerged under 21 feet of water because of flooding in Cincinnati's lower west side in early 1937, Schott and fellow pitcher Lee Grissom rowed a boat over the outfield wall to the entertainment of onlookers.

In St. Louis, a Pittsburgh rookie by the name of Cy Blanton out-dueled Dizzy Dean to the tune of a 3–2 triumph, and sent the Cardinals into the "second division" (which, in times gone by, meant fifth place or lower out of the eight teams) with a 5–6 record. Blanton was now 3–0 on the year, which included a one-hit shutout of the Cardinals and veteran lefthander Bill Hallahan back on the 19th. Interestingly, the young phenom Blanton, a native of Shawnee, Oklahoma, was once the minor league property of the Cardinals. Blanton's stops in the St. Louis farm system included Springfield, Independence and Joplin, Missouri, Hutchinson, Kansas, and Greensboro, North Carolina. It was while pitching at St. Joseph, Missouri, that Blanton was discovered by Pirates' executive Bill Benswanger. Benswanger found out that Blanton, at that time, was the legal property of the Tulsa ballclub, a team that was part of the Pirates' system. He was immediately purchased from Tulsa and sent to Pittsburgh.

After the game, in which Dizzy was toppled by the 26-year-old Blanton, Breadon announced that no lights would be installed in Sportsman's Park, with the first after-dark game was still on the horizon for late May in Cincinnati. The Browns of the American League owned the ballpark in St. Louis, but with statements like this from Breadon, it was obvious that the tenant Cardinals ran things.

And in Philadelphia that day, Sportsman's most famous victim was making his presence known again. Earle Combs proved that he was indeed back from the head injury he sustained in St. Louis the previous summer—his grand slam gave the Yankees a 7–5 win over the A's.

Several problems—not just outfielders crashing into the concrete wall—seemed to have been surrounding the ballpark in St. Louis, highlighted by the Cardinals' poor start to the year. But those problems took a dollar-and-cents form on the 29th of April, when trade unions decided to boycott Cardinals games because of an impolitic public statement made by team captain Durocher. The crux of the matter centered on the Forest City Manufacturing Company, the dress factory where Durocher's wife was employed as a designer. The Ladies' Garment Workers Union had been on strike since January 1935, and Durocher allegedly commented to a picketer that "You are walking the streets for nothing, and while you are starving, my wife is getting as much in one day as you would in a week." The insulted picketer, Doris Smith, confronted Leo verbally—then physically—and was thereafter arrested and fined $240 for disturbing the peace. The union was outraged—not just with what they felt was unbecoming conduct by Durocher, but how his actions might undermine their cause.

Furthermore, when it was discovered that the Browns and Cardinals employed non-union ticket takers, ushers, and vendors, the unions decided to picket in front of entry areas to the ballpark. Fortunately for Breadon and the Cardinals, the team would be out of town on a road trip through the 17th of May; it was hoped by Breadon and Rickey that cooler heads would prevail in the interim, and no detrimental effect would be felt at the box office. Nonetheless, the 70,000-member union said they would organize a boycott of the Cardinals' games until a settlement was reached. The boycott, they asserted, would not only be performed by themselves but also by anyone whom they could influence. Still, it was believed that an apology from Durocher would satisfy those who were angered.

"I have nothing against the union, and don't understand why I should be singled out," Durocher stated in his defense. "To the best of my knowledge, I have done nothing to apologize for." So, Breadon and Rickey waited nervously for the team to return home.

Some thought that the fighting spirit that Carleton displayed in Cincinnati was just what the Cubs needed; as chance would have it, another brawl was in store for them back home. "There have been many who, in seeking to find what is wrong with the Cubs, have spoken of the unpopularity they enjoyed as tough guys under the direction of [former manager] Joe McCarthy," wrote Burns. "It has been said the reason the Cubs haven't been like the Cubs of pennant years is that they have become too friendly with other players in the league.

"The outbreak in Cincinnati, after which the Cubs came from behind to win, caused exponents of this theory to chortle. After yesterday's [April 29] demonstration, the theorists were shouting I-told-you-so's from the housetops." It was indeed a day which made the scrap in the Queen City look like a pillow fight.

The Pirates were in town, and the fans who saw the lengthy two-hour, forty-one-minute game (albeit typical—and almost short—by today's standards) could certainly say they got their money's worth. Things started getting hot in the fifth inning, when a double by Pittsburgh's Cookie Lavagetto scored Traynor to give the Pirates a 6–2 lead. As Jurges took the throw from the outfield and placed a tag on Cookie, the two got their spikes tangled and Lavagetto came up swinging. Both benches cleared, and at the head of the Pittsburgh charge was former Cub pitcher Guy Bush. Few in baseball came tougher than him, and he immediately sought out Joiner, one of the many people with whom the salty Bush had a problem. Before Joiner could react, he was the recipient of three right hands from Bush, one that gave Joiner a bloody nose and one that opened a separate gash on his cheek. Bush was ejected and hauled off by his teammates, and Joiner was similarly banished for nothing more than taking a beating. In defense of his pitcher, Grimm then went after Bush as he was being led from the field, but finally thought better of physically assaulting him. Jurges and Lavagetto were also banished as the umpires attempted to clear the mess.

Some claimed that the hostilities between the two teams—especially Lavagetto's rage—could be traced all the way back to spring training in 1934, when Billy Herman and Lavagetto jabbed at each other. Herman, for some reason, had been tossing Cookie's glove far into the outfield after each inning (in the day when players left their gloves on the field, rather than bringing them into the dugout). In retaliation, Lavagetto had placed used chewing tobacco inside of Herman's brand new glove. The incidents escalated into some fierce verbal attacks between the two.

The Pirate advantage swelled to 9–2 by the eighth inning, as the lone Cub runs remained the solo homers hit by Cavarretta and Lindstrom back in the fourth inning before the combat erupted. In the eighth, the Cubs strung together a few hits to make the score 9–5, but when Hartnett hit into a double play, it looked as if the rally would fall short. Woody English then launched his first home run of the season (it was also his first hit in five at-bats), and former Giant Johnny Salveson was brought in to relieve Waite Hoyt. After a couple of walks and an error by Arky Vaughan, the Cubs suddenly had the tying run as the plate. Tuck Stainback walked to make it 9–7, and that brought up Lindstrom

Billy Herman. (Chicago Historical Society and George Burke)

with a chance to make the reprisal complete. He smacked a single to tie the game, and Cuyler followed with his second hit of the inning to give Chicago a 10–9 advantage. They weren't done there, however, as the 18-year-old Cavarretta doubled to plate Lindstrom and Cuyler and make the score 12–9. Unlucky Gabby struck out next, and Hartnett became one of the very few men in history to cause all three outs in an inning. It took French, Carleton, and finally Bryant to close things out in the Pirate ninth, as they scored two to comeback to 12–11. With the tying run for Pittsburgh at second, Traynor saw strike one, fouled off strike two, and took the third pitch. Hartnett was so confident the pitch was strike three, Burns witnessed, that he had "waddled 15 feet away" by the time Umpire Klem had officially agreed and raised his arm.

It was a stirring win for the Cubs, and few in the stands or the clubhouse doubted that the inspiration came from the fighting spirit shown in the fifth inning. As suggested by their on-field aggressiveness, the Cubs had seemingly awoken from their hibernation, and the National League standings in the morning papers of May 1, 1935, looked this way:

	W	L	Pct.	GB
New York	7	3	.700	—
Brooklyn	9	4	.692	—
Chicago	8	5	.615	0.5
Cincinnati	7	7	.500	2
St. Louis	6	7	.462	3
Pittsburgh	6	8	.429	3.5
Boston	5	7	.417	3.5
Philadelphia	2	9	.182	5.5

Leading hitters for the Cubs entering May were Herman (.385), Lindstrom (.308) and Galan (.300), while Klein (.280) was starting to heat up after a slow start. In Boston, Ruth continued to hold his own, with six hits in nineteen at-bats (.316), including his two home runs. And after nine straight wins, the Giants finished the month by losing to the Dodgers in their first trip of the year to Ebbets Field. It was the worst form of a haunted house for the Giants; for although the New York collapse actually happened at the Polo Grounds in late September '34, Ebbets represented the triumph of the underdog Dodgers. The Giants did look spooked—they kicked the ball around for three errors that helped pave the way to a 12–5 win for Stengel's men. It was, according to McGowen, "Some of the most jittery Giant defensive play seen in a long time … these misplays sent the 17,000 fans into a state bordering on delirious." Brooklyn, as it always had been and would be, was a unique baseball place in the 1930s; the downtrodden, the marginalized, the underdog always barking for respect. "Brooklyn is the last frontier of baseball fiction," described Joe Williams of the *New York World-Telegram*. "the lone surviving outpost of big league romance. Across the bridge baseball is still an Olympian game, and the men who play it still gods." It was more than a full year after the insult, and the Brooklyn loyalists did not let Terry forget his fateful words at last year's spring training. After the game, firecrackers were tossed quite close to him from the upper deck. To be sure, Flatbush was still a place the Giants hated to visit.

The Night the Lights Went On

Looking to cash in on the momentum, the Cubs sent rookie Roy Henshaw to the mound in the second game of the Pirates series. He was fresh off the University of Chicago campus, and it was his first major league start. Henshaw, being quite cerebral, was known to study various writings on pitching into the early hours of the morning. Scheduled to throw for Pittsburgh was Bush, but because of the recent fight, he was slapped with a five-game suspension and $50 fine by Frick not long before the game began. Jurges also was docked $50, but his internment would last only three games. And Joiner, his face battered after the onslaught by Bush, was given his walking papers by the Cubs. He was put on a train to Los Angeles, and would pitch for the Angels of the Pacific Coast League. Henshaw was extremely effective, scattering eight hits and going the distance for a 3–0 shutout. It was the Cubs' third win in a row, and their seventh in their last eight games. Galan was the offensive star with a pair of doubles. The final game of the series was rained out and the Cubs packed up and headed to Philadelphia to take on the Phillies. It was the start of their first long trip east of the year, and they were scheduled to play three in Philly and New York, four in Boston, and three more in Brooklyn before heading back home.

The Cubs had remained relatively healthy through the first few weeks of the season, except for Demaree. Grimm ordered him to stay home from the eastern swing after a bout with pneumonia necessitated a trip to the hospital. As for the Phillies, their main casualty was their player-manager, Jimmie Wilson. After Wilson was struck in the head on a pitch by Huck Betts of Boston back on April 29th, he stayed in the hospital for four days before catching a train back to Philadelphia before the rest of his players arrived. Doctors had advised Wilson to stay on the bench for about a week before playing again, as his eye was discolored and his temple still puffed as he headed home. In New York, Yankees' skipper McCarthy—former head man of the Cubs—had been laid up at his room at the Hotel Croydon on East 86th Street with a bad case of the flu. He had not managed the club for three days and he received visits from many people, including Ruppert. "He's a very sick man," the colonel announced simply. Coach Art Fletcher had been running the club, and the Yankees were on a Midwestern swing through St. Louis, Chicago, Detroit, and Cleveland.

Rain on Saturday, May 4 nixed the opener of the Phillies series, and was transferred to June 12. It was the third straight day of non-activity for the Cubs, but that was just fine with Philadelphia. It turned into an extra day's rest for Wilson, who split time with Al Todd as the team's catcher in addition to being the manager. There had been talk in the Philadelphia papers that the Cubs and Phillies were looking to strike a trade while together, and speculation was that English would be left in town and pitcher "Fidgety Phil" Collins would go to Chicago. Grimm vehemently denied the rumors, however, and no deals were made.

The Cubs idleness then stretched to four days, as another contest with the Phillies was added to the ledger for the Cubs next trip in June, which would be a six-game series in a four-day stay. The town awash had reminded old-timers of the 1911 World Series in Philadelphia, when the A's and the Giants had to wait a full seven days to play the fourth game of their series because of inclement weather.

All hope of playing in Philly on the current trip was lost the next day; the field remained soaked, and the Cubs, with their belongings still mostly packed from when they arrived, walked to the train station three blocks away from the Baker Bowl and got on the rails to New York to give it a try with the Giants. Since he had gotten his normal rest anyway, Warneke was announced by Grimm as the starter for the opener in the Polo Grounds, with the hard-luck French being pushed back once again. It had been a week since Warneke had last thrown, in the 12–11, fight-marred contest with the Pirates. He was most frustrated, however, that he didn't bring along his numerous homemade instruments on the soggy trip to help pass the time.

The weather was no kinder up the road; the rain that held the Cubs captive in Philadelphia followed them to New York and washed them out for the sixth straight day. Even in a new city, the players were getting restless. There was nothing to do except sit around the lobby of the hotel and wait for word of a possible break in the weather. It wasn't even the current boredom that had them most despondent; it was the prospect of all the make-up games being piled up for later in the summer, with strain on the pitching staff surely to accompany the numerous doubleheaders on the horizon. While the players lazily watched the ceiling fan go round and round in the lobby, Cubs assistant coach John "Red" Corriden regaled the troops with the Biblical tale of Noah's Ark. "We won't be tied with *that* record for thirty-four more days," Corriden said cheerily. "which I figure will bring us up to the afternoon of June 10, which is a travel date between St. Louis and Philadelphia. If we get back to Philadelphia again without playing a game, then maybe we'll beat Noah's record, for they always call off Tuesday dates in Philadelphia—even if a sprinkling wagon happens to drive past the joint."

Now more curious about who this Noah fellow actually was, the players straightened up out of the lobby sofas and drew closer to Corriden. He went on to describe the man with the ark as "one the few square shooters who was tipped off about the flood, unlike Mr. Grimm."

When they finished listening to the story, the Cub players turned their attention to the news in the papers out of Boston. Although Ruth had continued to play well for the Braves, the aches and pains were starting to mount and his playing time was gradually diminishing. "He's swinging only two bats instead of his customary three when warming up," one writer noticed. And despite his batting success, Ruth had been directing displeasure at National League managers who, in recognition of the Babe's limited running ability, had been placing their first and second basemen beyond the infield dirt. The strategy was working; second basemen were throwing him out on groundballs with throws from right field.

Then, the deal that Judge Fuchs had in the works was revealed: if Ruth continued to make the turnstiles click with his play, Fuchs would be able to maintain ownership of the club, in which case he promised Bill McKechnie that he would continue on as field manager. If the Babe and the club continued to slide, Fuchs would be forced to turn over controlling interest in the team to organization vice president Charles Adams (to whom Fuchs owed considerable debts) by August 1. In such a scenario, Adams made clear, he would make McKechnie his general manager and the Babe would be given the field manager's position. "It's all up to the Babe," an unnamed source within the Braves' organization revealed. "If he plays regularly he'll save Fuch's financial skin at the expense of his own managerial hopes. If he doesn't and the club fails to pull in the money, Fuchs goes out and Ruth gets in as manager." Adams, whose interests were varied, owned a large grocery store chain, two professional hockey clubs, and the Suffolk Downs Race Track. It was predicted by most on the inside that Fuchs would be able to pay the money that was in arrears and keep the club. Such a scenario would leave Ruth out of the managerial picture indefinitely, as his playing career would fade as well.

Ruth had certainly cooled at the plate, and in a recent game with many curious onlookers, Dizzy Dean struck him out with ease—right after Dean had hit his own home run over Ruth's head in left field. "I threw that third strike as fast as I could right down his alley and he missed it by considerable," he said in typical Dean description. "Honest, I was pulling for him to slap it into the bleachers. But that don't mean anything, him strikin' out—he's still the Babe, and if you've got any brains you don't trifle with him twice." The writers were not surprised with Dean's skill at the plate, which he had demonstrated many times before. "Dizzy of the Deans is out to help himself with the war club any time he ambles to the plate," noticed John Kieran.

"Mizzle and drizzle. Everybody is going crazy," Burns reported for the *Tribune* from New York, as he and the Cubs sat inactive for the seventh consecutive day on May 7. "And John Corriden, who coached at third base in the good old days when the Cubs played baseball, sobs because he knows that in a week the players will have forgotten all the secret signs it took him all spring to teach them." (Not to mention tales from the book of Genesis). Trying to keep his sense of humor, Grimm sought the silver lining amidst the storm. "Looks like we came to town under a cloud," he told the press. "Maybe it'll help get rid of all those dust storms I'm hearing about." Grimm, like Warneke, was looking for some kind of cheap instrument to play—his beloved banjo was back home in Chicago as well.

Perhaps having the worst time of all was the Cubs' traveling secretary Bob Lewis, whose plans for the team's accommodations and transportation seemed to change hourly. He had contingency train tickets for the team to Boston scheduled at three in the morning the next day; the Cubs had never left for anywhere at three in the morning, but needed to in the event that the Braves could schedule a doubleheader. Unfortunately, an ominous weather report for Boston (a region previously spared from the storms) suggested that the Cubs could possibly be idle for yet another four days. "Everything's a bargain for the fans," Burns announced, advertising the numerous two-game days coming up later in the year. And as bad as things had been for the Cubs, they were equally troubling for the Philadelphia. The Phillies hadn't played since April 29, and were saddled with eleven unscheduled doubleheaders in the future due to the rain.

The Phillies were keeping busy off the field, though. They finally found a taker for Phil Collins in the Cardinals, as the St. Louis ballclub—in what was described in the Philadelphia papers as a "straight cash transaction"—paid Phils president Gerald Nugent an undisclosed sum for the six-year veteran. Despite not being released to the press, the figure was believed to be between $7,500 and $10,000. In addition to trimming a sickly budget, it was part of a youth movement by the Phillies, who were looking to develop some younger pitchers for 1936. "We have only until May 15 to cut the squad," Nugent explained, "and Jimmie [Wilson] jumped at the first favorable opportunity to let Collins go. We still have ten pitchers left and the sale brings us right down to the National League limit of twenty-three, which we are forced to reach by the 15th." The 31-year-old Collins lived in Chicago, and reportedly would have welcomed a deal that would have sent him to the Cubs. The deal certainly fortified the St. Louis staff, but even before the move, Dizzy Dean was back to his old soothsaying tricks, predicting that the Cardinals would win a hundred games and that the favored Giants had no chance in catching them. The biggest threat to the Redbirds, according to Ol' Diz? "The Cubs, for sure," he claimed. "I'm figuring them very low when I say Warneke will win 22, Carleton and French 18 each, Root 15 and young Henshaw ten. That makes them second." Some, however, were less than impressed with the Deans' start to the 1935 season—such as Kieran. "Dizzy was set back a couple of times and Paul lost a game," he pointed out. "The way Dizzy was talking through the winter, the family wasn't to lose a game until along in July when maybe an outfielder would lose a close one in the sun."

Kieran righted himself quickly, adding, "Still, Manager Frisch probably will hold onto the Dean boys for a while. They may round into shape."

The first day in Gotham turned out to be a wash, too, as the Cardinals and Dodgers were rained out in Brooklyn as well.

At Ebbets Field, it was to be the first battle between Paul Dean and the Stengelmen since Paul threw a no-hitter against the Dodgers the previous September. It was the second game of a doubleheader that day, and Paul's famous brother garnered a complete game win in the first tilt. Following the feat, the celebratory St. Louis locker room produced one of Dizzy's most cited phrases, when he found his brother through the cheers and told him, "Gee Paul—you shoulda told me you were gonna throw a no-hitter. If I'd a-known, I would've thrown one, too!" So baseball fans around the New York area would have to wait another day—until Wednesday, May 8—before another stab could be taken at playing some games. The weather conditions weren't unique to the Eastern Seaboard, however. "More bargain day attractions were added to the rapidly mounting list," mourned James Dawson, "by the rain which prevented all of yesterday's [May 7] games in the National League and one in the American League ... although the fan profits from the alarming number of postponements the early season has brought, the teams involved are not so fortunate. Idle days have extended over such a protracted period now that the athletes are chomping on the bit." For the players, it was again down to the lobby for an update, back to the room, down to the lobby, back to the room ... and the story dragged on and on. Encouragingly, Grimm and Terry received favorable forecasts for the 8th, and it looked as if the games would finally take place. The games couldn't start soon enough for the Cubs, who sent two unbeaten pitchers—Warneke (3–0) and Lee (2–0)—into the twin bill.

The first games back from the torrents of nature for the Cubs were important on many fronts; not just simply from the perspective of playing again, but also from the standpoint of the standings. Although being early in the season, the two games were symbolic to both the Giants and the Cubs, to see if the latter, marching into the vaunted Polo Grounds, proved to belong with the former and the Cardinals in the National League race. As a result of the ever-changing schedule, it was believed by local writers to be the first time ever that a "western" club had played a doubleheader in its first trip of the season east.

It was indeed a grand day to play, as "welcome sunshine flooded the park," according to the *New York Daily News*. A total of 24,785 paying customers settled in for the two games.

Not showing any rust on his part, Cuyler gave the Cubs the lead in the second with a solo home run, which reached the upper deck in right field—an estimated 295 feet away. But the Giants quickly snuck back ahead, as Joe Moore returned the favor with a two-run shot in the bottom of the third. Parmelee, who Cuyler had long called "the toughest pitcher in the National League" was the starter for New York. Parmelee could handle the bat, too, and he almost drove his counterpart Warneke to centerfield along with the ball, smashing a run-scoring single in the fourth for a 3–1 New York lead. This score proved to be the final, as Parmelee allowed only three hits in being the only Giants hurler to beat Warneke in the last two years. In 1934, he had also knocked the Cub ace out of the game with his bat when he bashed a grand slam. The other two Cub safeties in the first game were singles off the bat of Jurges, and Grimm's hopes of the big hitters making a resounding return to the lineup were dashed.

Terry had Hubbell available to seal off the nightcap, but instead chose to go with rookie Clydell Castleman. The Cubs had a chance to score in the second inning when Hartnett drove a ball over Hank Leiber's head into the vast pasture in center field at the Polo Grounds. It might have been an inside-the-park home run, but Gabby was out of breath by the time he pulled into third. He was left stranded as the Giants pitched around Jurges to get to Lee, who was called out on strikes. In the first game, Leiber had robbed Hartnett of an extra-base hit in the fourth inning in almost the exact same spot, leaping against the fence for a fine catch. New York produced all the runs they needed in the third, as Ott came to the plate with Terry and Moore on base. The high-stepping slugger blasted a long home run to right, a blow that hit the façade of the roof and gave New York a 3–0 advantage. It was Ott's eighth homer on the year, which put him on top in the National League in the category and also gave him the league lead in hits, passing Terry. The Cubs gained a run in the sixth with Lindstrom's second homer of the year, a line drive into the left field seats. Their other score came in the next frame, as reserve catcher Wally Stephenson was sent to the plate for Lee. The crowd in New York gave some polite applause, for when the name "Stephenson" was announced, they figured it was the former Cub great Riggs Stephenson making an appearance. Young Stephenson looked like old Stephenson as he drove the ball to right-center for a triple and crossed home when Bartell booted a grounder off the bat of Galan. But that was it for Chicago, as the rookie Castleman was nearly as effective as Parmelee in Game One. He scattered five Cub hits in going the distance for a 6–2 decision and the doubleheader sweep, rivaling Blanton for honors as the top rookie hurler in the National League. "Look at the build on him," Terry said of Castleman. "He's all power. He's got grand control. He is the fastest man on my staff on some days."

The Giants had yet to lose at home on the year; Terry's men had registered nine wins and two darkness-shortened ties at the Polo Grounds.

And the entertainment was great in the other borough as well, as the Dodgers beat Paul Dean and the Cardinals in twelve innings, 3–2, when Danny Taylor and Joe Stripp knocked back-to-back doubles for the win. Work in practice had apparently paid off for the Brooklyn players; for Taylor, the team's hitting-cage magistrate, had been collecting fines of 25 cents for each extra swing taken in batting practice. To date, he had collected $28 and was looking to throw a huge team party in the near future with the revenue. The big hits in the game came off Hallahan, who along with Ed Heusser had relieved Paul. In the third, Dean was pitching to Taylor when he protested a ball called by umpire Dolly Stark. When Dean tried to show Stark up by turning his back and tossing his glove in the air, Stark rushed the mound to inform Paul that he was ejected. Dizzy then ran from the dugout to protect his brother from further penalty, and he and Frisch had to restrain Paul for eight minutes before he left the field and play was resumed.

It was then off to Boston. The Cubs took on the Braves (the only team in the National League in 1934 against whom Chicago had a losing record) with more drama unfolding behind the scenes. Just a couple of days after taking a "wait-and-see" attitude to the future of the club's ownership, Judge Fuchs followed suit on the local predictions. He announced that he planned to buy the remaining shares from Adams and his partner, V.C. Wetmore, on August 1. In addition, Fuchs revealed that he had been offered a new spot on the Massachusetts bench, but refused the assignment to continue his interests in baseball. The decision sealed McKechnie's and Ruth's fates, as McKechnie would remain manager as promised and Ruth's career remained indefinite. There had been more speculation in recent days that the end was near for the Babe, as sickness had hampered his ability to play regularly. The papers had also implied that there was a growing dislike between Ruth and Fuchs, but the Babe categorically denied it. "The press report that there is dissension in the relationship between Judge Fuchs and myself is unfounded," Ruth said. "Judge Fuchs has kept faith with me. I have been trying to play ball with the most severe cold when I should have been in bed.

"If I had been in better health I know I would have done greater justice to him and the ball club. After my treatments are concluded I will demonstrate that I am far from through, in spite of those who have been impatient and unfair in their predictions."

When the Cubs came to town, it was the first time since the "Called Shot" World Series of 1932 that Ruth had faced the Chicago Nationals. Looking forward on the schedule, the Babe licked his chops about coming to Wrigley. "I'd pay half my salary if I could bat in this dump all the time," he was quoted as saying before the 1932 World Series began.

Yet another legend nearing the end of his career was on the Boston roster, and in the opener against the Cubs, he made his first game appearance in nearly two years. Walter "Rabbit" Maranville, an infielder who had broken into the big leagues with the Braves in 1912, was inserted in the fourth inning when secondbaseman Les Mallon was ejected. His entry set a National League record—it was the 23rd season in which Maranville had appeared. The 43-year-old had missed all of the 1934 season with a broken leg, but had played 143 games at second base in '33 at the age of 41. The 1935 campaign would be the Rabbit's last; he played in 23 games to wrap up a career that included over 2,600 hits and nearly 300 stolen bases. In June of 1925, Maranville had been named the manager of the Cubs—and a few nights later, the fun-loving Rabbit and three Cub players were thrown in a New York City jail on disorderly conduct charges.

It was up to Carleton to get the club back on track, and he relished the opportunity. Since leaving St. Louis, he wanted to prove that he could be a leader on a pitching staff, and this certainly was an occasion when Grimm needed him to step up. Recent history was on Tex's side, too, as he had beaten the Braves six times in as many tries during the Cardinals' championship run in 1934. Carleton would be getting his first shot at Ruth, and interestingly, reports surfaced during the week about possible improprieties surrounding the Carleton-Malone "trade" in the off-season in conjunction with Ruth's acquisition by the Braves. Some other owners had heard, from "underground but reliable" sources, that a gentlemen's deal had been struck among the National League clubs and the Yankees. In losing Ruth to the Braves (and thus giving the National League a large gate attraction), it was claimed that the Yankees received Malone after he passed waivers—for that purpose—by all of the NL clubs. This was vehemently denied by the owners and Ford Frick, and the matter was considered closed.

So Carleton, an indirect pawn in the drama, took the hill as the Babe batted third in the Braves' order, which had been his typical slot during the season when healthy. Coming up in the first inning against the Cubs, there was no pointing to the bleachers (unlike the last time he faced the North Siders), alleged or otherwise. He tapped slowly to Cavarretta at first, who was most intriguing to the East Coast fans because of his youth and his sudden supplanting of Grimm at the position. The Cubs opened the scoring in the fourth when Galan doubled, was sacrificed to third by Herman, and sent home on a fly ball by Klein. The home crowd cheered wildly when Maranville laced a single past the head of Carleton in the eighth, but it was only the fourth hit off Tex and he and the Cubs had maintained a 2–0 lead. The next batter was Ruth, and along with the Rabbit, the fans hoped for game-saving heroics from the old pair. Ruth caught hold of a ball and propelled it over Klein's head in right, appearing to have launched a typical Babe four-bagger. But Klein executed a quick 180-degree turn, dashed back to the wall, and made the grab as he jumped into the barrier. The catch deflated Boston's hopes, and the Cubs plated three more runs in the ninth. Wally Berger's home run in the bottom half spoiled Carleton's shutout as he finished off a 5–1 success.

Meanwhile, back in Chicago, the White Sox lost at home for the first time on the season, ending a string of eleven straight victories at Comiskey Park with a 10–1 loss to the Red Sox. The defeat also pushed the Pale Hose from first place in the American League, as Cleveland ascended to the top spot with an 11–4 record; the Sox were now a few percentage points behind at 13–5. In other American League news out of Chicago, the apartment of AL umpire Clarence "Brick" Owens at 531 Fullerton was robbed, the bandits making off with $1,000 worth of coats and diamonds. Ironically, all of the goods stolen had been gifts given to Owens by the American League for his services.

Like the other clubs around the league, the Cubs were under an obligation to pare down the roster to 23 players by May 15. To this end, and in a move stunning to the Cubs' fans, Grimm decided, on May 10, to put himself on the "Voluntarily Retired" list. It was not an irrevocable decision; Grimm could decide by the 15th to make another transaction to meet the player limit. Burns, however, was quite sure that the die had been cast. "Though Charlie has five days to change his mind," he wrote, "and he has been known to change his mind as many as 25 times in five days, it is believed that today's decision will stick." It did not come as a complete surprise, however, on two counts: one, that Grimm had not rebounded from his 0-for-43 start to the season (including spring training), which had him considering retirement as soon as a suitable replacement was found for him. This point led to the second reason, which was the emergence of Cavarretta as an able heir—despite being only 18 years old. Cavarretta's confidence received a boost by the decision as well, for it showed that he had proven himself to the organization. After going 0-for-8 in the first two games of the season, Grimm had exclusively turned over the first baseman's job to Cavy and no one else was there to challenge the youngster. "The young Italian is not murdering the ball as yet, but is playing first base with aplomb and a surety that has not weakened the Cubs' defensive strength," wrote Carmichael in the *Daily News* about Cavarretta on May 11. "In fifteen games he has made one error of commission and none of omission." Grimm's sacrifice of his own roster spot meant that he could keep the rest of the club intact. He could return when the rosters were expanded on September 1 or after waiting the mandatory sixty days after placing one's self on the retirement list.

Perhaps the Cubbies recognized French's need to get a win in the second game of the series, as they jumped on Boston starter Bob Smith for five runs in the first inning. Though French would not be around at the end, Root finished strongly for him—French was the victor in a 14–7 decision in which Lindstrom pounded out four hits and Herman, Klein, and Cuyler had three each. Included in Klein's barrage was a 450-foot home run in the seventh inning, "one of the longest ever seen here according to old settlers," the *Tribune* revealed. Warneke made it a clean sweep in the finale with an easy 4–1 win, which was also his current record for the season. Warneke also contributed four singles, driving in the Cubs' first run in the fifth inning and their last one in the eighth. Tempers were boiling over on the struggling Braves ballclub, as McKechnie was tossed by umpire Cy Pfirman in the fifth when he protested the call made when Hartnett picked Berger off third base. And Ruth, looking weaker and weaker, struck out both times he came to the plate and was replaced in the sixth by reserve outfielder Joe Mowry.

The hot streak continued in a three-game set at Brooklyn, as Chicago took the first two behind Lee and Carleton for five in a row. Root lost the last game of the series, and the team finished the eastern swing with a 5–3 mark on May 15. The Dodgers acquired pitcher George Earnshaw that week from the White Sox for $7,500 to augment the staff, but the 35-year-old did not arrive in time to face the Cubs. Earnshaw had been off to a slow start for the Sox, whose removal helped them reduce to their roster limit. And in Detroit on the 15th, Lou Gehrig stole home for the fifteenth and final time of his career as the Yankees shut out the Tigers behind Charlie "Red" Ruffing, 4–0. And the Giants, though maintaining a fast start, suffered a serious setback when All-Star infielder Travis Jackson broke his thumb in pre-game practice but still played against the Pirates. When X-rays after the game revealed the fracture, it was imagined that Jackson would miss at least a month. Terry had trimmed the New York roster to the required 23 men at the last minute. Adolfo Luque voluntarily retired and was named a coach with the team. In addition, utilityman Joe Malay had to be sent to Fort Worth of the Texas League to arrive at the correct number.

As the Braves commenced a "western" trip (i.e., Chicago, Cincinnati, and St. Louis), word leaked that Ruth may be putting himself on the list for the voluntarily retired as well. While denying that his relationship with Judge Fuchs had waned, it was evident that the situation between Ruth and McKechnie had become broken beyond repair. While neither man would say it publicly, a gulf of mistrust had formed between the two. Ruth also denied that he planned on quitting immediately, but he did admit that, health-wise, he did not feel up to par. "I will say that I have not been myself a whole lot so far this spring," he told the papers, "and unless I am able to shake the present cold that has severely handicapped me for several weeks, there is a possibility that I will ask to be put on the voluntarily retired list … one result [of the cold] is that my eyes have been giving me a good deal of trouble. They water considerably and my failure to hit up to my past records undoubtedly is due to this ailment."

As for his desire to manage, Ruth made it clear that he had no intention to push McKechnie off the mountain. "You won't see me taking somebody's job away from him," he cautioned. "When my playing days are over, it will be time enough to make public what my future will be."

For the Cubs, the energetic run through the East had them within striking distance of the top spot as they headed back home. The standings:

	W	L	Pct.	GB
New York	15	6	.714	—
Brooklyn	15	9	.625	1.5
Chicago	13	8	.619	2
St. Louis	13	11	.542	3.5
Pittsburgh	13	13	.500	4.5
Cincinnati	9	13	.409	6.5
Boston	6	14	.300	8.5
Philadelphia	5	15	.250	9.5

Arky Vaughan of the Pirates was the league's leading hitter at .404, while Hartnett (.325) and Galan (.307) led the Cubs. As a team at .277, Chicago was well outdistancing the next club, Pittsburgh, which was hitting at .268. Ott's eight home runs continued to stand up in that category in the league, as he and Terry were being forced to shoulder the offensive load for New York due to more injuries on the club. In addition to Jackson, Bartell was felled on May 18 as he busted an ankle at Cincinnati. Terry had him sent back to New York for examinations, and the diagnosis revealed not only a bad sprain but also a chip of the bone. Doctors told the club they didn't expect Bartell to play for another three weeks. Secondbaseman Hughie Critz was suffering from a bad skin infection on his hand and was unable to grip the ball. With all the casualties, Ott moved in from the outfield to play third, the veteran Koenig fulfilled his promise as a valuable backup at short, and rookie Al Cuccinello—brother of crosstown infielder Tony of the Dodgers—handled the chores at second.

The first stop for Ruth on what some considered his western farewell tour was St. Louis and he had to split the marquee with the on-going union protest against Durocher and the Cardinals. Breadon nervously awaited the gate totals in his office, but was relatively pleased when seeing the attendance results of the first game back for the Cardinals—a 7–1 win for the Braves in which Ruth went 1-for-4 with a single in the fifth inning. "Yesterday, our first home game since the boycott was called, we drew 2,700 paid fans and 1,200 'knot-hole' boys," Breadon reported. "That's an average weekday crowd here. Whether the boycott will cut attendance if it continues, I don't know.

"There's nothing we can do about the Durocher case. The club is not involved in any way, and we certainly need Leo at shortstop. What are we going to do about it? Nothing. We're just going right along, doing the best we can." Breadon obviously ignored the Ruth factor in the attendance, which under normal circumstances, would have made it more than the average weekday crowd that it was. The boycott had grown to include the Bartenders Benevolent Union, the Protective League, and the Ticket-Takers and Ushers Union in addition to Durocher's original nemesis, the International Ladies' Garment Workers Union. William Brandt, the secretary of the Central Trades and Labor Union, which oversaw them all, stated that the boycott would continue until a settlement was reached with Durocher and the club. Brandt had authorized the boycott after the union's 70,000-plus members voted to approve the action. The reason the bartenders, ticket-takers, and ushers were involved was that Breadon refused to recognize their unions in the first place.

And it wasn't a convincing performance by Ruth, as far as the papers were concerned, towards his efforts to remain as a player. "A more or less vain attempt to convince the baseball world that he isn't through," one St. Louis writer remarked.

Back home at Wrigley, French got the homestand off to a good start on May 17 with a 5–0 shutout of the Phillies. The win pulled the Cubs to within one game of the first place Giants, and Lindstrom missed his first game of the year due to a death in his family. That day, Phil Wrigley unveiled his new plan for Ladies' Days at the ball park. Fridays had always meant free admission for women at Wrigley Field (until the practice was stopped in the 1970s due to complaints from women's groups), and Wrigley announced that the practice would continue. However, as opposed to sending out 20,000 tickets at once, the club would now deliver them in groups of 2–3,000 only. In other cost-cutting measures, Chicago police that day also had broken up what was becoming known as the "Wrigley Field Parking Racket." In what sounds like a story from modern times (with prorated prices, of course), several young men and boys had been charging fans coming to the park twenty-five cents to "watch" their cars for them. "Motorists refusing to pay tribute found their tires deflated," the *Tribune* noticed. In some cases, cars with keys left in them were missing at the end of the day, even some of those that were supposedly being "watched." The issue came to a head when fans were complaining of the slow traffic along Addison Street, which was caused by the youths standing literally in the middle of the street in an effort to guide cars into their lots—again, something that rings remarkably familiar of today.

But the traffic was unusually heavy coming in from the north on this day. Up in Evanston, Ohio State University track star Jesse Owens was making his Chicago-area debut in a quadrangular meet at Northwestern University against Northwestern, the University of Wisconsin, and the University of Chicago. The Buckeyes cruised to victory behind Owens' four first place finishes, one of which set a world record (220-yard low hurdles in 22.9 seconds—and only the third time he had ever competed in the event) and another that tied a world record (100-yard dash in 9.4 seconds). In addition, the other two firsts by Owens, only a sophomore, set Northwestern meet records (220 yards in 20.7 seconds, and 25 feet, $5^1/_{16}$ inches in the broad (long) jump). He would soon return to his summer job for income, working the warm months at a Cleveland gas station to support himself and his family. By the time the 1935 track season was through, Owens competed in 52 events and won a medal every time—44 firsts, six seconds, and two thirds.

May 18 was the beginning of one the great forgotten stories in baseball of the 1930s. The starting pitcher for the Phillies was William "Bucky" Walters, who in the off-season was getting the idea to scrap his third base job with Philadelphia and become a pitcher full time. He had played the hot corner since entering professional baseball in 1930, and played sparingly with the Braves and Red Sox before joining the Phillies in the middle of the 1934 season. Although he batted a career high of .260 in finishing off the season with Philadelphia, he found his true calling on the mound. Manager Wilson agreed, and starting with the 1935 campaign, Walters would go on to win 198 games and fire 42 shutouts with the Phillies, Reds, and Braves before retiring in 1950.

Walters' very first shutout came this day, as he scattered seven Cub hits over ten innings in a 1–0 whitewash. Having Walters pitch obviously allowed Wilson to put another competent bat in the lineup—the pitcher accounted for two of the team's hits off the Cubs' starter Henshaw. Walters batted seventh in the lineup, an atypical sight for the pitcher, and the former Giant shortstop Blondy Ryan got the dubious nine hole. Although the rain had ended, Chicago had not escaped bad weather entirely; the unusually cold temperatures for mid–May had encouraged only 7,000 spectators to come to the park. And another small gathering of 8,500 saw the home team drop the last game of the series 3–2 on a three-run homer by light-hitting second baseman Lou Chiozza and Phillies' starter Syl Johnson striking out ten. Galan tried to rally the team with a two-out triple in the ninth, but was left stranded when Herman popped up to third baseman Mickey Haslin to end the game. In addition to some untimely hitting, sloppy defense seemed to be costing the Cubs a few games lately, including this one, as noticed by Arch Ward. "No fewer than eight times this season, counting spring training," he claimed. "Bill Jurges and Augie Galan, who are roommates and pals, have let pop flies drop between them for base hits, much to the distress of certain Cub pitchers." Grimm heard about Ward's comments, and told him he thought the miscommunication was due to Galan's "squeaky" voice, which Jurges could not hear when being called off by the outfielder.

Next, it was the Braves coming north from St. Louis, and in Chicago, like everywhere else, fans were hoping to get one last glimpse of the Babe. Rumors continued to swirl about his impending retirement—perhaps any day now—and crowds formed at every stop the Boston players made on the road. While the Phillies and Cubs were finishing up their series, advance word had reached Chicago that Ruth had a 50/50 chance of playing in the opener the next day at Wrigley. Still battling sickness, Ruth said that it would be a "game time decision" and he would not be able to tell before then. Despite the Braves losing the last game in St. Louis 7–3 to Dizzy Dean, Ruth showed enough energy to make a diving catch off the bat of Rip Collins in the first inning. His bat continued to suffer, though, as he went 0-for-4 against Dean and a cumulative 1-for-10 in the series. St. Louis papers reported after the game that Bobo Newsom of the Browns—Dean's old pal in local furniture marketing—was sold by the struggling franchise to the Washington Senators for $50,000. Later in the month, the Browns would accrue more cash with the sale of second baseman Oscar Melillo to the Red Sox while also acquiring outfielder Moose Solters from Boston in the deal. Hornsby was quickly gaining respect around baseball in yet another skill—that of trading. Not only had he gathered over $100,000 for the club among the deals, but he also had decidedly-better players as well. In addition, he had been offered $35,000 from the Indians for catcher Rollie Hemsley, and $20,000 more from the Tigers if he wanted to ship Solters off again.

Ironically, the day after the Melillo deal was done (May 28), Newsom had his kneecap broken after being struck by a line drive off the bat of Cleveland's Earl Averill in the third inning. At the time of the injury, Newsom wasn't aware of its severity and he managed to finish the game, but, it ended his season. Even more ironically, another liner off Averill's bat would ultimately accelerate the dissipation of Dizzy Dean's career; in the 1937 All-Star Game, his smash struck and broke Dean's big toe on his right foot, which later caused an alteration of his delivery after a premature comeback and consequently an irreversible sore arm.

Also on May 19, Gus Suhr of the Pirates injured his hand in a game against the Dodgers in Pittsburgh, and Traynor had to take his place at first base. The following day, Traynor placed Suhr in the outfield for one inning, in part to keep alive a consecutive-games streak for Suhr that would ultimately reach 822 straight contests, a National League record at the time.

Ruth did indeed take the field for the first game of the series in Chicago and lasted a total of five innings. He caught four fly balls—three of them off the bat of Galan—and he was replaced by Hal Lee. At the plate, Ruth was walked by Bill Lee his first time up, popped up to Herman on his second trip, and ended his day by grounding into a double play. His teammates didn't fare much better, as the Cub twirler Bill Lee held Boston to six hits in a 5–0 shutout, powered by a 3-for-4 day by the rising Cavarretta. And only 6,000 showed up to the contest, suggesting that word was getting around that the Babe Road Show wasn't all it was cracked up to be.

Things looked to continue that way the next day, as Carleton was not only undefeated on the season (3–0) but also had beaten the Braves in his last seven tries. In fact, one had to go back to September 9, 1933, to find the last time that Tex had lost to Boston. But all good things must come to an end, as did Carleton's string of success on this day. He held the Bostonians in check through four innings, and so did his counterpart to the Cubs, Fred Frankhouse. The Braves then stuck Carleton for two runs in the fifth and

Bill Lee, who in 1935 emerged as an ace of the Cubs' pitching staff in just his second major league season. (Chicago Historical Society and George Burke)

the righthander returned to the hill for the sixth frame. Leading off the inning was Ruth, again hitless on the day to that point, and he began to receive jeers from the Chicago fans reminiscent of his 1932 World Series spectacle. Inspired by this or something else, he mimicked his glowing act from that October by launching a long home run to right field for a 3–0 Braves lead—his third home run of the year (and first in over a month) and his first hit in five games against the Cubs in 1935. "It was of the best Ruthian brand," Burns reported in the *Tribune* for Chicagoans unable to be at Wrigley that day. "It hit a building across Sheffield Avenue. Randy Moore also knocked a homer in the same inning, but it didn't make nearly as much mileage as the Babe's." Fabian Kowalik and Hugh Casey came to the rescue for Carleton, and Frankhouse limited the Cubs to one run, created by Hartnett and Cavarretta pairing doubles together in the seventh. There was mounting concern about Cuyler and Klein, as the normally-slugging outfielders were batting .232 and .235, respectively, with only two home runs each. While most attributed Klein's lack of power to his adjustment to the more distant walls of Wrigley than those of the Baker Bowl in Philadelphia, people were not sure what was wrong with the talented Cuyler.

"Well, give me a lot of pitching and just a little hitting and I'll never complain," Grimm offered to the press. "Cuyler's in one of his slumps. I know he'll come out, but in the meanwhile we miss those blows. Chuck Klein hasn't got his eye on the ball yet. When he starts banging out some long ones, we'll be better off."

Therefore, with the Braves in town, the Cubs' management paid more attention to star outfielder Berger than to Ruth; it was rumored that the Braves were putting Berger on the selling block to save some cash, and several pennant-contending teams had taken interest. He was a proven commodity, hitting 34 home runs, driving in 121, and batting .298 for Boston in 1934. "Hence the scramble for Berger, a scramble in which the Cubs undoubtedly will back their checkbook against the field any time," Carmichael wrote in his column. "Berger would be a valuable acquisition to any team in the league, particularly to the Cubs, who have an outfield in name only."

Who the Cubs would send east in a trade, in addition to a bag full of cash, was open to conjecture as far as Carmichael was concerned. "Money for Berger ... though the Braves could use the cash ... would hardly suffice in itself. A player or players would have to go along with the dough and they would have to be of such ability as not to give McKechnie the notion he was being fleeced."

Apparently no help was needed in St. Louis, as an incident the same day proved that the Gas House fire still burned. Dizzy Dean had to be escorted by police from the field at Sportsman's Park after a "near riot broke out," according to the Associated Press. Brother Paul was pitching against the Phillies, and after sending a high, hard one toward the head of Chiozza in the fourth inning, Philadelphia third base coach Hans Lobert starting giving Paul some flak. As Dizzy raced to the scene, Paul got ready to square off with Lobert, but umpires and other players were able to separate them. Peace seemed to be restored until things exploded again in the fifth. Paul nailed Al Todd with a pitch, and Todd immediately dropped his bat and headed for the mound. Todd, considered one of the stronger players in the league, had replaced Jimmie Wilson as the catcher after Wilson had removed himself in the first inning with an injury. Dizzy again rushed to his brother's aid, and was followed once again by players from both dugouts. Dizzy and Todd exchanged a few blows, and the cops dragged the elder Dean off the field to the cheers of the scant crowd of 2,500. It was suggested that the hostilities between Diz and Todd went all the way back to their days together in the Texas League in 1930. Lobert was booted the next inning by umpire Charles Rigler, after he protested about Cardinals' hitter Spud Davis stepping out of the batter's box.

As the Phillies left town for Cincinnati to play major league baseball's first night game, the team made it clear they had enough of the Deans and their attitude. "It's getting so that you can't get a hit off either of the Deans without getting beaned the next time up," Wilson told the press as he got on the train. "They started throwing at us down south [in St. Louis], and Paul resumed it in Philadelphia less than two weeks ago and pulled the same stuff Tuesday.

"Well, the Phils have declared war on the Deans, and there's no foolin' about it."

May 22. The day had finally come for boxing fans of Chicago, as the eight-match competition between the boys from the city and Italy was set to get underway at the fabulous Chicago Stadium. The Italian pugilists were described by Ward as "the strongest fighters ever sent out of Europe, according to those who have seen them in training." Ward also reminded readers that, since the *Tribune* had started sponsoring international matches with the Chicago Golden Gloves team in 1931, no collection of pugs from Chi-town had ever been defeated. Boxers from France, Ireland, and Poland had all been previously beaten by the Chicago club, and Germany was only able to score a 4–4 draw with a decidedly weak Chicago team in 1932. As vaunted as the 1935 Italian outfit was, the powerful Chicago boys were still the favorites—at least locally. "It will take Europe's strongest and bravest to conquer them," Ward concluded.

Confidence remained high on the Italian side as well. "If France, Poland, and Ireland, who were defeated by your Golden Glovers, were pleased with their treatment, we will be doubly so," said one of the boxers, Francesco Campello, about the hospitality shown to the foreigners by Chicagoans. "Because, you know, we intend to win. Other countries could praise Chicago's sportsmanship even in defeat. Think then how we can praise it in victory." Then, pausing to reflect, and then adjusting his tone to one more serious, he added, "It is almost unbelievable the cordiality Chicago has extended to us. When I am in France, England, or Germany it is different. Chicago makes me feel I am at home. None of us ever shall forget it."

At 9:45 P.M. on May 22, "the house lights went out" at the Stadium (as Chicago Bulls' radio announcer Jim Durham would always say even years later at the location, when the Bulls' starters were introduced before a game to basketball fans at the arena). A spotlight then shone on the center entrance at the north side of the building, parallel to Warren Avenue, as the eight Italians made their way towards ring under moderate applause. Upon coming through the ropes, they stood at attention towards the east, in honor of their country. Then, as the massive Stadium organ blared out "The Stars and Stripes Forever," the Americans made their appearance. Wild cheers from the 23,256 spectators rocked the building in what Ward described as "the biggest emotional spree Chicago has enjoyed in years." A total of 104 radio stations were set to broadcast the updates throughout the country, in addition to countless scribes at their typewriters and newsmen manning their film. The Italians drew first blood, winning the 112- and 119-pound matches. As the punches flew throughout the night, the hometown kids of Chicago gained the upper hand and landed victories in five of the last six bouts against the Italians, which gave them the overall triumph as well.

Boxing fans then turned their eyes to June 13, when Jimmy Braddock would take on Max Baer for the heavyweight title. Soon after, on June 25, the Franco-American rivalry would be quickly renewed as Louis prepared to oppose Carnera in Yankee Stadium in another heavyweight bout.

Walter Johnson, who earlier had made public his doubt of Ruth's abilities, soon found himself living in a glass house. A rift had arisen between Johnson and his third baseman, Willie Kamm, and the problem had reached the point where Judge Landis was asked to step in by Indians president Alva Bradley, but he refused. "It falls upon the manager as a practical proposition to act in cases where even honest differences arise," Landis decided. "This is so because the responsibility is his and with the responsibility must go the authority." Kamm, a 35-year-old veteran of the American League since 1923, had played in only six games by May 23, on which date Johnson announced that he was "sending Kamm home for the good of the ballclub." Was Kamm suspended, the local press wanted to know? "No, I'm simply giving him a railroad ticket to Cleveland," Johnson said as the club was playing the A's in Philadelphia. "What happens to him there is up to Bradley and [general manager] Billy Evans." The main problem, Johnson said, was that many of the younger players were complaining to him about Kamm, saying that Kamm was "cramping their style" by offering too much advice. Kamm admitted that he had tried to help the rookies, but that this was the first he had heard negatively of the matter. A week later, Bradley gave Kamm his release, but left open the possibility of Kamm returning to the organization as a scout if he found no other jobs in baseball that appealed to him. This scenario played out, as Kamm did eventually assume scouting duties with Cleveland.

Johnson's own job consequently became tenuous. The incident suggested to some that he was losing control of the team; one Cleveland reporter complained that, so far on the year, Indian players had been incapacitated due to "sunburn, rabbit bites, and stomach aches," among other minor ailments. Rumors even persisted that the end had already come for Johnson. "No, I haven't resigned, but they can fire me if they will," he said defiantly to the media about his bosses, while the Indians were in Chicago to face the White Sox. "Yet, I'd do exactly the same things over again a thousand times because, deep in my heart, I know I'm right. I have no regrets." When Bradley was asked if fault had been found in an investigation by Landis, what would have been done? "There is only one thing I could do, and that would be to dismiss Johnson and hire a new manager." It had been reported earlier by the Associated Press that Bradley—had Landis found that Johnson overstepped his authority as manager—would have dismissed Johnson immediately.

Although John Carmichael thought that both Ruth and night baseball would be good for the National League, he made it clear that he felt the latter wouldn't be necessary if the former was in better shape. "For one thing, the National League has Babe Ruth. For another, it has night baseball. There would have been a day, no doubt, when if the National League had Ruth it wouldn't need the added stimulant of evening baseball. But Ruth's sun is apparently near setting, and to give him a hand in balancing the books the league will try its own hand at experimenting with some midsummer night's dreams." Night baseball in the big leagues was the brainchild of Larry MacPhail, the innovative general manager of the Reds, who was always looking for a new challenge. One of MacPhail's first moves was to convince progressive Cincinnati businessman Powel Crosley, Jr., a man who MacPhail knew would be open to the possibility of night baseball, to buy the team in 1934. Crosley was immediately excited about the idea and encouraged MacPhail to pursue it.

To be sure, baseball after dark was not a new thing in professional baseball as a whole; all teams in the International, Pacific Coast, Western, and Middle Atlantic leagues hosted night ball in 1934, along with several teams in the American Association and the Texas and Southern Leagues after Keyser's experiment in Des Moines in 1930. Resembling transport trucks coming from a sawmill, long vehicles carrying portable light standards traveled with a few black teams so that multiple games could be played in place to place on a given day. But for the time being, only Cincinnati in the major leagues had permission to hold seven night games in 1935, one against each of the other National League clubs (the visiting clubs had the right to refuse to play at night, but all accepted the invitation). Strangely ominous to those walking by on Western and Findlay avenues, arc lights were installed at Crosley Field for a cost of $50,000. Upon ignition, club officials promised lighting "twice as brilliant as that of any other ballpark in the country." Not a large feat, since most of the minor league and semi-pro fields using lights were of very poor quality. The Reds brass also claimed that the lights, installed by the Cincinnati Gas and Electric Company under the advisement of General Electric, were six times as powerful as any lit football stadium in the nation—and that one could read the newspaper four blocks away from the center of the field.

"I was opposed to the idea at first," a transformed Frick said of night baseball. "I have now been forced to admit its possibilities."

Rainy and cold weather pushed the scheduled night game back twenty-four hours, and the original date of May 23 became May 24 as the day for all to remember. A total of 12,000 fans had purchased advance tickets for the event, while Reds officials were hoping for the capacity of 30,000, or perhaps more, by game time. When it was all ready to go, the actual assembly was in the 25,000 range with just over 19,422 entering as paid customers.

The Reds and Phillies were granted an extra-long batting practice before the game, which was followed by a merry bugle corps and fireworks show. Some of the nation's greatest radio stations got set to broadcast the action, including WGN, WLW from Cincinnati, WOR in New York, and Detroit's CKLW. The stations were also the founding partners in the Mutual Broadcasting System, which would preview the growth of network broadcasting in the years to come. Walter "Red" Barber, in only his second season of broadcasting major league baseball, was at the micro-phone. He had arrived in Cincinnati the previous season after being at WRUF in Gainesville, Florida, where he had worked for four years. The magical hour was at hand, and when President Roosevelt pressed the gold-plated telegraph key from the White House, it gave MacPhail the signal to throw the switch. A total of 958,000 watts shining from eight 100-foot towers lit up southwestern Cincinnati in a glorious blaze.

Interestingly, it was discovered by the sportswriters that, for most of the players on the field, it had been their first night game—amateur or professional. That being the case, most of the writers expected it to be an error-filled ballgame and consequently would hasten the call for night baseball in the majors to be short-lived. "Night baseball seems to be on its way out," no less an authority than *The Sporting News* had predicted the previous year, "and its mourners will probably be few." In leading the Reds, however, Dressen made his best effort to piece together a lineup with the most night game experience. The Reds and Phillies disappointed the foes of the whole idea, as they played a mistake-free game. While cam-eramen and the fans had a tough time adjusting their sights, the Reds rode Derringer and a scant four hits home to a 2–1 win. Not only were there no errors, but the glove work bordered on magnificent. "The the-ory that the players cannot see the ball well under the lights was shot to pieces by the staging of some of the finest defensive plays seen here this season," reported Jack Ryder, who covered the Reds for the *Cincinnati Enquirer*. However, a poll taken of fans soon after the game by another Cincinnati newspaper showed a general disinterest in games after dark.

How did Jimmie Wilson feel about night baseball coming to the major leagues, and his team being on the short end of the first such con-test? "It's all right, if the fans want it. But I'd rather play in the daytime."

Earlier that afternoon, it was announced that players for the All-Star Game would be chosen by the manager of each side instead of giving the fans the vote through the newspapers. It was feared that the vote was becoming a popularity contest with undeserving players carried by repu-tation getting the nod. In the 1934 game, when Hubbell made a mock-ery of the American League's best hitters, Lefty Grove was chosen by the public to start the game for the AL, even though he had hardly pitched to that point in the season due to an operation he needed on his ailing pitching arm. Therefore, Frisch from the Cardinals and Cochrane from the Tigers would get recommendations from the other managers in their respective leagues, but the two men would have the final say on the twenty players to represent each side on July 8 in Cleveland. The final rosters were due in the league offices by June 28, and one of the conditions was that each team in the majors had to be represented by at least one of its players.

The Giants had arrived in Chicago on May 23, after the last game with the Braves—and perhaps Chicagoans' last chance to see Ruth—was washed away in bad weather. The Cubs found themselves with a record of 15–11, three-and-a-half games behind New York for first place and just a half game from second place, occupied by Brooklyn. The Cubs had spoiled their chance to do some damage in New York, and they were swept by the Giants in the doubleheader back on May 8 that followed the long, rain-induced layoff. It was the opinion of many, including Burns, that the Cubs were not driving in enough runs. "Vice President Grimm will be juggling his lineup in a desperate attempt to get somebody who can use a bat in the so-called power spots," he wrote of the team's lack of punch. Hartnett and Lindstrom led the club with three home runs each, Klein and Cuyler still had their two, and English, Demaree and Cavarretta added one apiece for a team grand total of thirteen. The changes for the Giants opener would be drastic indeed: Klein and Lindstrom found themselves on the bench, while Cuyler was dropped from fifth to seventh in the batting order. Hartnett, the only starter hitting over .300, was put in the third slot as Cuyler switched with him. Lindstrom had been taking time away from Hack at third, but that was about to change.

"Hack's light has been hidden under a bushel most of the time this year," Burns added. "But Stan has happily kept to his knitting, possibly anticipating the decision that Grimm made yesterday [to give him a shot at the permanent third base job]."

Day games went on as usual at Wrigley Field on May 24, as they would for the next 53 years. The Cubs had taken the first game of the series with the Giants the previous day, with Charlie Root coming to the rescue of French in the fifth inning. Larry had left the bases loaded with nobody out, but Root permitted only a sacrifice fly thereafter to stem the tide. Later, Cuyler stepped in the batter's box in the bottom of the eighth with the game tied. A fierce wind had been swirling off Lake Michigan all day, and routine pop flies fluttered like knuckleballs to create a sea of misadventures for fielders. Cuyler got hold of a pitch from Chagnon and sliced the ball through the gusts towards Leiber in center field. Leiber darted one way, then another, and then another, trying to follow the zig-zagging path of the ball. Both he and the ball fell to the earth, and the speedy Cuyler circled the bases for an inside-the-park home run and a Cub lead. Subsequent hits by Jurges and Galan, with a sacrifice bunt by Root in between, provided an insurance run in a 6–4 win. Root credited his newfound strength to a recent shipment of fresh chewing tobacco that had arrived for him.

The Giants wasted no time righting themselves in the second game, chasing Henshaw in the first inning on five runs en route to 20 total hits and a 13–0 shellacking. The loss dropped the Cubs into third place behind Brooklyn, as momentum from the previous day had been squandered as well. They had no chance against Schumacher, as the thrower allowed only four Cub hits, three of which were singles. "Rarely has he performed any better than he did today," Drebinger asserted about "Prince Hal." The bad news mounted for Chicago—it was learned that Bartell, Jackson, and Critz were all recovering from their injuries sooner than expected, and might re-join the New York club within a week. Bryant and Casey had mopped up the mess after Henshaw made his quick exit. Warneke and Hubbell were slated to pitch the finale, which Burns predicted "should prove a happy contrast from the flop which 6,200 paid to witness yesterday."

With nice weather and the stellar pitching matchup, the crowd doubled to nearly 12,000. The Giants scored the initial go-ahead run in the fourth after umpire Cy Pfirman reversed a decision he had made. With Cuccinello on second, Hartnett thought he had picked the runner off with a quick throw. Pfirman called Cuccinello out, but apparently didn't see Herman drop the ball and the Giants stormed out of the dugout in protest. Pfirman consulted with fellow man-in-blue Rigler, and together decided that Cuccinello was safe. The Cubs had to return to the field from their premature trip to the dugout, as they thought the original play had ended the inning. It was as if all nine of them had been connected by a bungee cord to Pfirman, as they turned and sprang back at him. With Cuccinello restored to his place, Moore promptly singled him home for a 2–1 lead. Once again, it was a paltry offensive showing for the Cubs, who managed only four hits—only one more than the number of errors they committed—as the Giants escaped Chicago with another win, 3–2. Warneke had beaten the Giants in two out of every three decisions in his career to that point (14–7), but poor breaks cost him on this day. The Giants had a solid record of 6–3 on their current road trip, and were beginning to entrench themselves atop the standings.

That was Saturday, May 25, and newspapers around the country were still buzzing about the nocturnal affair at Cincinnati when an even bigger bombshell hit the next afternoon. It was what National League fans had been waiting to see, even more exciting than the idea of games being played after dark. The great one, who was hanging on to his uniform by its last threads, gave those in the stands at Forbes Field in Pittsburgh a dose of yesteryear. George Herman Ruth took his place in the batter's box and clouted a first-inning home run off Pirates pitcher Red Lucas, scoring himself and Urbanski. When he hit another long one off Guy Bush in the third inning, the crowd worked itself into a frenzy as he took his steps around the basepaths as slow as ever. He was greeted by teammate Les Mallon at home plate, whom he drove in and who had waited patiently to greet him. The Pittsburgh crowd stomped and cheered for Ruth when he appeared again in the fifth, and lined a single to score Mallon again for his fifth RBI on the day. His final at-bat came in the seventh, and the house knew that something special was yet to come. Ruth caught hold of another fastball from Bush, generated one more mighty cut from his massive frame, and crushed a ball to right-center that was surreal. It kept going and going, drifting into the bright sky. It ultimately cleared the pavilion—the first ball ever to get over the roof at the Pittsburgh park. The ball then took one hop off the street and rolled into Schenley Park off in the distance. "Baseball men said it was the longest drive ever made at Forbes Field," one writer reported. It would be the last home run for the greatest hitter of them all, number 714, the *coup de grace* for the old knight. When the ball was finally found, it was unofficially estimated by a Forbes Field employee to have landed 600 feet from home plate.

Ruth was replaced in right field by Mowry, as the applause thundered one more time. The hapless Braves still could not win the game, as Traynor homered for his own club in an 11–7 Pirates win.

Then, just as suddenly as he had discovered the fountain of youth, the signs were turning negative. It had not been reported on a wide scale how Ruth's condition had deteriorated even further—not just physically, but in his own confidence. The day after his great performance, he struck out three times against the Reds' Si Johnson in Cincinnati in what had been proclaimed as "Babe Ruth Day." A paid crowd of 24,360—larger than the paying total at the night game and Crosley Field's third largest on the year—saw his other at-bat result in a weak pop foul. The following day, the 27th, he was limited to appearing as a pinch hitter in the ninth inning and drew a walk. Then the most damaging blow came the next afternoon, when in the fourth inning, he fell on the infamous "terrace" in left field at Crosley Field, a gradual rise that met the outfield wall four feet higher than the rest of the playing surface. He had been going after a fly ball and his legs tangled beneath him. It was believed that he removed himself from the game more out of embarrassment than injury; Ruth knew that his body wasn't performing up to his standards.

The team went on to Philadelphia, where in the opener of the series—also proclaimed "Babe Ruth Day"—he was held hitless in four plate appearances against Orville Jorgens of the Phillies. The next day on the calendar was Thursday, May 30, (Memorial Day—the holiday was always placed on this date; it wasn't until 1971 that Congress decided it should be the last Monday in May), and the fans at the Baker Bowl were looking forward to a full day of enjoying the supposedly rejuvenated Babe with a doubleheader on tap between the two teams.

Ruth was in the starting lineup for game one of the series. In taking his first swing of the day, he gounded out to Dolph Camilli at first after an offering from pitcher Jim Bivin. It would be Bivin's only year in the big leagues, which he would finish with a 2–9 record and a 5.79 ERA in 162 innings. After limping though the first base bag and being called out, Ruth once again removed himself from the game. Nobody realized it at the time, but it was his last appearance in the major leagues.

Back in Chicago, it seemed as if there were eight other teams picking at the Cubs during the season: the seven actual clubs and Mother Nature. Just when Bill Lee was trying to get the team back on track beating the Dodgers at Wrigley, the rains came again—this time washing out two consecutive days. It was the ninth and tenth postponements for Chicago in the month of May, and a total of twelve for the year. Two more doubleheaders with Brooklyn needed to be arranged for later in the season, and the team could do nothing but board the train for Pittsburgh in preparation for a series with the Pirates beginning on May 29. Carleton had waited two days in Chicago to face Mungo, the Dodgers' ace, but Tex was put on hold and instead was slated to duel Ralph Birkofer in the Steel City. But alas, the Alleghenies were getting another bath as well, and the Cubs spent their first day there looking for a restaurant instead of the ballpark. "If you think we seem to be so tired of it all, you're wrong," informed Burns as he lazily pecked at his typewriter from his Pittsburgh hotel room. "We are studying to be writers on crop prospects ... since March 1 we have done practically nothing but come in out of the rain, from the shores of California to the rockribbed coast of Massachusetts."

So more free time was at hand for the club, and one thing Grimm didn't need was more time to worry about his offense. A doubleheader was to be played the following day, Thursday, May 30 (the day Ruth took his last swing). Cholly wasn't so jolly, for if the club did not start swinging the bats with more effectiveness, harsh changes were going to be made. The first, he announced to the team, would be making the players arrive at the park an hour earlier for extra work. Batting practice for the Cubs at Wrigley Field normally began at eleven, but would start at ten on the next homestand if the fellows didn't shape up.

It was obvious that the Pittsburgh fans (as well as Grimm) were anxious to see something, as a paid crowd of 40,430 on the holiday—the biggest National League gathering ever in Pittsburgh history, aside from a couple of World Series games—came to see Blanton hurl against Carleton. Blanton was still the sensation of the league, a prodigy that appeared destined to cement himself in the Pirates' rotation for years to come. Before this date, he had pitched nine straight complete games, so it was much to his, the Pirates' and the Cubs' surprise when he was chased in the fifth inning after giving up ten hits and staking Chicago to a 5–2 lead. But Tex had the day's shortest outing, as Henshaw came in during the first inning after four consecutive hits off Carleton and scored the game's first two runs. Bush was strong in relief for Pittsburgh, striking out ten Cubs in going the rest of the way. But Henshaw was his equal, riding out the duration for a 6–4 triumph for the visitors. The bats didn't come through for the Cubs in the encore, as Lucas—described by Burns disgustedly as a "broken down pinch hitter"—flashed enough stuff to post a 4–1 win for Pittsburgh and a split of the day. After a one-game reprieve, the bats went back into hiding as Chicago managed only six widely-scattered hits. In beating French, Lucas would have earned a shutout if not for back-to-back errors by Suhr and Vaughan in the second inning.

Earlier in the day, the umpires had been worried that old hostilities would flare between the two teams, but the only scraps were found in the stands. A few rowdy spectators had to be banished for the public safety, but the men on the field acted amiably towards one another.

Big crowds had been expected all around baseball for the workers' day off, and sound weather was finally showing up and doubleheaders were scheduled at most of the big league stadiums. At 10:30 that morning, the ticket windows were opened at the Polo Grounds for the twin bill between the Giants and the Dodgers. The Dodgers were holding on to third place, and had assumed a new role as a force in the standings. "We don't have to prove we're in the league," Stengel claimed. "We proved that last fall." He was referring, of course, to his mighty revenge against Terry and his comment from the spring. Word was spreading around town about the "Bums," and people were beginning to take notice—such as Kieran. "When they get a spot of pitching, the Dodgers are as tough as any tribe on the National League range," he warned. "Thus Mr. Casey Stengel, who once wore a sparrow under his cap, now has the pennant bee buzzing in his bonnet."

What about the Giants, Casey? "Oh yes, they've still got to prove they can win the pennant," he admitted. "And confidentially, I think they'll do that."

All of the reserved seats for the match up had been sold out two weeks in advance, and now the remaining 45,000 general admission and bleacher seats were available to the public. Waves of humanity gradually drifted inside the big horseshoe, and by the first pitch of game one at 1:30, 63,943 had squeezed together as the rafters creaked in protest. It was the most people to ever watch a baseball game in the National League, besting by over a thousand a doubleheader at the Polo Grounds the previous September when Dean and the Cardinals had raided the city. An additional 15,000 hopefuls were turned away at 1:00, a half-hour before the game, and police even had to chase away onlookers who were loitering on the train tracks which were suspended over and beyond the outfield walls. Among the throng inside the park was a sizable contingent from Brooklyn, of course, and they carried a Flatbush tradition up to Harlem by lighting several firecrackers in the stands (even in the midst of the dense crowd). It was the last bit of excitement for Dodger fans on the afternoon, however. "A great day for Terry and his men," celebrated McGowen in his article in the *Times*, as the Giants swept the games 8–3 and 6–0 to solidify their hold on first place and drop the Dodgers from third all the way to fifth. Ott hammered his ninth home run in the first game, still the most in the league and one more than teammate Moore. New York Mayor Fiorello LaGuardia smiled from ear to ear as he witnessed the blast, which went deep into the right field horizon of the yard.

The Cardinals were also re-asserting themselves in the first division, as they swept two games in St. Louis against the Reds in front of 18,000 at Sportsman's Park. Medwick contributed seven hits in the doubleheader win, including three doubles and a triple in the first contest. The win in game two was Dizzy Dean's sixth, and it leap-frogged the Cardinals over the Cubs into second place as May came to a close. Over 207,000 people made the turnstiles click on Memorial Day, certainly a happy sound for the league. And even though opinion polls had implied a general disfavor toward night games, on May 31 the Reds played the Pirates in another before 18,119 paid spectators—not terribly less than the paying crowd in the inaugural back on May 24—won by Pittsburgh, 4–1. The newspapers listed the standings on May 31 as follows:

	W	L	Pct.	GB
New York	24	9	.727	—
St. Louis	21	15	.583	4.5
Chicago	18	14	.563	5.5
Pittsburgh	22	19	.537	6
Brooklyn	19	17	.528	6.5
Cincinnati	16	19	.457	9
Boston	11	22	.333	13
Philadelphia	9	25	.265	14.5

The Yankees had taken over the top spot in the American League with a doubleheader sweep of the Senators on Memorial Day. Things had not been going well for the defending-champion Tigers; Cochrane, normally a happy-go-lucky guy off the field, was transferring his sour mood from behind the plate to the open street. "No sparkling raiment, no twinkle in his eye," noticed Kieran, as most of the fun in baseball looked to have departed for Cochrane. "The bones in his sun-baked face seem to be coming through his skin."

Confidence was high in Harlem, as the Giants were gaining strength with each passing day. They looked like a pack of federal agents on a manhunt, on a search-and-destroy mission for numerous foes, especially the Cardinals—the team that unsuspectingly had knocked them off the perch the previous year. Terry had long disposed of his fear of the Deans—or so it sounded. He pointed out that the brothers had so many endorsement deals that their minds couldn't be on baseball; they didn't have the time, what with their "pitches" for cereal, comic books, chewing gum, school notebooks, and countless other things. "You can see that," Terry said, in referring to the growing number of distractions for Dizzy. "Look at the way they [advertising suitors] swarm around him. He won't win twenty-five games this year—he won't have the time."

To which Dean replied, "He better mind his own business. He ain't so hot. He's having trouble himself." Perhaps only Dizzy knew what that trouble was, because the balance sheet showed Terry hitting .340 and his club in first place.

Alabama Gets Out, and So Does the Babe

It was now official: Babe Ruth was leaving the game.

The sudden setting of the final curtain on the game's greatest player set off a chain of strange events related to his departure. Early in the day on Sunday, June 2, Ruth announced to the press that he was quitting the Braves. Two hours later, it was learned that Judge Fuchs granted Ruth his unconditional release, which Fuchs thought would pre-empt the Babe's move. Upon hearing the news that he had been "fired," Ruth then told the papers that he was not retiring, but rather going on a "60-day vacation" after which he would entertain offers from any other interested clubs. He did make it perfectly clear that he was through with the Braves, and especially with Fuchs. "Unconditional?" Ruth smirked at the description of his walking papers. "That's great—I was going to ask for it anyway. Getting the release means I'm not going on the voluntarily-retired list." Things had quickly soured between the two men, with Ruth calling Fuchs a "double-crosser" and Fuchs labeling the Babe as an "imbecile" before the day was over. Walking off the field as batting practice began, Ruth's uniform had hardly been disturbed with sweat when he met reporters in the locker room. He led them into the trainer's office, and closed the door behind them.

"Fellows, you all know me, and we're pals," he began, as the sportswriters nervously began scratching with their pencils. "It hurts like hell to say what I'm going to tell you. I'm through with this club. Understand me, I'm not through with baseball if I can get anything worthwhile to do. I love the game. I still want to be a manager. But I positively won't be associated any longer with this man Fuchs.

"I thought in Pittsburgh, when I hit those three home runs, everything would be nice, but I was hurt in Cincinnati and couldn't get going again. Fuchs was nasty about it, but I was hurt and that's all there was to it. Tomorrow I've got to go to Haverhill [Massachusetts] with the club to play an exhibition game. Here's what happened: I got an invitation to go to New York to attend a celebration on the arrival of that French boat—you know the one I mean—the—yeah, that's it—the *Normandie*. I thought it would be a great thing for baseball, the publicity and all.

"I called up Fuchs and told him I thought it would be a great thing. He snarled at me and said, 'Nothing doing. You get out in uniform with the club for that exhibition game.' What do you think of that? I can't work with that kind of guy."

The Babe was then asked if he would return if Fuchs left the Braves. "You bet I'll come back. Just watch me."

Was Ruth concerned that he was losing his positions as vice president and assistant manager, in addition to his roster spot as a player, constituting a combined package that was to pay him $30,000?

"Vice president? Ha! Fuchs can take that vice presidency and—well, he knows what he can do with it. What the hell did it ever mean, anyway? It was a joke, a gag. I don't want another damn thing from him, the dirty double-crosser. I don't want to have anything more to do with a man like that. He says he loves baseball. Yeah, he does—like hell he does."

Ruth again denied rumors that there was hostility between himself and McKechnie. "I've been getting along fine with Bill," he said. "He knows me now, and he knows that I'm a gentleman. I wasn't trying to steal his job like a lot of people said. Bill is my pal." Ironically, as Ruth was wrapping up his comments a few moments later, McKechnie and Maranville knocked on the door, entered the room, and wished him well in his future pursuits. "Sorry to see you go, Babe," McKechnie said, extending his hand.

Fuchs believed that Ruth was up to his old carousing tricks. "Manager Bill McKechnie told me he couldn't have Ruth come and go as he pleased," Fuchs said, telling his side to the Boston writers. "He couldn't expect to have any discipline on his team under those conditions. You notice that as soon as Ruth made his announcement the Braves returned to their old form and starting winning [they had beaten the Giants on June 2]." Fuchs also said he didn't care if the Babe came and played in the exhibition game at Haverhill—but it wouldn't be in a *Braves* uniform.

It had been revealed that Ruth privately threatened Fuchs back on May 12 that he would leave the team, but little more was made out of it.

Then, amazingly, McKechnie turned face and claimed publicly that

Ruth was the reason for the downfall of the organization. "While his right hand was still tingling from Babe Ruth's hearty farewell handshake," one writer tried to understand. "McKechnie laid out for Fuchs the reasons that Ruth was 'a detriment to the ball club' and that this, a team without Ruth, was the moment they had awaited for the process of rebuilding."

McKechnie made his true feelings quite clear. "I must state publicly, in justice to the action of Judge Fuchs with reference to Babe Ruth, that on Friday and Saturday of last week I pointed out to Judge Fuchs that the main trouble with the ball club was that it was not able to properly function with Babe Ruth playing in the outfield," he said simply.

"Unless Judge Fuchs could convince Ruth to retire," he continued, "I would be unable to get any real discipline or revive spirit as manifested by the club previous to the acquisition of Ruth."

As it turned out, Ruth did not make the trip to Haverhill, but rather went to New York. The Braves did play the exhibition game, beating the Pawtucket Industrial League All-Stars 9–4 in front of 2,000 fans. The Haverhill Kiwanis had made plans for the game for over five months, and thought that the presence of Ruth would be a great financial and emotional boost for the community. In the end, it turned out to be just a normal exhibition. Even with Ruth in New York and nothing much to do, it was reported that no other clubs expressed an immediate interest in him. "There was no stampede for his services after he filed his ultimatum with the New York Yankees at the end of last season," the Associated Press pointed out. "And there will be less demand for him now in light of what happened this spring."

Frick, a longtime friend of Ruth's, wasn't very optimistic either. "I'd like to see the big fellow get a break," he said. "But I do not know of any further opportunity for him now, at least in the National League. He failed to take advantage of the opportunity given him in Boston. There was every reason for him to buckle down, keep himself in shape, obey orders and make a real future for himself there, but he didn't do it." Public opinion had turned on Ruth, to be sure. Not long afterwards, it was reported in the Boston papers that a local businessman had looked to turn a profit by purchasing 500 Braves tickets, having Ruth autograph them, and then re-selling them. When Ruth refused, the man went to Fuchs and said that Ruth had actually refused autographs to children he knew. Even though the man's story was ultimately dismissed, such talk was wrongly circulating around town and hurting Ruth's reputation unfairly. To help make amends in the public eye, Ruth later announced that he would return to Boston on July 9 to play in a charity game. Upon leaving the Braves, Ruth didn't even bother to pick up his last paycheck for about $1,500. "Fuchs can use it to buy cigars," Big George said in one last crack.

It was ten years ago to the day that his career had been resurrected. Ruth was reinstated June 2, 1925, by Yankees' manager Miller Huggins after a two-month suspension.

Ruth left the game with 76 records, including the most appearances in the World Series—three times with the Red Sox, and seven with the Yankees.

Also on June 2, pitcher George Pipgras was released by the Boston Red Sox, and he soon became an American League umpire. Interestingly, Fred Marberry would do the same thing two weeks later after being let go by the Tigers (although Marberry would make a brief comeback in 1936 with the Giants and the Senators).

Heading into June, many of the key Cub bats were still looking to warm up. Almost all of the accusing fingers pointed at the outfielders, and with good reason. Cuyler's batting average was down to .231; Stainback, .235; Demaree, .237; and the mighty Klein, who many thought was bringing a pennant with him from Philadelphia when the 1934 season began, was hovering at a weak .232 and the former Triple Crown winner still only had two home runs to his credit. Lindstrom (.253) and Herman (.254) weren't exactly tearing it up either, and Grimm continued to juggle the lineup to find a solution. "The fact that Red Lucas held them to six hits in the second game [at Pittsburgh]," Burns continued to lament, "threw Vice President Grimm right back into a sweat over the pitiful feebleness of the gents who actually get negotiable money for hitting. When Augie Galan dropped to .297 on Thursday [May 30], Grimm found himself without a .300 outfielder in a troupe of five."

If the hitting was to turn around soon, there was a tall order to start the month. In town for the Cubs' first home doubleheader of the year were the Cardinals, and Wrigley's largest crowd so far on the year—20,693—was on hand. The Cubs grabbed the lead on Paul Dean in the second inning of the first game, as Hartnett slammed a long home run, his fourth of the year, over the wall in left. The score bounced back and forth from there, and Dean and Warneke battled into extra innings. In the eleventh, the Cubs looked to be headed to victory when Galan opened the inning with a triple to straightaway center field. Dean, now cool with experience in his second year, intentionally walked Herman and Hack to load the bases for Hartnett, who promptly bounced into a doubleplay. Dean won the game for himself in the twelfth, when he doubled to start the frame and ultimately scored on a sacrifice fly by Frisch, leading to a 4–3 final in favor of St. Louis.

Defense was the doom in the second game for Chicago, as three first-inning errors by Hack, Galan, and starting pitcher Lee contributed to three runs and an eventual 4–1 win for the Redbirds. As a result of the sweep, the Cubs were now in a virtual tie for fifth place with Brooklyn, but still dangled by three percentage points above the Dodgers and the "second division."

The balance was soon reduced to a single percentage point, as Carleton got wild and helped blow a 5–1 lead to his former team in the ninth inning the next game. With one out, he issued his seventh walk to Rothrock after Martin had reached on a single. The Cardinals had been chirping on plate umpire Ziggy Sears, after Herman had walked in the fifth on a couple of close pitches. The game was held up for five minutes as Sears removed his mask, sauntered over to the Cards' dugout, and exchanged words with Frisch, Durocher, and the usual St. Louis provocateurs.

Charley Gelbert then proved he was back from his leg injury by beating out an infield hit to load the bases. Medwick singled home a run, at which point Grimm summoned French to face Rip Collins, who, although being a switch-hitter, was weaker from the right side in facing the Larry the lefty—at least, that was Cholly's strategy. Collins—a close contestant for Dizzy Dean in the chase for the 1934 National League Most Valuable Player Award—fouled off the first pitch, and then caught hold of the next from French for a grand slam homer and a 6–5 Cardinal lead as the "boos" were hurled down from the grandstand. To secure the win, Frisch brought in Diz in the bottom half to relieve Hallahan, and then retired Lindstrom and Klein with Hartnett the potential tying run left stranded at second. Afterwards, most of Burns' anger was directed at French, who he thought was failing as "the answer to the Cubs' fifteen-year prayer for an able lefthander." The Cubs were 7–12 at home since their trip to the east coast, said to be a stretch of bad home ball not seen since the "pre–McCarthy days," as the *Tribune* alluded to the successful years of the late–1920s.

Consolation was found in the finale, as Root ended the Cubs' four-game slide—and stopped the Cardinals six-game winning streak—with a fine outing for a 6–2 win on June 3. In addition to quieting the St. Louis bats, Root used his own for two hits, including a home run with two out in the bottom of the eighth for the final Chicago run. Hack got his first homer, and Cuyler showed signs of life, too, as he added two hits and was robbed of a probable triple in the sixth on a great running catch by Terry Moore.

When the Cardinals railed east from Chicago for Pittsburgh, things were again at a boiling point between Dizzy Dean and several of his team-mates. The main enemy had been Medwick; the two had never been fond of each other, and they had to be separated more than once during the game on June 3. Dean accused Medwick of loafing on a play in the third inning when a pop fly to left field fell for a hit, which led to four Pirates runs and an eventual 9–5 win for Pittsburgh. Dean, noticeably disgusted with the perceived lack of effort on Medwick's part, made it clear to his other teammates that *he* would stop giving any effort as well. Diz then started yelling in protest at Umpire Rigler, who was well-familiar with the Cardinal temper; just last year, he swung his mask during an argu-ment with Frisch and opened a gash on the chin of the St. Louis skipper (this occurred in a game with the Cubs, when Hartnett blatantly missed Medwick with a tag on a play that would have won the game for St. Louis, but Rigler called Medwick out).

The rest of the Cardinals thought that Dean had quit trying in the middle of the game, and consequently Diz and several other players had to be separated in the locker room. Afterwards, Frisch was furious with his pitcher; it was yet another example of the eccentricity that the man-ager had to deal with, which was becoming more and more common since Dean joined the Cardinals full time in 1932. Even en route to the Car-dinals' championship in 1934, a majority of players on the team had grown more than weary of Dean's attitude. Frisch said to Dizzy, loud enough to be heard by the others, that he would be suspended and fined $5,000 if he ever again showed disrespect similar to that displayed to Medwick, or if he so blatantly gave less than his best effort. "It was an unwarranted display of temper and a most unfair thing for Dean to do," Frisch told the papers. "He came in [the dugout] after the four-run inning and made slurring remarks about the ball club. Naturally, the fellows who have been hustling their heads off resented this and they challenged him. He wasn't doing his best out there, and he knows it. He has twice in previous games with the Pirates disobeyed my instructions and pitched wrong to Arky Vaughan, with the result we lost both games. He seems to think he can throw the ball past the good hitters just because he's Dizzy Dean. That's not baseball, and he can't play that way for me."

Despite his frustration, however, Frisch considered the matter closed. After Dean apologized to Medwick and the rest of the team, Frisch was confident that he would not have to carry out his articulated threat of a suspension and fine.

A quick two-game sweep of the Reds by the Cubs, 10–2 and 5–2, and the Chicago team was off to St. Louis on a train that left after mid-night on June 6. Henshaw was the benefactor of the offensive deluge in the first game, and he felt that it was about time; he jokingly nicknamed himself the "NRA Pitcher," which he said stood for "No Runs Again" when he pitched (although that was the case for most of the Cubs' moundsmen so far on the year). There was to be a third game in the series, but once again there was a cancellation, this time due to "rain, cold, wet grounds, high winds, and the prospect of no customers." The Cubs would not be back home until the 28th, as the battling Cardinals were first on the list of a long road trip. The tiny crowd of 1,229 paid folks that saw the last game against Cincinnati was the lowest total at Wrigley Field in ten years. They released together a hearty cheer on the final play, a foul pop-up chased by Cavarretta down the right field line that bounced out of his glove and into the waiting mitt of his johnny-on-the-spot neighbor, Herman.

Perhaps the lack of interest was due to the recent success of the South Side club. The White Sox were hanging on the heels of the Yankees, with a second-place record of 23–17 on June 6, ahead of preseason-favorite Cleveland and reigning–AL champion Detroit. Much of the Sox's performance was attributed to the pitching of a young rookie named John Whitehead. On the 6th, Whitehead lost to the Browns 2–0, and it was his first defeat on the year after winning his first eight major league starts — a feat for which no sportswriter could recall anyone setting down a precedent.

Signing a convicted felon to a professional baseball contract was *faux pas* for most owners; like on many other topics, gentlemen's agreements pushed the possibility aside for fear of public relations damage to be done with such pursuits. The Detroit Tigers raised a lot of eyebrows in 1971 when club officials, including manager Billy Martin, went to Jackson State Prison in Michigan to offer a tryout to a man named Ron LeFlore, an inmate convicted of armed robbery, who, nonetheless, "was better than everyone at every sport he ever tried — even ones had hadn't tried before," according to a boyhood friend. LeFlore was given a special weekend furlough from his sentence to leave the prison, so that he could meet the club at Tiger Stadium to show off his skills. After hitting a few balls into the upper deck, throwing bullets to third base from the center field wall, and scorching a path in the sixty yard dash, LeFlore saw his prison stay expedited. He was signed by the Tigers and soon became the Most Valuable Player in the Florida State League, followed by appearances in the major league All-Star Game beginning in 1976. LeFlore's tell-all autobiography, *One in a Million*, is aptly titled; in fact, the last sentence of the book contains part of a speech he once gave to inner-city youth in Detroit: "If you get caught using drugs or stealing, you're going to go to prison, just like I did. But don't get the idea you'll be as lucky as I was. There won't be a major league baseball team waiting to sign you when you get out. Just because it happened to me, don't you expect a miracle, too."

But back in May and June of 1935, another convict with legendary amateur athletic feats received a chance to play professional baseball. Edward "Alabama" Pitts arrived at Sing Sing prision in 1930, the result of an armed robbery committed with an accomplice in New York City against grocery store owner John Costello. The two perpetrators were in the Navy. Pitts and his partner had gotten away with $75 and a gun from their victim, but were quickly apprehended by the police. Like LeFlore, Pitts excelled in baseball and football while in prison (LeFlore especially gained the interest of nearby Hillsdale College football coaches, whose team once played a squad of prisoners at Jackson). Pitts, an outfielder, was signed to a contract by the Albany Senators on May 22, 1935, three weeks before he was to be released from Sing Sing.

On the morning of June 6 the 24-year-old Pitts, having served five years of his eight-year sentence, departed the prison dressed in a sharp three-piece suit and fedora. He said goodbye to supportive warden Lewis Lawes, who would later write the landmark book *20,000 Years in Sing Sing* and become a leader of many reforms of the penitentiary system. Lawes oversaw the massive detention center—already 110 years old in 1935—that stretched for nearly 150 yards along the east bank of the Hudson River in Ossining, New York.

Pitts was to be part of the Albany team that was playing the Syracuse Chiefs that evening in Syracuse. But he was greeted with an unfortunate order from Judge W.G. Bramham, president of the National Association of Minor Professional Baseball Leagues. Bramham had suddenly voided the $200-a-month contract under which Pitts was to play, stipulating that no felon would be allowed to participate in minor league ball and that such an allowance would be a "detriment to the game." Some looked to Landis for a statement on the issue, but he had none "until the matter is brought to me or my secretary," the major league commissioner said. It was gametime, 8:30 P.M., and Pitts was still dressed in his suit awaiting an appeal of the decision. Bramham's edict held, but Pitts was still brought out to home plate and introduced to the crowd of 2,000 by Matthew Cadin, formerly the chief of police of Syracuse. The audience stood and gave a vigorous cheer, and the players from both sides formed a semi-circle of support around Pitts. The game went on without him, and tears welled up in Pitts' eyes as he watched his would-be teammates hitting practice fungoes before the game. Later, he rested in a box seat to watch the game. "This is the latest I've stayed out at night for a long time," he joked as the ninth inning neared its completion.

"If organized baseball admits Alabama Pitts," pondered Arch Ward in his *Tribune* column on June 8, "wonder what it will say to some of the Black Sox who have been trying to get back. They too, it seems, have paid for their crime." He was of course referring to eight players from the 1919 White Sox, who were banned from baseball for life by Landis after being tried (and acquitted) in a confidence game for a conspiracy to fix the World Series against the Reds.

Pitts got back on the team bus the next day, and the club headed back to Albany to prepare for a series with Buffalo. Even though his routine would be the same (dressed in street clothes up until game time, waiting for possible word that he could play), he planned to stay with the team. Part of the deal from Bramham was that Pitts was allowed to practice, albeit behind locked gates at Albany's field. There was one more major appeal to be had, and then the decision on his playing status would be final. Tempting job opportunities were plentiful for him elsewhere, as calls from barnstorming baseball teams from New York City, Philadelphia, Schenectady, and Dayton were being heard. In addition, the New York Giants and the Philadelphia Eagles of the National Football League were inquiring about his services as well. But Johnny Evers, the general manager of the Albany club, was not letting Pitts go without a fight. The 54-year-old Evers—he of the famed Cubs' double play trio of "Tinker to Evers to Chance" and native of Troy, New York—vowed that he would make Pitts an "assistant business manager" if that's what it took to keep him on the team's roster. "This man is going to play even if it forces me out of baseball to put him in the lineup," Evers said.

Things turned in Pitts' favor the very next morning, as Bramham got a telegram from Dizzy Dean and Pepper Martin, in which the Cardinal stars made a plea to allow Pitts to play; another came from heavyweight boxing champion Max Baer, who was preparing for his June 13th title defense against Jimmy Braddock; yet another came from a newspaper reporter in Decatur, Illinois, stating that at least two players with criminal records from the Three-I League (which stood for Illinois, Indiana, and Iowa—a prominent Midwestern Class "B" league until it folded in 1961) had been signed to professional contracts even before they had been paroled; and there were hundreds of others, all with the same general message to Pitts: "Good luck." An attorney from Wisconsin offered his legal services free of charge to him. A letter of support even came from his victim of five years prior, Costello, who thought Pitts should be given a chance. "If the parole commissioner thinks it safe to send Pitts out," Costello said graciously, "it ought to be safe for baseball players. My sympathies are entirely with Alabama in this controversy."

Most importantly to Pitts in a formal sense, however, his request for a hearing was approved by Warren Giles, the executive committee chairman of the NAMPBL. Giles immediately sent a telegram with the news to Evers, which also stated that hearing would probably take place as early as the following week in New York City. The minor leagues would continue to honor the ban on Pitts, Bramham still asserted, until the matter was decided once and for all by Landis. The appeal was brought to Landis' office on June 10, but because the judge had fallen ill, his doctor had ordered him away from all work for a week; thus, the matter had to wait. The wait was imagined to wind up being longer than that, as doctors had also recently discovered that the baseball czar had high blood pressure. The toughest wait on the matter appeared to be for Evers, as the gritty old ballplayer made another bold, succinct statement. "If Landis rules against us, we will abide by his decision, but I shall sever all connections with the game I love and to which I have devoted my entire life. That is a sweeping threat, but I mean every word of it."

Evers also warned that denying Pitts a chance would not only be wrong, but would have denied the game its greatest player in the past and be dangerous for the future. "This man's record is as clean as anyone's in this room except for one false step," he continued to the writers. "I think he would be a credit to the game. One of the greatest characters in baseball came out of a reform school, but no one refused the fans he attracted. When this boy Pitts is turned down, the fellow in prison will say, 'Well, what's the use?'"

Lawes, the man who monitored Pitts for the past five years, echoed the sentiment. "I feel this decision is far reaching, not only as far as Pitts is concerned, but because it strikes at the very foundation of prison administration and the rehabilitation of inmates," the warden stated. "It will have a profound effect on many men still in prison who hope to become decent citizens. Letters I have received in great numbers show 90 percent of the people are in favor of Pitts being allowed to play. Even policemen think he should be given a chance."

Another telegram of support came from Jimmie Wilson of the Phillies, who wanted Pitts' services in Philadelphia right away. "I would be glad to have Pitts on my ball club," said Wilson, whose Phils—with a sickly record of 14–25—needed any kind of boost, and were only a few games away from taking Boston's place in the National League cellar. "I need a good, hard-hitting extra man. If Pitts can fill the bill, there's a suit waiting for him at the clubhouse. I don't care what he did. He has paid his debt to society and that is finished. He should not have to pay interest until he dies."

Warneke and Lee, the same two men who had been rocked by the same club the previous week, were Grimm's choices to start the double-header opener in St. Louis on June 7. The Cubs did not need another postponement, but they got one—even though the skies were a perfect blue in St. Louis. With the lack of meteorological forecasting technology currently enjoyed today, the *rumor* that storms were headed towards St. Louis caused Cardinals officials to call off the first day of contests. An overnight shower had slightly dampened the field, and the men in charge thought that much more rain was on the way. But there was hardly a cloud in the sky, and Grimm and Hartnett consulted local linksters for the nearest golf course north of St. Louis.

If the Cubs had known what was in store for them, the day off would have been likened to a worrisome trip to the dentist for the following afternoon. They suffered a pair of painful one-run defeats, 5–4 and 6–5, as the Gas House Gang thrilled the home crowd by winning in dramatic fashion both times. In the first game, a two-out double by Galan in the eighth scored Cavarretta and Klein to tie the game at four, as Jurges was halted at third while carrying the go-ahead run. In the bottom half, Carleton relieved Warneke, who had been sloppy in allowing earlier runs to score on a wild pitch and his first error in two years. Carleton effectively retired the Cardinals, but the Cubs were unable to score in the top of the ninth against Paul Dean. Leading off the final St. Louis attack was Martin, the "Wild Horse of the Osage," the man who symbolized a mixture of dirt, muscle, and baseball as he went head-first into most bases. Entering the day, Martin, at .377, was second in hitting in the National League only to Vaughan of Pittsburgh. He lined a sharp single to center and took his normal aggressive turn around first base, and the crowd howled with excitement. Next was Rothrock, and he tried to bunt a ball that was high and out of the strike zone. It was a successful pitch by Carleton, as Rothrock popped the ball into the air in front of the pitcher's mound. Carleton dove for the ball as Martin froze at first, waiting to see if the ball hit the ground. It did, but for some reason Carleton threw toward Cavarretta at first instead of getting the force play at second. His ill-advised throw became ill-executed, sailing over Cavarretta's head and down the right field line as the Cubs' bullpen scrambled to get out of the way. Martin kicked it into fifth gear as only he could, and circled the bases with fury, coming "home with the winning run before a Cub player could lay hands on the ball," moaned Ward.

Lee spotted the Cardinals an early 5–0 lead in the second tilt, but the Cubs fought back to tie, highlighted with doubles by Lindstrom, Cavarretta, Stephenson, and Herman. Neither Warneke nor Paul was through with his work on the day, as they respectively relieved Casey and Bill Walker in the eighth inning. Dean got three straight outs in the Cubs' turn, after Cavarretta rattled a ball off the right field screen to tie the game at five apiece. Warneke was more focused in this stint, retiring the St. Louis hitters through the tenth inning. With the Cubs unable to cross the plate in the eleventh, Collins strode to the plate with a chance to complete the sweep. Collins, a native of the Pittsburgh area, was in the process of building a fence made of broken bats around his new home in Rochester, New York. It was a frightful scene for the Chicagoans to see him coming to the plate, for it was only the previous Sunday that he brought the end of the doubleheader at Wrigley with a grand slam. It was not an old film but seemed so, as he measured one pitch from Warneke and launched it over the pavilion in right field. The ball scooted along Grand Avenue as the fans back inside looked out and cheered wildly, sending them home on the streetcars with a 6–5 win.

"In this manner, dear neighbors," Ward summated, "did our Cubs take their long threatened dive into the second division of the National League."

After the game Joiner, who had just returned to the club for a short time, was sent back to the Pacific Coast League by the Cubs, destined for San Francisco.

Meanwhile, the Yankees were playing in Fenway Park against the Red Sox, when Boston outfielder Carl Reynolds collided with Gehrig while crossing the bag at first base. Gehrig got up holding his arm in agony, and it was thought he had a separated shoulder. He came out of the game, and it looked like his consecutive games streak—currently at 1,552—would end. Fortunately for baseball history, the Yankees and Red Sox were rained out the next day, and there was an off-day for travel the next. This gave Gehrig sufficient time to rest the shoulder, and though still having pain, he would be ready to play in St. Louis on Tuesday the 11th against the Browns.

The single game on Sunday the 9th promised to draw a big crowd to Sportsman's Park, because of a three-fold reason provided by Dizzy Dean. Number one, he was pitching; number two, he was facing the former teammate whom he disliked the most, Tex Carleton; and number three, there was interest to see just how his mates would perform behind him, considering his outburst against them in Pittsburgh. The Cardinal players themselves weren't sure what to expect from the fans, but most thought that the crowd would be angry with Diz as well. They were right.

When Dean emerged from the dugout to take the mound in the first inning, he was greeted not only with derisive comments but also hurled lemons. The remaining players were safe, and it was obvious for whom the projectiles were intended. There was no question that Dean's teammates had put the incident behind them. They scored in every inning against Cubs starter Charlie Root—only the tenth time in baseball history that such an onslaught had happened—and Diz himself contributed three hits to the team stockpile of 21 in a 13–2 rout of Chicago and the series sweep. Gelbert got four hits in his first four trips to the plate, the day after he had made his first start since 1932; Rothrock also got four safeties, and would have had two more if not for great defensive plays by Herman and Galan. Rickey commented upon the performance with words of encouragement about his star pitcher. "In spite of all his talking, we like Dizzy and he likes us," the "Bushy-Browed Mahatma" said, as St. Louis writer Bob Broeg always referred to Rickey. "We won't sell him for any amount of money. We expect to go ahead with our team as it is in our fight to retain the league championship." Rickey was speaking to the press from the campus of Ohio Wesleyan University, from which his son and daughter were graduating that day, and of which he was a trustee.

Grimm was afraid that obsessive pinochle playing was causing his team to lose rest, and thus contribute to the poor on-field performance recently seen. In today's professional baseball world, managers take the good with the bad in regard to players' endless devotion to video games; they like the fact that the entertainment keeps players out of the bars, but sometimes get concerned about the possible sleep deprivation that might result from the addictive activity. Nocturnal pastimes were more of an issue when ball games were played exclusively in the daytime, and Grimm was getting the same feelings with his club. While he ordinarily didn't try to regulate the players' personal habits, he applied some regulations to the card-playing cohorts.

Grimm had nothing against pinochle itself; he loved to play the game, and often joined the others in a match. But he was afraid that so much time spent on the game would take away valuable discussion opportunities about baseball, such as the opponent's next starting pitcher and the like. Grimm encouraged the chums to talk about these types of things as the club made its way to Philadelphia in preparation for a six-game series in four days, the result of the rainouts from the previous month.

Henshaw surrendered seven runs in the first two innings at Philadelphia, which was too much to overcome despite Hartnett's one home run and Galan's pair in a 10–4 loss. "Charlie Grimm's pinochle wizards, traveling under the name of the Chicago Cubs, were licked again at baseball today," concluded the *Tribune*. Grimm was seriously considering some kind of deal before the trading deadline of June 15 to rattle some cages on the lethargic club.

But he did some more direct cage-rattling in the locker room before the June 12 doubleheader at the Baker Bowl. In the veteran players' assessment, it was the most scathing outburst they had ever remembered from Grimm. Although the press had been told to remain outside the room, Burns and the others kept their ears near the door. "He told two members of the team, whose names are scattered through the record books, that he would not take them back to Chicago if he could find any team that would offer anything," he reported. Burns did not reveal the individuals' names, but it was clear that he was referring to Cuyler and Klein. Cuyler had improved slightly in recent days to raise his average to .264, but his position in centerfield had, for the most part, been usurped by Lindstrom. The heralded Klein was still plodding through the mire at .240, only six points ahead of Jurges' figure for the lowest among the regulars. But Grimm took the opportunity to blast the whole team, and he threatened to ban card playing altogether for it was suggested that a poker crew had also been assembling on most nights, long after the pinochle club had gone to bed. In addition, it had been rumored that one of the players had been accused by the others of literally putting cards up his sleeve, and Grimm said enough was enough. To illustrate how serious the problem was perceived to be by team officials, club treasurer Boots Weber and Phil Wrigley himself were immediately heading east to join the trip. Since it was thought improbable that the two were making the thousand-mile trek to lecture players on gambling habits, it was assumed that they were seeking to make an instant trade involving Klein or Cuyler, or both.

The tension that overspilled in Grimm's diatribe made an impact, especially on those to whom it was most directed. Klein doubled his home run total on the day from three to six, with a blast in the first game and his first two trips to the plate in the nightcap. But Klein's take was not even half of the team's output, as the Cubs slammed seven homers on the afternoon. The result in the first game was a 15–0 destruction of the Phillies, with French the beneficiary. It was as if a wave of frustration was released out of the clubhouse door, for the Cubs scored nine of the fifteen runs in the first two innings. Longballs by O'Dea and Cavarretta, in addition to Klein, were the hallmarks of the first contest in which French permitted only five Philly hits. But Carleton could not keep the momentum going in game two, as he was shelled early and often in an 11–8 loss, the final two runs given up by French who was summoned in the eighth after his magnificent performance earlier in the day. The energy from Grimm's speech turned out to be short-lived, and after the game several of the veterans wondered what would become of their futures.

That evening, the journeyman Braddock shocked the boxing world with a 15-round decision over Baer for the heavyweight championship. Attention was then turned to the upcoming Louis-Carnera bout, the winner of which was believed to be advancing toward a shot at the "Greatest Title in the World." But they all couldn't escape the long shadow of the most beloved retired champion—former heavyweight boxing king Jack Dempsey announced that, in a few months, he would establish a restaurant in New York. When it did open for business, Dempsey cheerfully greeted each customer to what would become a wildly-popular establishment and even donned the chef's hat from time to time. Dempsey had briefly tried his hand at being a farmer in the San Joaquin Valley of California, but soon became bored with his 166-acre peach orchard outside Fresno and sold it.

Wrigley and Weber arrived after the doubleheader split, but still came in time to see plenty of baseball as the clubs got set to play another twin bill the following afternoon. Warneke started strong, leading the Cubs to a 12-6 victory in the first one, and Galan capped off a fine day in front of the boss with heroics in the second affair. With two out in the ninth and Klein on second, he smoked a pitch from Walters over the right field wall for his third homer of the series. While Klein added his seventh homer in the first game, Cuyler went 0-for-3 in the nightcap after sitting out game one—and the talk intensified about his impending departure.

Hopeful they could take the finale and win the series against the seventh-place club, the Cubs and Kowalik battled Curt Davis. With the game tied at three in the Phillies' half of the fifth, Wilson put his team ahead with a sacrifice fly to score George Watkins. Galan, who caught the fly, fired the ball towards third to prevent Johnny Moore from advancing from second base. Hack abandoned the base for some reason, and the ball went bouncing towards the Cub dugout. Wilson argued successfully with umpire Charley Moran, claiming that the ball got into the dugout and that Moore should be awarded home. Nearly the entire Cubs bench then charged Moran, disputing the final resting point of the ball. The only thing Chicago gained from the debate was the banishment of coach Roy Johnson. Galan scored in the seventh on Hack's third hit of the game, but the Cubs could get no closer. The game ended 5-4 in favor of Philadelphia, and the series ended in a draw. For the six-game set, Galan amassed ten hits, including the three home runs and four doubles. With Klein knocking four round-trippers himself, these two men appeared to be set in the outfield for the future, while Cuyler awaited news of a trade. Herman was also an offensive force against the Phillies, as he slapped out 13 hits—and six doubles among them, which raised his batting mark up to .279. And Hack, at .312 and a point ahead of Galan, was now the leader among the starting players.

The club was then off to Brooklyn for a four-game series, trying to separate itself from the Dodgers on the list of teams. After Lee beat the Dodgers 9–4 behind 18 Cub hits, Grimm had an appointment at 9:30 that morning (June 15, the trade deadline) to talk deals with Stengel. Grimm did not keep the appointment, however, as coffee with Phil Wrigley took precedence. Apparently, Wrigley used the opportunity to talk Grimm out of any trades, warning Charlie that a move made in anger might be one he would later regret. Certainly Cuyler (and until recently, Klein) had been a disappointment but since the centerfielder was a proven star player, it was reasoned that he should get an extended chance. That week, Wrigley began having dinners with each of the players individually, and Cuyler was his first guest. So the roster stood pat for the time being, as midnight of June 15 came and went. The National League standings the next morning looked like this:

	W	L	Pct.	GB
New York	33	14	.702	—
Pittsburgh	32	22	.592	4.5
St. Louis	30	21	.588	5.0
Chicago	25	23	.520	8.5
Brooklyn	24	24	.500	9.5
Cincinnati	20	29	.408	14.0
Philadelphia	18	29	.382	15.0
Boston	13	33	.282	19.5

"From this vantage point, only one team is in position to thumb its nose at the calendar. That is the New York Giants," wrote John Carmichael that day in the *Chicago Daily News*. "From stem to stern Bill Terry has a high class ball club, completely equipped as to pitching and reserves. There isn't a weak spot on the club, and if injuries to Jackson, Bartell, Crtiz, etc. are Bill's quota for the season, then he has little to worry about." After a complete collapse the previous September, the Giants were returning to their consistent selves, having yet to lose more than two games in a row for the season. Over in Pittsburgh, Arky Vaughan of the sizzling Pirates was batting an even .400 to lead the league, with 76 hits in 190 at-bats.

After the trade winds blew through without a storm, the bats stayed

hot and the Cubs beat the Dodgers again behind Carleton, 6–2, in front
of 7,500 at Ebbets Field. It was Carleton's first win since May 15, which
was also in Brooklyn against the Dodgers. Still among the hottest sluggers in the lineup was Hack, who shot up to .340 (good for sixth in the
league) with eight hits in his last eleven at-bats. He also stole a base during the win, as catcher Al Lopez catapulted his throw into centerfield
that brought a fury of "boos" from the sparse crowd in Flatbush. Hack's
hitting torrent would be outdone the same day (Sunday the 16th), however, by Washington Senators outfielder John Stone. Stone rapped out
his twelfth hit in two days against the Browns in St. Louis—including
two triples, two doubles and four singles in the Sunday doubleheader,
while scoring five runs.

The Cubs made it three in a row, thanks to two homers by Klein—
which pushed his total to nine, and scored Lindstrom on each—in a 5–3
triumph for French, his fifth win. It was Klein's sixth round-tripper in as
many days, and the Dodgers lost for the seventh time in their last eight
tries. Stengel knew he had to break things up, and to this end, he even
took the atmospheric matters into his own hands. After the third Chicago
win, he found Grimm and told him that "better pack them trunks of
yours, for if there is as many as three drops of rain between now and 3:15
tomorrow, there won't be no game." The Brooklyn area got more than
three drops, which strengthened Casey's case. As a matter of fact, all
seven major league games scheduled for the day were rained out.

The Stengelmen had their desired day off, and the Cubs headed off
to Boston in an effort to keep their good fortune going in a doubleheader
against the Braves. And to be sure, Wrigley was coming along with
them—no way he was leaving now, lest he break up the winning streak.
"Mr. Wrigley hasn't taught any of his athletes anything about the tech-
nical side of baseball," pointed out Burns. "But being the gent who pays
the salaries, his presence in the presidential box has done wonders at keeping the fellows going. He appears to be helping the spirit of alertness
around the ballclub immeasurably ... if things keep up, he has no greater
chore than seeing that Chicagoans again start to drop in at Clark and
Addison."

After Boston, the Cubs had five games to play in New York against
the Giants, and Wrigley said he would stay for those, too. New to the
traveling party in the past couple of days was Wrigley's brother-in-law,
A.G. Atwater, who in the following year would meet and begin courting
film star Dorothy Lee (they eventually married, but then separated after
three years). For something to do on the trip, Wrigley had taken it upon
himself to inspect the locker rooms of each of the stadiums the Cubs

visited; he wished to improve the health standards of the dressing rooms back in Chicago, as several of the players had been complaining of bouts with athlete's foot.

Over in Harlem the previous day, Alabama Pitts was getting his first taste of the big leagues—albeit as a spectator. The former felon took in the Cardinals-Giants game sitting next to his erstwhile warden Lawes, Lawes' daughter, and Evers. While watching the game, Lawes mentioned within earshot of a reporter that an ex-convict was on the field as they watched, but he did not name which Cardinal or Giant it was. Afterwards, Pitts and Evers were interviewed over NBC radio, and the would-be manager once again put out a public plea in the direction of Landis for Pitts' reinstatement. When asked about his prospects for taking the field, Pitts appeared to be more concerned with a potential reinstatement having the proper reflection on what Lawes had done. "Irrespective of myself, I wouldn't want to see it harmful to Warden Lawes," he spoke on the airwaves. "I wouldn't want to tear down in a few weeks the wonderful work the warden has done in the past thirty years in building the self-respect of men." Everyone would have to wait the weekend for Landis's decision. It was expected on Monday, June 17.

"Not only for myself would I like to earn my own living," Pitts added, "but for the sake of future hopes of other men who might be in a like situation."

Monday finally came, and Landis issued his decision. It was decreed that Pitts would indeed be eligible to play, but only in regularly-scheduled Albany games and in no sideshow exhibitions for money-making purposes, as directed in the last part of the judge's written statement:

> Pitts will be allowed to play, on condition that a new contract be executed by the Albany club and Pitts containing a covenant that during the year 1935 Pitts shall play only in regular league games and shall not appear in or at exhibition games, this condition being imposed because it is distinctly in Pitts' interest that mere notoriety be not exploited and capitalized.

This statement constituted the sole amendment to Pitts' original contract with the club, which he would finally sign on June 19 and would pay him a salary of $200 a month. Pitts was elated, and his response to Landis's conclusion was brief. "I'm sure Judge Landis will never regret having made that decision, and I know I am going to make good in organized baseball. He's a great man; I've always heard about his fairness. That's all." Pitts gave a tear-filled speech of appreciation to the Albany Rotary Club, and the local businessman gave him a rousing ovation.

George Wriston, president of the local Kiwanis, claimed that Pitts "would be an asset to any town." Added Evers, "I've had many thrills in baseball, but this is the greatest thrill I've ever had in my life." He mentioned that Pitts would probably be given his first starting assignment the following Sunday, June 23, so that he could have his first game in the daylight and not be subjected to the league's poorly-lit fields in a night contest for his first at-bats. And though unlikely, Evers announced that he would pursue a full pardon for Pitts of his crime.

"Naturally, I am pleased," chimed in Lawes, who was gaining more and more popularity for his progressive advances in the correction system. "It is encouraging to administrators as well as all the men in prison."

Some were concerned that Pitts, with relative inactivity in the past few weeks, would not be ready to jump in and play effectively with the Albany club—an idea that was refuted by Albany's field manager, Al Mamaux. "Those who think Pitts' training has been neglected are going to be fooled," he said. "He is better today than some of the outfielders I have seen in the International League." Bramham and Giles, who had their edicts overruled by Landis's decision, declined to comment on the final outcome. While Pitts was cleared to play on Sunday the 23rd in the Albany game against Syracuse, he had yet another hurdle to clear down the road: the International League had teams in Toronto and Montreal, and Pitts would need to obtain special permission to cross the border into Canada when Albany played there in early July.

Bad weather chased a few away, but 8,000 were curious enough to come to Hawkins Stadium in Albany for the doubleheader and a glance at the parolee. When he ran out to take his place in centerfield in the first inning, the crowd gave a supportive roar. He nailed two singles in the opener, and handled seven chances in center, including a couple of double-defying grabs in the gap off frustrated Syracuse batters, without a miscue, even though the home team lost the game. On the first play, he valiantly crashed into the left field fence; on the second, he ran through the right-center gap to outrace the slow-footed right fielder Hack Wilson to the ball, portly as ever and five years removed from his amazing 190-RBI year with the Cubs. It was rumored that Yankees manager McCarthy was interested in Wilson helping out the Yankees, but as Arch Ward pointed out, "Hack's batting average has faded to .280, and the McCarthy rumor to zero."

Pitts found the going tough in the second game, as former major-leaguer Flint Rhem shut down Albany to secure a sweep for the Chiefs.

The Cubs endured a tough split on their first day in Boston, as Warneke logged his sixth loss in a 2–1 decision to Bob Smith in the first game while Lee beat Huck Betts 3–0 in the second. Lindstrom assumed the duties in center field for both contests, as Cuyler saw duty only as a pinch-hitter in the opener, getting a single while batting for Warneke leading off the ninth inning. But after that it was three in a row for Chicago, starting with Carleton, who beat the Beantowners for the eighth time in his last nine tries on the 21st, followed up with a doubleheader sweep the next day. Little-used catcher O'Dea had four hits in the opener, including a triple that helped in a 6–4 win for French. Root won the nightcap 5–3, as Jurges was a perfect 3-for-3. The team then boarded the train to head back to New York, continuing the grueling trip with five more games against the Giants in the Polo Grounds. They were 10–4 so far on the eastern journey. That night, in their New York hotel room, Jurges and Herman were talking when they heard a noise outside the door. Jurges (understandably nervous in hotel rooms after his experience three years prior), still carrying on the conversation, walked over to the door and opened it—much to the surprise of two snoops, who were leaning against the door trying to listen in on the discussion, for whatever reason, and fell onto the floor. Herman laughed good-naturedly, but the angry Jurges chased them through the hallway and down the stairs. In 1935, it obviously wasn't so difficult for a person to ask for, and receive, the hotel room numbers of major league players.

Over in Pompton Lakes, New Jersey, Joe Louis finished up his training for his upcoming bout in Yankee Stadium against Carnera. Louis was not short on confidence, as he predicted a knockout at some point before the sixth round. "It will be as quickly as possible, in the first round if I can do so," Louis said about his intention of sending the Italian to the mat. "I never saw Primo fight, but I saw pictures of his fights. He appears easy to hit, but maybe I won't find it so easy." Carnera had previously been the heavyweight champ in beating Jack Sharkey on June 29, 1933, but lost it to Max Baer the following year when Baer put him on the canvas eleven times. Louis had gone through twelve sparring partners in his preparation (to whom he each paid $5 a round), and the current number was at three due to the punishment he was dishing out to his helpers.

The Cubs couldn't muster a single run for Warneke in Harlem, even though they collected 11 hits. Big Lon left the game, which turned out to be an 8–0 whitewash for Fitzsimmons and the Giants in the fifth. It was the fourth win of the season for "Fat Freddie," all of them shutouts. Among the witnesses of the slaughter was comedian Joe E. Brown, a baseball fanatic who was the guest of Ford Frick at the game and a companion of Dizzy Dean's at the 1934 World Series. Brown was not satisfied in just being a fan, however; he was looking to buy an interest in the Braves from Judge Fuchs.

A riveting comeback victory for the Chicagoans came the next day. Down 9–5 in the ninth, the Cubs drew to within two on a triple by Hartnett that scored Herman and Hack. Chagnon was summoned by Terry to relieve Parmelee, and he promptly retired the struggling Cuyler on a short fly to Ott in right. Then came Klein, who smashed a long home run over Ott's head in right, plating himself and Hartnett for a nine-all tie. The blast denied Parmelee of what would have been his seventh straight win against the Cubs. As the game was knotted into the tenth, Al Smith followed Chagnon to the mound, and Galan walked and waltzed into third on a single by Herman. With Smith being lefthanded, Grimm pulled the similarly-batting Hack in favor of Demaree, at which point Terry brought in the righthander Gabler. Demaree whacked the first pitch into center field for a single and the lead. Henshaw cleaned up in the bottom half, and Chicago had a 10–9 triumph. After the game, most of the players from both teams had dinner near the ballpark, and then made their way across the bridge to Yankee Stadium for the big fight that evening (portable lights had been brought into the stadium for the event, with the undercard beginning at 8:00 P.M.).

Louis was a 6–5 favorite entering the bout, even though Carnera outweighed him by almost seventy pounds (260 to 196). "At one time it reached 8–5," reported Harvey Woodruff for the *Tribune*. "Some smart money has lately appeared to support the Italian. Up in Harlem, the colored settlement, Louis is 7–5, owing to advance arrivals from Detroit and Chicago, with little Carnera money in sight." The match was expected to draw 60,000 attendees and gate receipts expected approach $300,000. There would be no radio broadcast of the fight, because promoters William Carey and Mike Jacobs chose otherwise when preparatory time became short in the weeks before the bout. But press credentials had been requested by over a thousand newspapers; among those granted were four from San Francisco, two from Los Angeles, three from Detroit, eight from Chicago, and "others from Minneapolis, St. Louis, Kansas City, Denver, Des Moines, Cleveland, New Orleans, and all points west and south with a solid quota from the east," said one reporter. They didn't see much of a fight—Louis easily knocked out Carnera in the sixth round.

The owners of Yankee Stadium and the Polo Grounds each received $16,000 for the fight; for even though the match occurred in the former, there was an agreement to split all revenue from non-baseball related showcases. This was done to prevent each from outbidding the other for events.

A week later, it was confirmed that Louis's next fight would take place in August in Chicago against King Levinsky, who himself was a Chicago native, and like Louis promised to provide a good local draw. One of the ballparks—either Wrigley or Comiskey—would likely hold the bout, but there was the possibility that the mammoth lakefront coliseum, Soldier Field, would get the honors if advance ticket sales were overwhelming. A promoter in Berlin named Walter Rothenburg was also attempting to stage a fight between Louis and German champion Max Schmeling, a bout that would have obvious racial implications after two years of Hitler's dictatorship in Nazi Germany. "For most Nazis, if Schmeling should beat Louis there would be no race problem," the *New York Times* reported on July 9. "But if he should be knocked out by the Detroit fighter, he might find himself unpopular."

As often happens with new-found fame, Louis also found himself with new-found "friends." One was Anthony Barrow, a barber from Chattanooga, Tennessee, who claimed to be Louis's cousin. But the relationship was going to be a lot closer that Joe realized—Barrow planned to "tuck away my shears and clippers, go to Detroit, and move in on Joe to help him spend all that money."

While the Cubs-Giants series continued, Terry announced to the papers that he had voted for Grimm and Dressen as Frisch's two assistant coaches in the All-Star Game. He said that Dressen was selected for his giftedness at stealing the opposing team's signs, but did not reveal his reasons for choosing Charlie. Terry also opined that Rip Collins of the Cardinals, and not him, should be the starting first baseman for the National League. It was also revealed that the ballots would exclude Klein, Cuyler, and Warneke from the game, all participants in the 1934 event (Klein and Warneke had been in the original 1933 game as well), while most felt that Hartnett and Herman stood a good chance and Lee an outside shot.

The teams split a doubleheader on June 25, 3–2 for New York and 10–5 for Chicago, perhaps a compromise from too much partying before, during, and after the boxing match the previous night. Herman opened the second game with his first homer of the year, the first of four hits in the contest for Billy after going 0-for-3 against Castleman in the opener. The Giants took that one when, in the tenth, Terry started the frame with a single, was bunted to second by Ott, and scored when Hank Leiber nudged a single over the outstretched arms of Cavarretta into right field. The Giants also took the last game of the series on the 26th, 5–2, as Schumacher crafted his eighth straight win and tenth overall on the year, and the Giants were over the .700 mark with a 41–17 record. Grimm was still doing some shuffling with the batting order, rewarding O'Dea with another start behind the plate and batting him in the cleanup spot (it was not in penalty to Hartnett's play, as he himself was batting .307 and leading the team with 33 RBIs). Gabby's understudy came into New York hitting .413, but was quickly returned to the bench with an 0-for-4 outing. Root had allowed only one hit and one run through six innings, after which the Giant bats came alive. It ended a long trip for the Chicago team, which they finished with a strong 12–10 mark. French was starting to make his mark on the pitching staff, as he picked up three wins on the eastern swing; it would have been four had the Cubs held onto his 2–0 lead in the ninth in the doubleheader opener on the 25th. Warneke, however, had dropped four games on the trip; he was struggling to regain his truly dominant 1934 form.

That day in Boston, with his Pirates playing the Braves, centerfielder Lloyd Waner set a record for that position with 18 putouts in a doubleheader, a mark for a twin-bill that still stands today. And in Cleveland, All-Star outfielder Earl Averill severely burned three fingers on his right hand in a pre–Fourth of July fireworks accident. Two days later, his consecutive-game streak would end at 673 which was second only to Gerhig's on-going run, due to the mishap,. The Indians' team doctor, Edward Castle, predicted that Averill would miss at least six weeks with the injury.

As the Cubs made their way back home, they and the rest of the baseball world were finding out the rosters for the All-Star Game, to take place two weeks later in Cleveland. The final picks made by Frisch for the National League, announced to the press on June 27, were as follows:

> Infielders—Terry, New York; Collins, Martin, Whitehead, St. Louis; Herman, Chicago; Vaughan, Pittsburgh
> Outfielders—Medwick, St. Louis; Paul Waner, Pittsburgh; Ott, Moore, New York; Berger, Boston
> Catchers—Hartnett, Chicago; Wilson, Philadelphia; Mancuso, New York
> Pitchers—Hubbell, Schumacher, New York; Jay (Dizzy) Dean, St. Louis; Derringer, Cincinnati; Mungo, Brooklyn

Two days later, Medwick celebrateed his selection by hitting for the cycle against Cincinnati, although Paul Dean dropped the 8–6 decision to the Reds.

Grimm and Dressen were in fact the assistant coaches chosen by Frisch, and the Cardinal skipper understandably chose his own trainer, Doc Weaver, to make the trip to Cleveland as well. In addition to Klein and Warneke, another conspicuous absence was Traynor, as the Pirate third baseman had (like the aforementioned pair) participated in the first two all-star games.

It was the Pirates who greeted the Cubs back on Addison Street, as Pittsburgh had just taken over second place behind New York with a doubleheader sweep of Boston the day before. It was the first time the Cubs had been in Chicago since they left the night of June 6 for the East, and the comforts of home were a most welcome sight. And despite the long trip, Burns reported, only two minor ailments had struck the team—Hack picked up a sore finger from a bad hop on a ground ball, and Lindstrom was fighting a strained hamstring caused by legging out an infield hit.

"Tiny Roy" Henshaw started the first one against the Bucs, which was ironic, as he was facing "Big Jim" Weaver for Pittsburgh. Henshaw, who would celebrate his twenty-fourth birthday the following day, was not daunted by the large man, and turned in the performance of his life. Up to the sixth inning, he had permitted no hits, when relief pitcher Mace Brown of the Pirates came to the plate. Brown lifted a pop fly towards Lindstrom in left-center, and Freddie, with his sore leg, gimped over to get under it. He was there in time, but somehow it dropped through his hands to fall freely to the ground, and Brown pulled into second base. Henshaw recovered to strike out Woody Jensen, and Bud Hafey popped up to Cavarretta to end the threat. He breezed through the seventh and eighth as well, and when Paul Waner grounded out to end the ninth, Henshaw was the first Cub to fire a no-hitter since Jimmy Lavender in 1915—or so he thought.

In the days before such decisions were always immediately made public, the official scorer had given Brown a double on the muffed play back in the sixth inning, when nearly everyone in the park had been sure that Lindstrom was charged with an error. The Cub players, who moments earlier had stormed out of the dugout to congratulate Henshaw, were furious about the ruling when they returned to the clubhouse. Lindstrom himself, though pointing out that he did run a long way for the fly ball, admitted that he got two hands on it and did expect to be logged with a miscue. Burns fairly pointed out that, if the scorer had made the opposite call—as what normally would have happened with a pitcher halfway through a no-hit game—he would have received criticism in simply another form. In any event, it was still an inspiring 8–0 win for Chicago, and Hartnett drove his seventh homer to straightaway center as part of the offensive outburst. It capped off a grand day for the All-Star catcher. Mrs. Hartnett gave birth to their second child that morning, a daughter who was now the sibling of Charles, Junior.

The stellar pitching continued, as French and Warneke dominated in a twin-bill to the tune of 1–0 and 2–1 scores, respectively. The Sunday crowd of 17,400 appreciated the fine ball played. The shutout for French was his third on the year, his fifth straight win, and seventh overall; Warneke's sixth victory snapped his personal four-game losing skid. Their backup support was outstanding as well, as Burns claimed that "no Cub infield in history ever played better baseball than the Cub quartet yesterday." Jurges, Herman, Cavarretta, and English (subbing for Hack) had flung themselves over the dirt all day long (especially Herman, who stymied Pittsburgh with twelve assists in the first game alone). The only run in the opener resulted on a error by Pittsburgh starter Waite Hoyt, who was matching French pitch-for-pitch into the twelfth inning. Lindstrom then doubled (after being hitless in his four previous at-bats on the day), and Klein was walked intentionally after Stainback was inserted by Grimm as a pinch-runner for Lindstrom. English then laid down a bunt between home plate and the pitcher's mound, on which Hoyt pounced as he turned and whipped the ball towards third. His throw misfired so terribly, however, that third baseman Tommy Thevenow didn't even make an attempt for it. The ball wound up in the box seats behind him, and Umpire Quigley pointed towards home which directed Stainback to end the game with the winning run. Klein's eleventh homer was the difference in the nightcap, as the Cubbies had now beaten Traynor's club six times in their last seven tries. Henshaw had shut them out in the last two contests, so the run the Pirates scored in the second game of the doubleheader was their lone tally in four games at Wrigley on the year.

The Cubs were 9–3 in their last twelve games, and the doubleheader sweep vaulted them over the Pirates and Cardinals into second place, as the standings on the morning of June 30 displayed:

	W	L	Pct.	GB
New York	42	18	.699	—
Chicago	36	27	.571	7.5
St. Louis	36	28	.562	8.0
Pittsburgh	38	30	.558	8.0
Brooklyn	29	32	.475	13.5
Cincinnati	28	36	.437	16.0
Philadelphia	25	37	.403	18.0
Boston	19	45	.296	25.0

After Bill Lee lost the last game of the series against the Pirates in Chicago, the Cubs got on the train to Cincinnati, where they would play the first night game in franchise history on Monday, July 1, against the Reds.

And Alabama Pitts was finding that life "on the outside" was no bowl of cherries either—after one week of play in the International League he was batting .156 and had let his fielding percentage slip under .900.

Cubs Out After Dark

Even though it seemed that the grizzled veteran had been to the four corners of the baseball world, this would be the first-ever night game for Charlie Grimm. He would follow the managers Wilson and Traynor, as he planned to insert players with the most under-the-lights experience into the starting lineup. This would include Demaree and Stainback in the outfield and Bryant on the mound—for two reasons: Clay had pitched many night games while in the minors in New Orleans, and conventional wisdom of the era suggested that his main pitch—"a low hard one," as Bryant called it—would be toughest to see after dark.

The *paid* crowd at Crosley Field for the event was 19,516, the largest so far of the three night games. A brass band concert opened things at 7:00, as pre-game practice was just beginning. The glowing moons were turned on at 8:30, just after a brilliant fireworks display "comparable to those at the World's Fair," a writer for the *Tribune* marveled. The contest didn't begin until 9:00, for the reason that a darker hour would provide a better performance from the lights.

Billy Herman, like most of the Cubs, had the experience of only a few night games—and none in the past five years. But he displayed an immediate comfort. After Galan grounded out to open the game, Herman laced a single to center and quickly scored on a double by Cavarretta, who had been elevated by Grimm to the number-three spot in the batting order as reward for his steadily-climbing average, at the very moment .297 after the run-scoring hit. O'Dea, another night-game veteran playing in lieu of Hartnett, then chased Cavy home with a single. After Demaree popped out, Klein crushed a 375-foot triple down the right field line to score O'Dea, and Dressen replaced starting pitcher Schott with Don Brennan.

Unforunately, Bryant didn't last much longer. After allowing a run in the Reds' half of the first, he began the second by walking Brennan and giving up a single to Billy Myers. Henshaw came to the rescue, silencing the Cincinnati bats the rest of the way with the exception of a lone tally in the sixth. Herman, Cavarretta, O' Dea, and Klein had all struck again with hits in the Cubs' fifth, opening up a 7–3 lead at that point. The final was 8–4, as Herman went 4-for-5 with two triples and O' Dea drove in three runs with three consecutive hits.

Although the Cubs did fine with the batting end of things, they much preferred to play defense under natural sunlight. "We like to hit under the lights," Hack said, "but it will be all right with us as fielders if we never play another night game." Henshaw had made the only error, which occurred after his first pitch when he induced a dribbler off the bat of Lew Riggs and threw wildly to second in hopes of starting a double play. Despite only just the momentary lapse in execution, the Cubs nervously scrambled after batted balls all night in the dimmed view.

With their evident general disdain for night games, major leaguers were making fans wonder if the players were becoming too preoccupied with their own safety. And that same week, the Yankees' George Selkirk, who had replaced the legendary Ruth on the hallowed grounds in the Bronx, was apparently growing tired of running into the outfield wall. He suggested that each park install a six-foot wide cinder path to border the field—a sort of "warning track," as he called it—to let a player know he was nearing the barrier. It would be another fourteen years, however, before the owners visualized enough benefits to have them installed in all major league parks.

Hartnett used the refreshing night off to spark the offense the next afternoon, as his single, double, and eighth homer—pushing his average to .338—helped Tex Carleton beat the Reds 9–3. His homer flew out to dead center field, over the 25-foot wall and 407 feet from home plate. With sacrifice bunts and walks mixed in, Hartnett had hit safely in 11 of his last 13 at-bats, the homer in the first inning being his sixth straight at that point. Carleton (6–3) held a shutout until two were out in the eighth inning, and it was almost two years to the day that Carleton had his legendary battle with Carl Hubbell. The two pitchers had hurled scoreless ball for seventeen innings, after which the Giants scored a run on their eighteenth chance. Hubbell found the strength for one more "goose-egg," as he amazingly wound up pitching virtually two shutouts in the same day but only getting credit for one 1–0 win.

The Cubs were now 17–7 since Grimm overturned the money-changers' tables at the hotel-room poker games back in Philadelphia.

Grimm also announced after the game that Wrigley Field would surely have lights in 1936—despite the protests of nearly every player on the team about night baseball. "Whether they like it or not, they are going to get it," Cholly informed the media.

Lee again couldn't finish up successfully on a "getaway" day, as he started a 4–3, ten-inning loss in the last game of the series, a defeat that was charged to Bryant when he surrendered Ernie Lombardi's eighth homer of the year (while in New York, the Giants' shortstop Bartell somehow managed to play ten innings without ever touching the ball on defense). The team started back for Chicago, where the Cardinals would be waiting at Wrigley over the Fourth of July holiday. But as the team was preparing to leave, something didn't appear right; Grimm was seen running back and forth from his hotel room and the train nearly left without him. As it turned out, the train would be leaving without Cuyler and his $12,000 salary. The veteran outfielder, being gradually squeezed out of playing time between fellow old-hands Klein and Lindstrom and young pups Demaree, Galan, and Stainback, got his unconditional release from the club, "without even a wrist watch as balm to his feelings," the *Tribune* noticed. "When Riggs Stephenson, another old Cub favorite, was given his release last winter, Owner P.K. Wrigley presented him with a watch which he claimed retailed at $350." On one of those trips back to his hotel room, Grimm met Cuyler there and presented Kiki with the severance papers, already signed by club vice president John Seys. Cuyler was confident that other teams would be interested in him, and he was right; the Reds, Braves, Phillies, Browns, White Sox, and several others inquired immediately after getting the wire. The courting telegram from the White Sox, simply saying "See us when you return to Chicago," arrived in Cuyler's hands before he even packed to leave Cincinnati; Hornsby, who had managed Cuyler previously, wanted to sign him for the Browns right away—but had to check the team's bank account first.

"There are only a half-dozen players in the National League who are faster than me right now," Cuyler claimed. "I hate to leave the Cubs as I have been with them so long and our relations have been very pleasant. They have no need of six outfielders now that they have two youngsters coming along, and Lindstrom is out there [in center field], so I had to go. That is baseball."

This was Cuyler's fourteenth year in the majors, and his eighth with the Cubs. At the time of his release, he held a .313 career batting average, including a .268 mark for 1935.

His answer came a couple days later on July 5, when the Reds won his services. The White Sox were indeed the other finalist, but Cuyler's reported demands—a salary of $14,000 plus an additional $5,000 as a signing bonus—scared off White Sox manager Jimmie Dykes and the rest of the Pale Hose front office. "We were willing to pay Cuyler good money for the balance of the season," said White Sox vice president Harry Grabinger, "but our need for outfielders wasn't pressing enough to warrant meeting his figures. Even if we had signed him, he would have had to wait for a chance to play. The present Sox outfield is functioning well enough to suit Dykes." There was, however, an open slot in the Cincinnati outfield—and a large amount of open salary as well—with the recent retirement of Chick Hafey, who had stepped down due to illness. Hafey had found disfavor with the Reds' brass, as in late June he left the team unannounced and headed to California to be among family members to recuperate from the sickness. Hafey would miss the remainder of the 1935 season and all of 1936, but would return for one final year with the Reds in '37, during which he hit .261 in 257 at-bats. For his career, the Berkeley native batted .317, including a National League-high .349 with the Cardinals in 1931.

While it was doubted that Cuyler was receiving from the Reds the kind of money he was requesting, it was thought to be equal to or greater than the $12,000 he was getting from the Cubs. Another major factor in his choosing Cincinnati over the White Sox was his desire to stay in National League, in which he had played exclusively.

One week before the All-Star Game, only 6,000 out of 67,276 reserved seats in the main section of Cleveland Stadium remained available at $1.35 apiece, and were located in the vast upper reaches of the left and right field corners. A total of 10,913 bleacher seats were being saved for a day-of-game sale, which would go for fifty-five cents each. In addition, Evans was planning on selling around 3,500 standing-room entries in the upper deck, as well as 5,000 more—through special permission of Landis—in an area on the grass beyond the playing surface in center field. A special corps of 1,500 ushers and police officers were to be dispatched at the stadium; and if the crowd approached the possible 90,000, or even the expected 86,000, it was rumored that it would be the largest gathering to ever watch a baseball game. In July 1935, the record books had at that time acknowledged the September 9, 1928, doubleheader between the Yankees and A's at Yankee Stadium to be the biggest ever at 85,265, although this figure was in doubt due to the numerous non-paying customers receiving passes to the game that day; more credence for the mark was given to a smaller figure—80,184—who paid to see a doubleheader in Cleveland on July 31, 1932, between the A's and the Indians. For fear of exorbitant refunds necessary in the event of a rain-out of the All-Star

Game, the city of Cleveland took out a $12,000 insurance policy in preparation for such a contingency.

While the nation commemorated its 159th birthday, a glorious scenario for baseball fans was crafted in Chicago on the Fourth of July. The Cubs were weary as a result of their train ride from Cincinnati, but a season-high of 38,100 fans at Wrigley—more than twice the size of any crowd in the Friendly Confines to that point in the season—rolled out the carpet for their club upon arrival at the home park, as the rival Cardinals were on stage once again. It was indeed a full house, and in the midst of continued hard times, the citizens celebrated a truly American pastime on a truly American date. Things were not any easier than they had been a year ago; by the end of the month, the Relief Board of Cook County had doled out 20 percent more aid to unemployed workers than had been paid in July of 1934. As usual, however, people still found the time, money, and interest for baseball. It was a place where things were okay, with your value and your opinions worth as much as the person's sitting next to you.

It was frustrating to watch the boys, however, as the Cubs bowed twice to the champions, 5–3 and 6–4. Jesse "Pop" Haines, 42-years-strong, bested Root in the opener (who had relieved French, after hne gave up his first runs in 18 innings) while Diz picked up win number twelve against Warneke (his ninth loss) in the nightcap. A highlight for Demaree occurred in between the games when he received his trophy for being named 1934 MVP of the Pacific Coast League. And before the day's play started, a moment of silence was observed for the passing of Hank O' Day, who was both a National League umpire and Cubs manager. The sweep ran the Cards' string of consecutive wins over the Cubs to five, as Pepper Martin punctuated the Gas House honor by knocking over O' Dea on a play at the plate, jarring the ball loose. The Cubs' catcher saw some early holiday fireworks as he lay dazed, while Martin scored and triumphantly pumped his fist in the air.

There had been a Babe Ruth sighting on the Fourth, as he played in another ho-hum game with the locals, homering for the Westchester County (NY) "Married Men's" team against the local "Bachelors" in a 12–1 victory for the grooms. The next day, down in Brooklyn, brothers Tony and Al Cuccinello homered in the same game; siblings wouldn't sock long ones together for another fifteen years until Dom and Joe DiMaggio did it on June 30, 1950.

It would be an unusual one-day trip home, as the Cubs would have to travel back east to Pittsburgh for games with the Pirates before the All-Star Game in Cleveland on the 8th. Dejected from the doubleheader loss, the Cubs left town having fallen from second place at the start of the day to fourth at its finish, as the Cardinals were the closest to the Giants. "Close" was relative, however, as St. Louis was an imposing nine games behind New York at the season's halfway point.

After dropping a 4–0 shutout to the Pirates and Red Lucas (who didn't allow a Chicago runner to get to third) in Pittsburgh, the Cubs roared back with an extra-inning win by the score of 10–8 on July 6. The star of the contest was Cavarretta, as the rookie pounded out four hits to all corners of Forbes Field. With the All-Star Game approaching, Grimm felt justified in beckoning both French and Warneke from the bullpen in this game, which was authored by Carleton for the first seven innings. French was baby-sitting an 8–2 advantage in the ninth, when the Bucs exploded on him for six runs to gain a tie. Warneke then entered and shut the door, as both teams remained scoreless through the twelfth. Then, with Galan and Herman aboard in the Cub thirteenth, Cavy slapped his fourth safety, which not only scored Galan but induced an error from Thevenow that sent Herman across as well. Warneke had another strong inning in the bottom half, and all concerned were hoping that he was making the corrections necessary for a strong second half to the season, more like his usual self. "Way back yonder when the three-hour and ten-minute game was in its infancy," recollected Burns, "Guy Bush got around to the matter that has been stimulating his ambition all season—a start against his former buddies…. Guy did mighty well for five innings, then introduced his famous 'goose ball,' much to the delight of the Cubs, who knocked him out in the seventh.'" Indeed, the man who had surrendered Babe Ruth's final home run was definitely more interested in this contest; Bush considered himself a Cub through and through, as emotions ran high in his memories of the twelve-year tenure (1923 through 1934) that he spent on the North Side.

Earlier in the game, Carleton nearly fainted in the dugout after chugging around third base to score a run in the third inning. It was a hot, sultry day in the Steel City, and Carleton's teammates immediately came to his aid with water and ice. When umpires Bill Klem, Cy Pfirman, and George Barr soon came over and complained about the Cubs' delay in taking the field, the rookie catcher Stephenson brashly ripped the ball from Klem's hand—the most experienced and feared official in baseball—and heaved it towards the centerfield fence, giving his pitcher extra time to recuperate as the rest of the team laughed in amusement.

For the All-Star Game, Frisch had originally decided that Dean and Wilson would be the starting battery for the National League. While the selection of Dean raised no eyebrows, the Wilson choice was a surprise to some, due to some tension that arose between him and Frisch since

Wilson left the Cardinals after 1933. When Frisch took over the Cardinals in the middle of that season, he and Wilson verbally sparred over leadership issues over the team. The argument come to a head when Frisch reportedly scolded Wilson for arguing with an umpire, saying that only himself as manager would perform this "duty." But the fences seemed to be mended, at least according to what Frisch was saying. "Wilson is a smart catcher and belongs in there as the number one man," he affirmed.

But things made a turn for the worse in Dean's relationship with baseball, his manager, St. Louis, and now with St. Paul, Minnesota, as well. After the Cardinals concluded their series in Chicago against the Cubs, they got on the train for St. Paul to play an exhibition game there on July 5. Breadon and Rickey were notorious for squeezing exhibitions in wherever they could on the schedule, as it was an extra money-making opportunity. Most of the players did not care for these events; they usually weren't paid anything for the effort and would have preferred a day off from the grind of the regular schedule. Nonetheless, thankful to simply have jobs in the time of depression, they typically played the games for the grateful, out-posted fans in far-away places. Dean's personal resentment, however, could be traced back eleven months earlier.

Back in August 1934, the Cubs swept a hard-fought doubleheader from the Cardinals in Sportsman's Park, beating Dizzy and Paul Dean. Disgusted with the results, the Deans (with Dizzy leading the revolt) decided they would skip the scheduled exhibition game in Detroit the following day. They missed the train on purpose, and there was hell to pay when the club returned a couple days later. Frisch charged into the locker room and told them that they were both fined and suspended. Diz became so angry that he tore up his home and road Cardinal uniforms, knocked over most of the furniture, and, pointing a finger of warning around the room, vowed that he would never play for St. Louis again. The whole case was ultimately brought before Landis, as the Deans pitted themselves against the formidable legal team of Rickey, Breadon, Frisch, and a number of Cardinal players who "testified" that Dean's arrogance was beginning to alienate many on the club. The fines stuck, but were reduced after Diz made a public apology in the St. Louis newspapers (the club was more lenient on Paul, for they felt that Diz had an overreaching influence on him), and the suspensions could end whenever the Deans wanted to rejoin the team, which they did almost immediately. After this incident, no difficulties were displayed from either of the brothers until the questionable effort by Diz in the game on June 3 of the current season in Pittsburgh.

So it was imagined that the Deans had learned their lessons, at least as related to skipping exhibition games. Dizzy and Paul got on the train from Chicago to St. Paul, but that was about the extent of their physical exertion on the trip. Once again, they had protested going, and once again, Frisch threatened them with suspensions and fines. As the Cardinals took the field at St. Paul, the Deans never left the dugout—not to pitch, hit, coach the bases, or even wave to the fans. Dizzy, in fact, didn't even bother to put on his baseball shoes with his uniform. At the end of the game, the St. Paul fans booed loudly—and everyone knew why.

Frisch was clear about his feelings, but like Miller Huggins' attempts to "manage" Babe Ruth, Frisch was often left wondering what to do. "It was the worst thing I've seen in my baseball career," he said plainly. "I've been in baseball seventeen years, and my head is still on my shoulders. I suppose they [the Deans] think they are good. If a man doesn't think enough of his profession to take a bow before fans who drove forty or fifty miles to see him, I don't know what I can do about it." Frisch also let it be known that Dean was yanked from his starting role in the All-Star Game, and that honor was given to Derringer of the Reds.

"If he [Frisch] wants to keep me out of the All-Star Game, it's all right with me. It's his privilege," Dean told the press. Then, in an obvious reference to Breadon and Rickey, he added, "The Cardinals are a chain gang, an outfit that will send you back if you don't hit .600 ... look at [Pepper] Martin—he's got a busted ankle, and still they sent him to St. Paul to play ball just to grab some dough. They treat us like dogs."

Despite these comments, Breadon surprisingly deferred all punitive measures against Dean to Frisch's judgment—and the result was nothing. "It's all blown over, I tell you, there will be no penalty for the Deans. I'm sick of the whole matter," the Cardinal manager concluded. On July 7—the day before the All-Star Game—Dean appeared in a relief role in the first game of a doubleheader in St. Louis against the Reds. The 15,000 fans on hand at Sportsman's Park drowned him with "boos" when he came in for Jesse Haines in the fourth inning, but the cheers returned for the Arkansas boy when he delivered an RBI single in the Cardinal fifth, part of a five-run inning that keyed a 9–4 St. Louis comeback win. It was Dizzy's thirteenth victory on the year, and Paul raised his record to 8–7 by beating Derringer 5–1 to close out the day. It seemed all was okay once again, as the double-win by the Deans leap-frogged the Cards over the Cubs into second place as the All-Star Game arrived.

This juxtaposition occurred despite that fact that Lee had led Chicago into the second half with a 13–1 thrashing of the Pirates and Cy Blanton, as Jurges enjoyed a perfect 4-for-4 day at the plate as he and Hartnett charted a pair of doubles each. It had been Lee's first complete game since June 19, back when three weeks was a long time in between repeating such a feat. The team feared that Lindstrom, now having the lion's share of work in center field with Cuyler gone, had broken his finger on a pitch that hit him in the fourth inning; fortunately, an examination later revealed no fracture. Many of the Cubs made plans to stop over in Cleveland on the way back home, so that they could see their mates in action in the game of stars. At roughly the halfway point of the season, these were some statistics for the Cubs players:

	AB	HR	RBI	Avg.	Pitcher	W–L
O' Dea	75	3	16	.347	Lee	8–3
Stephenson	6	0	0	.333	French	7–5
Hartnett	228	8	43	.329	Carleton	6–3
Galan	310	4	33	.310	Henshaw	6–4
Hack	166	1	26	.307	Warneke	6–9
Herman	313	1	28	.304	Root	3–5
Cavarretta	277	4	39	.300	Kowalik	2–1
Demaree	72	1	14	.278	Bryant	1–2
Lindstrom	209	3	35	.263		
Klein	224	12	34	.259		
Jurges	234	1	26	.244		
Stainback	40	0	2	.225		
English	68	2	7	.176		

After the games of July 7 were completed, some of the National League stars from the western clubs (namely, the Cubs, Cardinals, and Reds) caught the same train to Cleveland. Along the way, the train stopped in a little Indiana town, and children gazed in amazement at the famous folks passing through and swooped upon them for autographs. Dean was happy to oblige, and humorously took the opportunity to try and turn the tables on Frisch, who was in the middle of getting dressed. As Diz signed the kids' tablets, he began to beckon his manager through one of the train's windows.

"Come on, Frank—these poor kids won't have no chance to see the All-Star Game, and they want to see you. Come on out and speak to them."

Frisch said softly through the window, so only Dean could hear, that he was tired and not dressed appropriately, and therefore asked that he be excused.

"Okay, Frank," Dean yelled back, eyeing an opportunity. "I've given you a fair chance and you've fallen down. I've gotta good notion to fine you."

What was that all about? the press wanted to know when they got to Cleveland. "Oh, nothing," Diz explained. "I'm letting him off with a warning this time."

Due to a bout with kidney stones, Harridge had to miss the game, but was replaced by Tigers owner Frank Navin as a representative of the American League. As Harridge recovered in his bed at St. Francis Hospital in Evanston, Illinois, he fought doctors' instructions to relax and listen to the game on the radio; he wanted to be in Cleveland. The day before, Navin and his fellow American League owners got together and agreed to raise the league's waiver price from $4,000 to $7,500, which placed it at the same level as in the Senior Circuit. This move was designed to stimulate more intra-league transactions, as teams would then be more willing to part with a player that might help a rival club, since the club offering the player would be receiving more money. Navin's star first baseman, Hank Greenberg, had socked his 24th and 25th home runs in a 16–1 thrashing of the Browns on July 5 in Detroit. The win had put the defending pennant winners within a game-and-a-half of the top spot in the league, held by the Yankees. And Greenberg's homers had put him within one of the record pace set by Ruth in 1927, when the Babe nailed sixty. Perhaps more impressive was the fact that Greenberg had become the first player to enter the All-Star Game with 100 RBIs (there was no All-Star "break" at this point)—no player would match the feat until Juan Gonzalez had 101 at the All-Star break in 1998. The Tigers would defeat St. Louis again the next two days for their ninth and tenth wins in a row, as they crept to within a single game of New York. Despite Greenberg's prowess with the bat, it was his glove that had caught the attention of Joe Cronin. "It's as big around as a catcher's mitt," Cronin noticed. "And about as thick as a flapjack, and covered with licorice juice." But even with his astounding numbers, Greenberg was not on the All-Star roster.

The idea for the All-Star Game was concocted, furthered, and mostly implemented by Arch Ward, as an idea to Harridge, just as Ward was serving as chairman of the "Century of Progress" exhibition at the 1933 Chicago World's Fair. "It has been a tremendous success from every angle," wrote Dan Daniel about the All-Star Game for the *New York World-Telegram*. "It is obvious that the contest should be an annual feature." While some originally thought that it was a passing novelty soon to be forgotten, the impending crowd at Cleveland proved that it was to be a worthy annual event. "In the short space of three summers," Ward wrote proudly, "the midyear interleague game has become the biggest attraction in baseball. No other single game of the year develops so many endless arguments." Evans, the Cleveland general manager, had also been one of the first supporters of the contest back in 1933—and his loyalty was rewarded with an opportunity to host the contest that would later become known as the "Mid-Summer Classic." Excitement for the matchup was clearly evident back in May, as Evans reported that 40,000 orders for advance tickets—from nearly every state in the Union—had already been received at that point.

Frisch then suddenly switched to Van Lingle Mungo as his starting pitcher. But when Mungo injured the index finger on his pitching hand, Frisch called on Warneke to take his place, despite his 6–9 record. Grimm refused to let Warneke make the appearance, however—not because he didn't deserve it, but because Lon had pitched the four-and-two-thirds innings in the 10–8 win at Pittsburgh on July 6. "It is useless to send him there [to Cleveland] if he is not going to be of any good to the team," Grimm explained. "If I could have dodged using him, I'd be glad to have Lon pitch at Cleveland." So, changing plans once again, Frisch's own Bill Walker from the Cardinals got the call instead.

The American Leaguers included pitchers Rowe and Tommy Bridges from Detroit, Lefty Gomez from New York, Lefty Grove from Boston, and Mel Harder from Cleveland; catchers Cochrane and Rick Farrell from Boston, and Rollie Hemsley from St. Louis; infielders Gehrig, Gehringer, Cronin, Myer, Foxx, and Ossie Bluege from Washington; and outfielders Bob Johnson and Doc Cramer from Philadelphia, Al Simmons from Chicago, Joe Vosmik from Cleveland, Ben Chapman from New York, and Sam West from St. Louis. Aside from Ruth and Greenberg, the other noticeable absence from the AL roster was Averill, as his firecracker mishap cost him an appearance. And many Chicago baseball fans felt that pitcher Ted Lyons, and not Simmons, should have been representing the White Sox; Lyons possessed one of the best records in the American League at 9–3. The second-guessers also complained about the selections at shortstop—Cleveland's Billy Knickerbocker and Philadelphia's Eric McNair were both hitting thirty points higher than Cronin and Bluege.

The game got underway at 1:30 P.M. Eastern Standard Time, as Governor Martin Davey of Ohio threw out the first ball (Landis followed with one as well). Ruth was watching with his wife from a box seat near the American League dugout, as he peered out over the only American League park in which he failed to hit a home run (the Indians moved into Municipal Stadium in 1932 after leaving League Park, which had been their home since 1901). As the Babe flipped through a game program, he and others noticed that the "autograph" page contained players' names that were misspelled; 50,000 such programs would be sold on the day. Also in attendance were the entire Brooklyn Dodgers and St. Louis

Browns teams, in addition to scattered players from the other clubs, including the Cubs; Kowalik, in fact, was put to work as he threw batting practice to the National League hitters.

Radio announcers positioned themselves behind the microphones. Among them was Bob Elson from WGN, Graham McNamee and Tom Manning from the National Broadcasting Company, and France Laux and Jack Graney from the Columbia Broadcasting System. The temperature was a bit cooler than expected—71 degrees at game time—and the attendance turned out to be a bit lower than expected at 69,831. Nonetheless, the figure was 20,000 more than the first All-Star Game at Comiskey Park in 1933, and 21,000 higher than the 1934 game at the Polo Grounds. It was understandable that the centerfield area was only a third full; the wall, at that point of the park, was itself 493 feet from home plate, not allowing much of a view. Walker, the last-minute selection as the National League's starting pitcher, created a fury in the pressbox as anxious sportswriters were thrown further off the scent when Schumacher was rumored the night before as another possibility for Frisch. Gomez was Cochrane's choice, as the lefthander "led all American League pitchers last season in everything except height and weight," according to Kieran. Martin led off the game for the Nationals with a single on the first pitch, and the scrappy Pepper fittingly stole second (earlier, he had scared away autograph seekers in pre-game practice by accidentally firing several balls into the stands from third base—also not unusual for Martin. With his throws even more wild than usual, however, some began to think that Pepper had some friends behind the dugout, and wanted to send them some souvenirs). After moving to third on a groundball by Ott, Martin was left stranded as his teammate, Medwick, struck out. Medwick's usual Gas House temper was not checked at the All-Star door, however, as he clearly kicked his leg at home plate umpire Red Ormsby—but caught himself before he actually struck him, protesting a check-swing that Ormsby ruled a full one for the third strike.

Batting fourth in the American League order was Foxx, beyond whom only Ruth had more homers in the history of the game. After Vosmik was retired, Gehrig forced Gehringer at second when Foxx came to the dish. With a full count, he caught hold of a pitch Walker left up in the strike zone—"a 3–2 cripple," as mocked by Irving Vaughan—and drove it far into the leftfield stands, giving the AL a quick 2–0 lead. After following up with another tally the next inning (Hemsley tripled to the leftfield wall, and was driven in on a deep fly by Cronin), the Americans allowed a run in the fourth when Arky Vaughan doubled, Medwick walked, and Terry singled for a score. It was all the visiting team would have, as Gomez labored six innings (still an All-Star Game record to this day) in shutting down the Nationals after which Harder closed things out for the final three frames in a 4–1 win. Foxx had picked up another RBI in the American half of the fifth, smashing a line-drive single off Schumacher's glove with the bases loaded, scoring Vosmik. Gomez got the victory, which he also did in the 1933 game, and would do again in 1937— also a record that still stands (Harder, additionally, was credited with the victory in a relief role in the 9–7 win for the American League in 1934).

Not much noise was heard from the Cubs who were present, as Herman went hitless in playing the entire game at second, while Hartnett caught only the last two innings and did not make a trip to the plate.

The box score:

National League	AB	R	H	RBI	PO	A
Martin, 3B	4	0	1	0	0	0
Vaughan, SS	3	1	1	0	2	2
Ott, RF	4	0	0	0	1	0
Medwick, LF	3	0	0	0	0	0
Terry, 1B	3	0	1	1	5	1
Collins, 1B	1	0	0	0	2	0
Berger, CF	2	0	0	0	1	0
b-Moore, CF	2	0	0	0	1	0
Herman, 2B	3	0	0	0	1	4
Wilson, C	3	0	1	0	8	0
c-Whitehhead	0	0	0	0	0	0
Hartnett, C	0	0	0	0	3	0
Walker, P	0	0	0	0	0	0
a-Mancuso	1	0	0	0	0	0
Schumacher, P	1	0	0	0	0	1
d-P. Waner	1	0	0	0	0	0
Derringer , P	0	0	0	0	0	0
Dean, P	0	0	0	0	0	0
Totals	31	1	4	1	24	8

American League	AB	R	H	RBI	PO	A
Vosmik, RF	4	1	1	0	1	0
Gehringer, 2B	3	0	2	0	1	3
Gehrig, 1B	3	1	0	0	12	0
Foxx, 3B	3	1	2	3	0	0
Bluege, 3B	0	0	0	0	0	0
Johnson, LF	4	0	0	0	4	0
Chapman, LF	0	0	0	0	0	0
Simmons, CF	4	0	2	0	2	0
Cramer, CF	0	0	0	0	0	0

American League	AB	R	H	RBI	PO	A
Hemsley, C	4	1	1	0	6	0
Cronin, SS	4	0	0	1	1	4
Gomez, P	2	0	0	0	0	2
Harder, P	1	0	0	0	0	1
Totals	32	4	8	4	27	10

National League	0 0 0	1 0 0	0 0 0—1
American League	2 1 0	0 1 0	0 0 x—4

NL	IP	H	R	ER	BB	SO
Walker (L)	2	2	3	3	1	2
Schumacher	4	4	1	1	1	5
Derringer	1	1	0	0	0	1
Dean	1	1	0	0	1	1

AL	IP	H	R	ER	BB	SO
Gomez (W)	6	3	1	1	2	4
Harder	3	1	0	0	0	1

a—Flied out for Walker in third. b—Flied out for Berger in seventh. c—Ran for Wilson in seventh. d—Grounded out for Schumacher in seventh. e—Martin. LOB—Nationals 5, Americans 7. 2B—Vaughan, Wilson, Gehringer, Simmons. 3B—Hemsley. HR—Foxx. Umpires—Ormsby and Geisel (A.L.), Magerkurth and Sears (N.L.). T—2:06.

Simmons, the only Chicago player to make an offensive impact in the game, actually had been the best hitter in the entire three years of All-Star play through 1935 as he carried an impressive .462 (6-for-13) batting average.

All the while, two indomitable athletes were proving themselves very much human. There was Gehrig, who was now 0-for-9 in All-Star competition; and presently in New York was Jesse Owens, who was beaten for the second time for the year in the 100-yard dash by Eulace Peacock of Temple University.

The game did not have a great trademark like the first two contests. In 1933, Ruth provided a dramatic homer; in 1934, Hubbell successively struck out the five biggest bats in the American League. But nevertheless, it was clearly evident that the game's popularity was increasing. "This is the greatest boost baseball has gotten in years," said Sam Breadon, who back in 1933 was one of a few National League owners who were staunchly opposed to the idea of an All-Star Game. All of the gate receipts, minus expenses and $10,000 given to both the National and American Leagues for their charitable funds, were donated to the Association of Professional Ball Players of America which gave support to indigent players for retirement needs—a final amount estimated by Evans to be nearly $60,000. While Boston was scheduled to host the 1936 game in Braves' Park, the financial instability of that organization caused many in power to question that decision and to table the issue for further discussion. The attendance record set in 1935 would stand until the 1981 All-Star Game, also played in Cleveland Stadium, which was witnessed by 72,000 spectators.

Yet, there was also a faction of National League owners and team presidents who still did not like having the game and were even calling to end it. Word had leaked that Terry instructed Frisch to "go easy" on Schumacher, in terms of the number of innings he should work; the Cardinals' skipper supposedly received similar requests from other National League managers as well. When news of these tactics reached the fans, the editorial sections of the sports pages were flooded with angry letters. They all demanded the full-fledged effort of both teams, to be alleviated by the suggested return of the vote for All-Star selections to the fans themselves. "This [having the fans vote for the participating players] was the basic idea behind the game in the first place," wrote Ward, whose pen was the genesis of the whole concept. "And the sooner its value to baseball is recognized, the better it will be for the All-Star Game and for the sport itself." Ward had another thought for future All-Star games as well—a "break" for all players surrounding the contest. "Having something to do with the interleague contest from its inception," he offered, "I would like to add the suggestion that next year and every year thereafter the major league schedule-makers arrange for an open date before the All-Star Game as well as the day afterward. This would almost eliminate the danger of either league using up its pitching talent in advance of the game, as the National League did on this occasion."

Ward also had a bite for Frisch, Dressen, and Grimm in what was their perceived soft-handing of the NL roster, particularly the pitching staff—Schumacher notwithstanding, for he was referring to the managers' use of their own hurlers. "The three National League managers may say that the All-Star Game didn't count for anything as far as they were concerned, but it counted heavily with the 70,000 who saw the game and the millions who listened in throughout the land. Whether the Cubs, Cardinals, and Reds are a game higher or lower in the standings at the end of the year will make little or no difference, but millions will remember that Grimm, Frisch, and Dressen either kept out of the game or nullified the services of Lon Warneke, Dizzy Dean, and Paul Derringer." A few in the New York press suggested that Frisch had limited Dizzy's work not to impose a form of "punishment" on him for his recent debacle on the St. Paul trip, but to give his marquee pitcher extra rest. Some of the stars didn't get the expected playing time, and some weren't there at all. "The names were on the list," added Kieran, "but they might just as well have been rubbed out."

But perhaps the most serious omission was Greenberg, and it was made by his own manager—Cochrane. How could that happen, asked Kieran, when "Lank Hank has been playing grand ball right in front of Mr. Cochrane's very own eyes day after day? It was all right, the critics admit, to pick Lou Gehrig ... but Greenberg deserved at least a part-time job at first base in this All-Star clash. He is leading both leagues away off in home runs and there is no one close to him in the little matter of driving in runs for his side."

Steve McKeever, president of the Brooklyn Dodgers, cited his own two reasons for discontinuing the event: that star players can get hurt, and that there is no "financial return for the participants." It was interesting that many team officials felt this way, because these same two reasons could have been applied to the numerous exhibition games that players were forced to conduct on off days—with the owners reaping the monetary rewards. "Please remember, Mr. Managers," reminded Joe Williams of the *New York World-Telegram*, "this isn't your game. It's the fans' game." Added Paul Gallico of the *New York Daily News*, "The only conclusion one can draw about the All-Star Game is that no one connected with baseball is in a terrific lather to run this affair."

As regular play resumed in the National League, the Reds hosted another night game on July 10. It was the Dodgers' turn, and the attendance dropped off sharply to 12,000. Those on hand, however, saw another fireworks display and, more significantly, the first home run in the major leagues hit after dark. Babe Herman—formerly a star with Brooklyn, most recently with the Cubs and Pirates, but acquired only a couple weeks prior by Cincinnati—sailed one into the right field stands in the seventh inning with two out and nobody on base. The Reds had long since passed their need for runs though, as an eight-run third led the way to a 15–2 obliteration of Stengel's cadre. Over in Pittsburgh, Schumacher—who in college was passed over by the Yankees after a scout said "he will never be a big leaguer"—apparently didn't work too hard in the All-Star Game, and he beat the Pirates for his eleventh straight win. And in the continuation of the American League schedule, the Tigers' winning streak ended at ten, despite a record-tying ten doubles in a 12–11 loss in Washington. Another streak would end the following day for Detroit, as outfielder Pete Fox failed to hit safely for the first time in 30 games.

The Cubs were looking to maintain the momentum they had begun before the All-Star Game, and the opportunity presented itself in a five-game series against the Braves in Wrigley Field beginning on July 10. The bruins smelled blood, as the struggling Boston club was falling deeper into last place. Chicago jumped on them with two wins, 6–4 and 5–3, the second of which was their tenth win over Boston for the year and Carleton's ninth in ten tries against the club, with Galan getting his 100th hit on the year. But alas, the energy was thought thwarted when the Cubs had to travel *on an off-day in the middle of the series*—July 12–to Madison, Wisconsin, to play in an exhibition against the Madison Blues of the Wisconsin State League. Not heading to Dairyland was Bryant, whose performance had become unsatisfactory in Grimm's eyes in the previous weeks. Instead, he was sent south to Birmingham in the Southern League, along with cash, in exchange for pitcher Clyde "Duster" Shoun. The Mountain City, Tennessee, native Shoun threw from the left side, and since not having seen him since spring training, Grimm liked the reports sent to Chicago on him. Shoun, however, would be sent back to Birmingham before ever getting a chance to "toe the slab" with the Cubs.

The Cubs beat the locals 2–1, as the little-used battery of Kowalik and Stephenson turned the trick. The team then made a u-turn and rumbled back down the tracks across the Illinois counties of Boone, McHenry, and Kane towards the city to finish affairs with the Braves.

The day trip had no bearing on matters, much to the chagrin of McKechnie's men. On July 13, Henshaw and Lee dominated in a doubleheader to the tune of 10–2 and 3–1 triumphs. The Bostonians were subsequently run out of town by the Cub bats in the finale 8–7 for a five game sweep, their seventh victory in a row (going back to the two wins at Pittsburgh before the All-Star Game), and thirteenth in fifteen games against the lowly Braves in 1935. It was another uninspiring performance by Warneke, however, as Grimm went back to him in giving French the entire series off. Warneke had been knocked out of the first game against the Braves, in which he fell behind 4–1 in the third inning before Root came to the rescue in shaping the 6–4 comeback win. With only three stanzas of work, Grimm reasoned, Warneke was given a quick chance to right himself in the tail end of the series. Given a 3–0 lead through five innings, however, he allowed the Braves to tie the game as Carleton entered. Tex held Boston in check, as he usually did, to gain the victory and run his record to 8–3, while Warneke was saved from yet another loss (as he was four days earlier by Root). On the day, Herman joined Galan in the hundred-hit club while Klein pummeled his thirteenth homer. It was a small Sunday crowd of 7,700, but it was assumed that many fans were saving their money for the following Sunday, when Terry's Giants would enter town and a figure five or six times that population was expected. For as hot as they were at the halfway point of their own schedule (behind the playing pace of most of the league, due to the numerous early-season rainouts), the Cubs still found themselves eight games behind the mighty New York club.

The only downer to the series was the discovery that Lindstrom had indeed broken his finger; it was estimated that he would miss two weeks of play.

In their own efforts to catch the Terrymen, the Cardinals were looking to continue the strong ball they had recently played. People were coming back through the turnstiles in St. Louis, and Breadon claimed that attendance was up sixty-five percent from the 1934 championship season. Thus, the last thing the Cardinals needed was more dissension from the Dean family. Paul had hardly been the pitcher he was in '34, when down the stretch towards the World Series, he was throwing as well as anyone in baseball—including brother Dizzy. Less than a year later, Paul was barely over the .500 mark. Things looked like they were turning around for him on the 14th, as Paul valiantly beat the Phillies 5–1 in the first game of a doubleheader in St. Louis. Diz was to take the mound in the second one, but instead complained of a sore arm and informed Frisch that he was not available. Once again, Dean had his Cardinal teammates sneering at him, for several of them testified the previous year that Diz got a sore arm "whenever he felt like it" during the tumultuous weeks following the Detroit exhibition fiasco. The Cardinals were most enraged this time, however, because they had witnessed Dean whipping balls from third base over to first in pre-game practice, showing no signs of a sore arm whatsoever at that point. It was an untimely move by Dean as well, for it was the day that the Cardinals were receiving their 1934 championship rings in person from Landis, raising the championship flag atop the center field flag pole, and being honored by the largest Sportsman's Park crowd of the year, 23,000. A few Cardinal players even suggested that Diz was jealous of the recent success of veteran pitcher Bill Hallahan, who had struggled during much of the Gas House Gang's run in 1934. Just a year earlier, Bill McCullough of the *Brooklyn Times-Union* had written of him, "Once the fastest southpaw in the National League, Hallahan has gone into a tailspin ... his toboggan slide has whittled Frisch's staff down to the Dean brothers, and nowhere do the books show a team winning the pennant with two pitchers." On the 13th, Hallahan— the old hero of the 1931 World Series for the Cardinals—shut out the Phillies on two hits at Sportsman's for the team's eighth win in a row.

Hallahan had not allowed a hit in the game until slugger Dolph Camilli singled in the seventh, as "Wild Bill" appeared to be re-establishing himself as a stopper on the staff.

This success by the veteran lefty perhaps helped lead to another incident the very day after Diz sat out his scheduled start in the doubleheader, as St. Louis played Boston on July 15. Dean said his arm felt better, so he went out and picked up another win in a 13–6 romp over the Braves. St. Louis had now ripped off eleven straight (Walker victoriously filled in for Diz in the second half of the doubleheader two days prior). After the game, Dean was to drive to Springfield, Illinois, for a church charity game appearance with Illinois Governor Henry Horner. Driving quickly up Route 66, Diz started to take his time as he got closer to Springfield. Upon getting to the event, he informed the audience—including Governor Horner—that, before anything else, he needed to immediately get something to eat, preferably the largest steak that Sangamon County had to offer. While that was somewhat understandable to a few of the people at the ballyard, he then disappeared for a long time into the streets of the town, and didn't return until an hour and a half later. The governor had long left, and the crowd that remained really didn't care if Diz was there or not.

And just one day later at Sportsman's Park, Dean received the trophy for being named the National League's Most Valuable Player in 1934. There was applause from the stands, but not like there should have been for a hometown MVP. His teammates appeared unimpressed, and most waited impatiently with hands on hips for the ceremony to be over. But Dean, at heart generally a good man, recognized the opportunity for contrition; while not apologizing for his recent behavior, he did tell the crowd that he hoped to finish his career in a Cardinal uniform.

The five-game sweep over the Braves had pushed the Cubs away from the Pirates and onto the heels of the Redbirds, as the standings on July 15th showed:

	W	L	Pct.	GB
New York	51	22	.698	—
St. Louis	46	29	.613	6.0
Chicago	45	32	.584	8.0
Pittsburgh	42	37	.531	12.0
Cincinnati	36	42	.461	17.5
Brooklyn	33	42	.439	19.0
Philadelphia	31	44	.413	21.0
Boston	21	57	.296	32.5

At this point, famed Manhattan oddsmaker Jack Doyle had the Giants and Tigers as less-than-even money to win their respective pennants, with Terry's club at 1–3 and Cochrane's at 4–5. Both were 9–5 choices at the start of the season. The longest odds for taking the title among the National League teams belonged to the Braves at 200–1, while the bookies currently gave Hornsby's lowly Browns a one-in-one-thousand chance of winning at all. They held a record of 21–54 and were a distant 27 games behind front-running Detroit in the American League.

The Cubbies then picked up a full game on New York on the 15th, as Herman's double in the tenth inning sent Galan across the plate for a 2–1 victory over the Phillies, Chicago's eighth in a row. French had his fourth shutout of the year in his grasp, but the Philadelphia run that scored in the first inning was of the unearned variety, courtesy of a throwing error by Stainback. Instead the win went to Warneke, who was in desperate need of one when he entered the game in the ninth (French and Grimm almost had to be separated, as the lefthander was angry that he wasn't allowed to finish the game). Afterwards, just when Dean was making his road trip from St. Louis to Springfield, it was rumored that Phil Wrigley had secretly and illegally bought Diz from the Cardinals, but the story—one that seemed to surface with one organization or another any time Dean and the St. Louis club were fighting—was quickly doused by Grimm. Jolly Cholly made it clear that Dean's presence might not be good for any team at this point. "We have not purchased Dean," the manager said unequivocally. "We are not negotiating for his services. We would not pay what the Cardinals want for him even if they could offer him for sale under baseball law. We are not sure that we would want a player of the type Diz has turned out to be, the Cubs being singularly free of temperamental prima donnas."

The St. Louis "non-donnas" had the Cards chugging along, moving to within four games of the Giants on July 16 as the venerable Jesse Haines beat the Braves, 2–1, for twelve straight. And rookie centerfielder Terry Moore was more than pulling his weight, too, as his homer in the ninth inning beat Ed Brandt and the Braves again by the score of 2–1 the following day, giving St. Louis thirteen consecutive wins and Hallahan his ninth in a row. When Paul Dean made it fourteen in a row, the Giants were beginning to have stark memories of their collapse to the Cards in '34. Hubbell kept them on track, however. The screwballer got his twelfth triumph in Cincinnati despite a barrage of soda bottles from numerous fans that littered the field, the result of a questionable call by umpire Beans Reardon that ended a Reds offensive threat. Cincinnati, in small part due to the novelty of the night games, was currently second to the Giants in National League attendance.

The Cubs could not keep pace with the Big Two, though, and the Phillies snapped the winning streak at eight games by taking two out of three at Wrigley. Henshaw was run from the mound in the second inning of the opener (a 7–5 loss), while Lee got nipped in the second game by Curt Davis, 3–2. Davis did not allow a Cub hit after the fourth inning in that contest. Root was able to salvage the finale, as Henshaw started once again and was knocked out of the box again, but had plenty of offense to support an 11–3 beating. The summer heat had come to Chicago, and the umpires tried to cool off between innings with bags of ice placed atop their heads. As had been the case at Wrigley every season before—and has been every season since—the southerly winds carrying the summer warmth started propelling the ball over the outfield wall with greater regularity. Klein, Demaree, and Hack all planted the ball beyond the confines during the day.

Overall, it was an unimpressive performance against a second-division club (Philadelphia was fourteen games under .500 at 31–45 entering the series), and Grimm and his mates knew that better preparation was a requisite with the Giants in town over the weekend of July 19–21.

"It seems to me that this would be an appropriate time," announced Arch Ward in his *Tribune* column as the New Yorkers came to town, "to stand up and give a hand to the youngest player who ever became a regular in the major leagues. Today happens to be the boy's birthday, his 19th. I refer to Phil Cavarretta, first baseman of the Cubs, who stepped from high school competition into the big leagues to take away the job of one of the best first basemen baseball has known." Indeed, Grimm had not given himself a start since the first week of the season, and the former Lane Tech star Cavarretta held firm at the position by hitting .299 with 43 RBIs on his 19th birthday, the 19th of July. The previous morning, he had been the special guest of the Humboldt Park Baseball School in Chicago. His popularity was growing, understandably among the city's fans especially, and he showed few signs of nerves as the pennant race started to heat up. As the Wrigley Field crowd gathered for the first game with the Giants, they saw Cavy get honored with a diamond ring from some grateful friends and a basket of flowers from his parents (it was surprising to some that Cavarretta accepted the bouquet on the field, notwithstanding the fact that it came from his family; flowers were considered bad luck in baseball, and many a floral giver has been turned away politely without explanation from a fearful player). Presenting Cavarretta to the crowd was Pants Rowland, the scout that signed him and who was surprised to learn that Cavy was 19 this day—not 18, as he had thought.

To begin what was expected to be a banner weekend for attendance, the Cubs were expecting approximately 20,000 free guests as a result of a Ladies' Day promotion on Friday the 19th. It was a critical four-game set (with a doubleheader slated for Sunday), and the salty veterans, Warneke and Schumacher, took the hill to get the battle underway. The Giants were slipping a bit, coming off a four-game split of a series in Cincinnati against the struggling Reds, a series that Terry had hoped to sweep going in. Warneke did some offensive damage almost immediately, producing a critical two-out, bases-loaded single which jumped the Cubs ahead, 2–1. He scored himself in the fifth for a 3–1 advantage, and later saw his mates send Schumacher to the showers with a six-run eighth inning. Doubles by Hartnett, Demaree, and Klein keyed the outburst, and the Cubbies shipped "Prince Hal" to the locker room. Ott hit his league-leading 21st homer to lead off the ninth, but it wasn't nearly enough; Warneke had an easy 9–3 win in front of a total gathering of 26,700. It was the first win for the Cubs in five tries against the Giants on the year, and the first time they had beaten Schumacher in three attempts. And St. Louis had finally been cooled off (in wins, if not in weather), so the New York lead stood at four games.

A passing thunderstorm delayed the start of Cubs-Giants game for an hour on Saturday the 20th. The game was scheduled for two o'clock, but the skies opened just minutes before the first pitch was to occur. When things got going the Chicago bats continued their assault. French bested Parmelee for his eighth win, 7–2, and the Cubs placed themselves in position for a momentum-turning sweep the next day.

It was Sunday, July 21, and Phil Wrigley was expecting the largest crowd of the year at his ballpark; he was not disappointed. A total of 46,168 paid fans—in addition to some freebies that put the complete sum over 50,000—crammed into the stands for the doubleheader, while thousands more were turned away, retreating back onto the streets in disappointment (it would be years later before the park was reduced to its current capacity of 38,902). Some who got inside were standing on the field of play, and the umpires stipulated that any ball entering the gallery would be counted as a ground-rule double. Still many others "watched from roof tops, porches, fire escapes and telegraph poles," according to James Dawson, who was covering the scene for the *New York Times*. Carleton—who played a part in several big victories over New York for the Cardinals in '34—kicked things off against Hubbell, the ace of the Giants' formidable staff. Terry's troops struck first, gathering four scores on Carleton in the first three innings and sending Tex out of the game. The big blow once again came off the bat of Ott, as his mammoth 22nd homer caromed off the upper half of the rightfield foul pole, teasing Sheffield Avenue as it bounced back into the stands. To the rescue came Root, as he had done many times before, and he held the Giants in check until the Cubs could scratch back to tie and send the game into extra innings. In the eleventh inning—after the Giants had failed to score for the eighth straight frame—Galan opened the Chicago attack with a double to the left field wall, and Herman followed with a bunt. At first, it looked as if Billy had pushed the ball too close to the mound, as "King Carlos" (still in the game, as was typical of his stamina) pounced on it and threw to third. The speedy Galan, however, got a great jump when he saw the ball hit the ground off Herman's bat, and beat the play with Herman safe at first. Cavarretta squeezed himself onto the bases next, as the thirdbaseman Koenig couldn't field his grounder cleanly while the other runners held. After Hartnett bounced to the mound to force Galan at home, Demaree whacked the first pitch he saw for a hit to center, and the Cubs won the day's opener, 5–4.

It looked like the second contest would be a squeaker as well. Holding a 5–0 lead going into the Giants' eighth, Lee surrendered a barrage of hits that quickly tied things up. He was replaced by Warneke, who refused to let New York take the lead. Sensing urgency, the Cubs' offense unleashed on Al Smith in the bottom half. Demaree stroked another hit, followed by one off the bat of Klein, and Jurges was intentionally walked to fill the bases for Warneke. Smith then hit Warneke on the foot—the last thing that Smith wanted to do—which scored Demaree for the lead. After a double by Galan the floodgates were flung wide open, and the New Yorkers went meekly in the ninth as they suffered an 11–5 setback, and Warneke was given credit for his tenth win (and second in the series). The main benefactor for the Chicago offense in the big inning was Chagnon, who relieved Smith and had been in Terry's doghouse recently for not pitching to hitters the way in which Memphis Bill had directed him.

The sweep provided the fourth and fifth wins in a row for the Cubs, in addition to thirteen in the last fifteen times they had taken the field. The most clear and present danger for Terry, however, was to the south of Chicago; for while the Giants were licking their wounds in the Windy City, the Cardinals disposed of the Dodgers twice in St. Louis, and for the second straight year, what had been building towards a seemingly-insurmountable Giant lead in the standings was down to a sliver—the Cards were behind by only a game-and-a-half. And Jolly Cholly's Chicago Cubs were now a mere four behind the leaders, a vast improvement from the 10½ games they found themselves trailing by after their work was done on the Fourth of July.

Chasing the
Galloping Hoodlums

Not wanting to break their luck, the Cubs took a page out the Gas House Gang's manual and kept wearing their dirty uniforms. The teams from the Empire State crossed paths over central Illinois, as the Giants fearfully entered St. Louis and the Dodgers came north to face Chicago. The Cardinals lost the first game of the Brooklyn series 3–0 to Johnny Babich, which snapped their win streak at fourteen, but then swept the Sunday doubleheader behind Haines and Dizzy Dean to make it sixteen triumphs in their last seventeen tries. Kieran was most apprehensive about his Harlem lads entering the Redbirds' nest. "If it gets down to a rough-and-tumble race, the Cardinals will be the favorites," he warned, the fore-casters in awe the old Gas House form being shown once again. "They are fast and rough and they boast about it. They swell with pride when they are referred to as the 'Galloping Hoodlums.'"

While it never stuck as long as their other nickname, the Cardinals temporarily enjoyed the title—and it was used quite frequently in the New York press for the next several weeks. It had also been a New York writer, Dan Daniel, who gave the name the "Gas House Gang" to the 1934 club during that year's World Series. A cartoon that accompanied Daniel's article in the October 9, 1934, edition of the *New York Telegraph*, which depicted the Cardinals as a slovenly, muscle-bound group crossing the tracks from the blue-collar Gas House district of a fictional town to play the Giants, the team illustrated with a silver spoon attitude and without much fight.

The inevitable didn't take long. In the first game of a twin bill on

July 23 Paul Dean beat the Giants to follow Hallahan's victory in the series opener. Dean's win made the Cardinals 18–1 in their previous nineteen games, while New York had faltered in nine of their past eleven, their worst slide since 1932. The Cards' voyage to the top of the standings lasted for only a few hours, for in the nightcap, Al Smith returned the Giants to first place with an 8–2 win. The games were played in front of a Wednesday throng of 31,000 at Sportsman's Park, the largest weekday crowd in St. Louis in thirteen years. There were three more contests scheduled in the important six-game series.

Another great race was taking shape in the American League, as the other pennant winner from 1934 had also regained first place. The Tigers defeated the Yankees 4–2 on July 24 at Yankee Stadium, which put them ahead of New York by a half game; Detroit, however, still actually trailed the Yankees by a fraction of a point in winning percentage. The teams had split a doubleheader the day before in front of the largest AL crowd of the year—62,516.

Due to the early-season storms back in April and May, Brooklyn had played only one game in Wrigley on the year; so, as in St. Louis between the Giants and Cardinals, the clubs would now hope to complete six contests in the next four days as the National League race was beginning to show its true colors. A total of 42 hits were made by the clubs in the opener, one of which included Klein's sixteenth homer, as Mungo became the ninth pitcher to work on the day and got his twelfth win in a 14–13 thriller. But the Cubs righted themselves to take two games on the 23rd, an 8–0 shutout by Henshaw over Babich (in which Klein hit number seventeen, and nearly missed number eighteen by pulling a ball foul onto Sheffield) and Warneke's nine strikeouts leading to a 6–4 triumph (his thirteenth) over Tom Zachary, despite the fact that Grimm and Lindstrom were ejected for arguing during the latter contest. They added another doubleheader sweep the next day in front of 12,300 fans, O'Dea winning the nightcap with a dramatic homer to right field in the eleventh inning to win 7–6. In that contest, a grand slam by the Dodgers' Danny Taylor had given Brooklyn a 6–4 lead over Lee in the ninth, but hits by Klein, Galan, and Herman in the bottom half made the game continue. Root was the winner in the first one, as Klein ripped another homer in a 9–3 decision. And Carleton finished off Stengel's club in fine fashion the following afternoon (Thursday, July 25), as Brooklyn lacked "pitching, batting power, and inspiration," according to McGowen. The Cubs won for the eighteenth time in the last twenty-one games by beating the Dodgers again, 4–2. Carleton was emerging as another strong force on the staff, allowing a mere single in the first six innings en route to his ninth win. He stayed in the game despite taking a hard line drive off the bat of Sam Leslie in the second inning. Watty Clark, the starting pitcher for the Dodgers, became only the second lefthander to complete a game against the Cubs on the year—and Hubbell had been the only southpaw to whom Chicago had lost in 1935 to that point. The victory jumped the Cubs (56–35) ahead of St. Louis for second place by two percentage points and a half game; the Cubs were now only three games behind the front-running Giants, with the Cards three-and-a-half back. The Giants had rebounded from losing the first two games in St. Louis to win the next four, which included victories over the four Cardinal aces of Dean, Dean, Walker, and Hallahan. In the fifth game of the series, Schumacher collapsed in the dugout after working six innings in the stifling St. Louis heat that reached 97 degrees on the field, but Allyn Stout filled in to seal the victory for New York.

The Reds were the next victims at Wrigley, as French dominated Derringer and the Reds for a 5–1 final on July 26. The victory was partly due to the old Cub friend Cuyler, ironically, who dropped a flyball in a crucial situation. The Red Stockings had a tough day, but not quite like the one experienced by Washington Senators pitcher Ed Linke in New York. In one of the strangest plays ever seen, Jesse Hill of the Yankees hit a line drive off of Linke's head, which was subsequently caught on the fly by catcher Jack Redmond. Straying off second base was New York's Ben Chapman, and Redmond quickly fired the ball to second for a most unusual double play. The Yankees were out of first once again after losing the game, and Linke was in Roosevelt Hospital in New York for a few days. But one month later, the act would be eclipsed in Boston. With the Red Sox batting in the ninth inning against the Indians at Fenway Park, Cronin lined a ball off the head of Cleveland thirdbaseman Odell Hale. The ball deflected on a nearly perfect ninety-degree angle to shortstop Billy Knickerbocker's glove, which launched a triple play, ended the game, and sent everyone away from the field speechless.

With the Reds struggling to find pitching to complement that of Derringer's, they were no match for the charging Cubs, as Grimm's men ripped through the rest of the series for three more wins behind Henshaw, Warneke, and Root. Not only had the Cubs been triumphant in 22 of their last 25 games, but they had won eleven times in the last eight *days* as well. The win by Root was his ninth on the year, which more than doubled his entire total from 1934. And over the past week, Hack had regained his hitting stroke by again surmounting the .300 mark to join Hartnett, Demaree, Herman, and Galan as starters above that figure. Galan also enjoyed a stretch of reaching base ten straight times early in

Augie Galan. (Chicago Historical Society and George Burke)

the series, and later ran the stint to fifteen out of sixteen plate appearances. To date, only Klein (18) had double-figures in the home run category; Hartnett was next with nine, while batting a team-leading .346.

On July 30, a sort of temporary Mason-Dixon line was drawn on the team as the Cubs were in Pittsburgh to play the Pirates, and hopefully keep the winning streak alive (Vaughan of the Pirates, incidentally, still topped the league in hitting at .393). Perhaps a lack of sleep had caused the edginess, as the team had left Union Station in Chicago at 11:15 the previous night, and the rougher-than-usual train ride had kept many of the players awake. Tensions had been rising for a while between Jurges, a Brooklyn native, and Stephenson, who was from North Carolina. It had all started a while back when Stephenson, who, being a rookie in addition to hailing from the Tar Heel State, unabashedly stood up and took his cap off each time the tune "Dixie" was played on the Wrigley Field sound system. Feelings were further exacerbated when Jurges' mis-play of a flyball cost another southerner, Bill Lee, a victory. Pitcher Hugh Casey then joined the fray, as he (of Atlanta) and Lee began giving unwelcome shooting tips to the shortstop. When Jurges and Stephenson had to be separated before the game in front of the dugout at Pittsburgh, then in the dugout, and once again in the clubhouse, Grimm decided that the latter was the instigator and Stephenson was released. He was sent back to Chicago on a train to await an assignment to the minor leagues. The breaking point for Stephenson came when he had heard, through someone on the team, that Jurges had said his "grandpappy chased Stephenson's grandpappy with a cornstalk." While no harm was thought to come out of the altercation, Jurges displayed otherwise when he arrived in the locker room the next day with a lump on his jaw. Walt Goebel, a player who was with the Los Angeles club in the PCL, was wired to come and take Stephenson's place.

As Stephenson was making his way to Tinseltown, citizens in the L.A. area were beginning to clamor for a major league team, and a new speed record was seen on the railroad. A car on the Santa Fe Railway between Los Angeles and Chicago reached a top velocity of 111 miles per hour, which—along with increased air travel, of course—encouraged baseball magnates to look into the possibility of a team on the West Coast. "Los Angeles has been demanding a place in a major league for a long time," Ward had written back on March 17, 1934. "But nobody gave the idea serious consideration until a leading journal printed an editorial saying it was high time something was done about it."

While various players took sides in the matter, things ultimately cooled off between the North–South factions—but the club did not. For after winning the opener in Forbes Field behind French (his 11th win), the Cubs were now a scorching 23–3 in their last twenty-six, and a single game behind the Giants after the day's play on July 30:

	W	L	Pct.	GB
New York	60	32	.652	—
Chicago	61	35	.635	1.0
St. Louis	55	38	.591	5.5
Pittsburgh	53	43	.552	9.0
Brooklyn	40	51	.439	19.5
Cincinnati	41	53	.436	20.0
Philadelphia	39	53	.423	21.0
Boston	24	68	.260	36.0

"But who fears the Cubs?" Kieran boldly challenged the readers a couple of days before. "Not the Giants, even if they *were* clawed severely in their last visit to the Windy City ... a good team, the Cubs. But Memphis Bill Terry said long ago that the Cardinals were the team to beat, and he still sticks to his word."

On July 31 in Cincinnati, the Cardinals got their chance to play in their first night game. Unlike the previous night contests, the Reds' administrators had found themselves with too many requests for tickets, and they oversold the park. Some had thought, however, that club officials intentionally re-sold reserved tickets when word arrived that trains carrying fans were late getting into town that evening. Nearly 42,000 fans (far over capacity) crammed into every available space—even onto the playing surface, where many were in the path of batted balls.

In the midst of the massive crowd that gathered, a female fan by the name of Kitty Burke slipped under the restraining rope that surrounded the field. The Reds were getting ready to bat in the bottom of the eighth inning, and Burke grabbed a bat from in front of the dugout before security personnel could apprehend her. She motioned to Paul Dean and commanded him, "Throw it to me, big boy!" With the rest of the crowd now amused by the scene, the ushers backed off as Dean playfully lobbed in a pitch with Burke in the batter's box. She swatted at the ball, and rolled one along the first base line. Sprinting out of the box in her high heels, Burke tripped and fell to the ground as Dean tagged her out while laughing hysterically. Frisch, who never hesitated to pursue any advantage for his team, rushed over to the umpire and demanded that the play be counted as the Reds' first out in the inning. While Burke would never appear in the box score of the game, her spirited interlude may have indeed helped the Reds to a 4–3 win over the Cardinals in ten innings. Because of the overflow crowd, it was estimated that forty-seven baseballs were lost into the populace at the game—a high number for a contest in that era—with "a wholesale value of about $58.75," according to Arch Ward.

In addition to the St. Louis club playing its first National League game under the lights, July 31 was also the day that Judge Fuchs finally surrendered his majority stock ownership in the Braves and went into retirement. Adams kept his 9,000 of the 14,000 shares of Braves stock in a personal safe, and was looking for what he described as "any reliable purchaser" to take over the club.

Also that same day, the Cubs were playing a doubleheader against the Pirates in Pittsburgh. After winning the first game, they could almost sniff first place near the end of the second. With two out in the ninth and holding a 5–4 lead, the Cubs were one batter away from being in a virtual tie with the Giants. It was then that Lloyd Waner doubled home Woody Jensen to knot the game at five. Two innings later, pitcher Ralph Birkofer slammed a long double to the flag pole to score Tom Padden, and the Pirates gained a split on the day with a 6–5 decision. To that date, Birkofer had managed only four hits for the season, all of them singles.

But a worse blow for Chicago occurred during the first-game win. Hartnett fractured his ankle in the fifth inning, but finished the game. Afterwards, the ankle was confirmed broken by J. J. Schill, a local physician, who announced that Gabby was on the shelf for at least two weeks. With O'Dea the only other catcher currently on the roster, Grimm swallowed his pride and immediately forwarded word to Stephenson for his return to the Cubs, less than twenty-four hours after he was sent away. Hartnett meanwhile, batting .347 at the time of his injury, boarded the next train back to Chicago.

Not having such a restful sleep that night was Stainback, as the imaginative youngster heard a riveter making noise at a nearby construction site from his hotel window. Stainback ran for cover in the hall closet, fearing it was a tommy-gun attack by gangsters; actually, it was only work that continued on new buildings at the nearby University of Pittsburgh campus. Teammates calmed him down by escorting him to a late dinner at Jake's Place in the Schenley Park area of the city; there, they were entertained by the eating exploits of Galan. The tiny 155-pound outfielder gleefully consumed four whole chickens that Lindstrom bought for him. Upon leaving the restaurant, Lindstrom was shaking his head. "I have seen all the great eaters in baseball—Shanty Hogan, Bob O'Farrell, Pat Malone, Hack Wilson," he said, stunned. "But in knife-to-knife competition, little Galan can lick all those big fellows at any table in America."

Warneke planned to be in top shape for his start in the series finale. Unlike Stainback, he had slept fine since 8:30 the previous night, citing the need for extra rest after his frequent use by Grimm in July. Warneke had gone 6–1 during that month, as he fought to return to the head of the pitching staff for the pennant drive. A win would have put the Cubs in a deadlock for first with New York, but Lon's plan was derailed by the league's top hitter, Vaughan, who again had topped the .400 mark with now less than eight weeks left in the season. His second-inning grand slam was part of a quick six-run assault by the Pittsburgh men, which was barely enough as Bill Swift hung on for another 6–5 Pirate win. The entire Cub bench rushed umpire Beans Reardon in vain, screaming that Vaughan's drive went on the outside of the foul pole. Chicago made a valiant comeback, which included a two-run triple in the eighth by Lindstrom, making his first appearance in a game since July 7. O'Dea and Cavarretta failed to come through in the ninth, however, with the tying run in scoring position. Vaughan was now batting .401, looking to be the first hitter since Terry in 1930 to go at least 2-for-5 throughout the entire season. And Jurges' old Southern pal was indeed back. "Reb Stephenson rejoined the club this morning and reluctantly used Union money to pay for his breakfast," Ward reported. "The young man seemed happy to be back, however, and may permanently reinstate himself if he is a nice boy while Gabby Hartnett's ankle is on the mend." The next morning, Stephenson and Jurges were seen having breakfast together, and were overheard to say that they agreed the Civil War was a "draw."

August in Chicago, 1935. Roller Derby had arrived at the Chicago Coliseum, thanks to a hasty plan drawn up by a man named Leo Seltzer while he scribbled thoughts on a cocktail napkin in the Ricketts Restaurant. The Cubs had also arrived in the National League pennant race, thanks to the plans devised by Jolly Cholly. He had not taken a plate appearance since the first week of the season, as Cavarretta was booking himself among the long list of Cub greats.

In the amateur athletic world in August, trouble was brewing as Berlin, Germany, was preparing to host the 1936 Olympic Games. A debate had been going on a long time in American circles on whether or not the U.S. should send its athletes to the games, in light of the anti–Semitic, anti–Catholic, and anti–African stances being taken by Hitler's Nazi party since his rise to dictator in 1933. On August 1, the new president of the American Olympic Committee, Avery Brundage, stood firm in his intent to send U.S. competitors to Germany in the following year. This stood in contrast to the position of his predecessor, Jeremiah Mahoney (a former New York State Supreme Court Justice), who severely questioned the integrity of the German government and the treatment of even its *own* athletes. Brundage, however, was willing to give the Nazis the benefit of the doubt. "Regardless in what country the Olympic games are held," he began to the press, "there will be some group, some religion, or some race which can register a protest because of the action of the government of that country, past or present. Pledges satisfactory to the international and American Olympic committees have been made by Germany, respecting the treatment of its own athletes as well as those of visiting countries.

"If it develops these promises have been broken, further consideration can be given to the subject [of keeping the U.S. athletes home] by the American Olympic Committee. So far we have had no reports whatsoever, official or otherwise, that Germany has failed to give Jewish athletes a fair opportunity to qualify for Olympic teams." Ironically, it would be Brundage who, 37 years later at the 1972 Olympic Games in Munich, announced that the "games must go on" after the murder of two Israeli athletes by Palestinian terrorists with six days left in the competition, leading to the deaths of nine more in a standoff with authorities.

"Superstitious souls urge that the Olympic games never be awarded to Germany again," Arch Ward would write in September 1935. "The last time they were scheduled for there, a world war broke out."

On August 2, the Cardinals were in Union City, Tennessee, and awoke on the train to find themselves entered in another of Rickey's exhibitions (they had just left Cincinnati after a series with the Reds). They were playing the local Greyhounds of the Class-D Kitty League, and it was a great treat for the residents of the isolated town. A total of 7,500 anxious spectators crowded into Union City's tiny Turner Field, at the time the largest crowd ever to watch a sporting event in western

Tennessee outside of Memphis. Diz and Martin took control of the public address system to provide the laughs via the microphone, and Dean later came down to take the Cardinals' final at-bat. He was struck out by Greyhound pitcher Newt Daniel, but St. Louis beat the home team 4–2. Later in September, the Pirates and Reds would swing through Union City for games against the Greyhounds as well (Earl Browne, who was serving as a backup firstbaseman for Pittsburgh during the 1935 season, would return to the Kitty League in the 1950s as a manager with the team in Owensboro, Kentucky).

The Cubs replaced the Cardinals in Cincinnati, a five-game stay before they would head home to Wrigley to face the Pirates and the Cardinals. They were dealt an 8–0 shutout at the hands of Schott and the Reds, on Grimm's third anniversary of being named the Cubs' skipper. His club, once holding a record of 24–3 at one stretch in July, had now lost their last three and fell two games behind the Giants. The Cincinnati officials had thought about playing the game at night, but decided against it in consideration of the mob that assembled for the night game with the Cardinals the previous week. Joining the Cubs in the middle of the series once again was Shoun, who had recently thrown two straight shutouts (and another game with only an unearned run allowed) for Birmingham in the Southern League.

French righted the Cubs off their losing streak with an 11–3 win over Emmett Nelson on August 3, but the team split a doubleheader the following day that included Warneke suffering his eleventh defeat, one more than he had for all of 1934. And Stephenson, looking to make some inroads with his fellow workers, celebrated his first professional start in game two by collecting three hits in leading Root and the Cubs to a 4–3 victory. Before this game, Stephenson had never made a start above Class D ball, but he skillfully handled the game behind the plate with ease. And Grimm was nearly ejected once again for arguing with umpire George Magerkurth, after Hack was called out at the plate in an effort for an inside-the-park homer. Before his big debut, it was Stephenson's nemesis on the club, Jurges, who made a crucial eighth-inning error in the first contest that allowed the Reds to claim that one, 5–1.

Grimm was having a particular problem with Magerkurth; the "guesser" (a derogatory term for the men in blue during the era) had also drawn the wrath of Frisch and Dressen on various occasions, although such spats were nothing new with these men. Magerkurth, a National League umpire since ejecting John McGraw in his first game in 1929, had developed a reputation as a surly official—and that was exemplified in his most recent confrontation with Grimm. After the issue was dead and

gone, Magerkurth continued to chase and bark at his two primary antagonists, Grimm and Stainback. Grimm felt it was uncalled for, but planned
to make no further issue of it—or Magerkurth's umpiring skill in general.
Nonetheless, Grimm's position changed the following day, August 5, in
the final game of the series at Cincinnati. As the Reds took their turn at
bat in the sixth against Carleton, Babe Herman watched ball four go by.
It got away from Stephenson, headed toward the stands, took a few hops,
landed in the third row of seats, and after a discussion that lasted five minutes, the umpires decided that Herman should have second base. Then
Grimm, surprisingly calm, let the crew know that if Herman went on to
score, the game would be played under protest. Lew Riggs soon after
doubled, which plated Herman and officially marked the game for review
by the league office. For the time being, it was a 3–1 win for the Reds,
giving them the series three games to two as Stephenson added another
three hits on the day. Magerkurth was most often called his nickname of
"Meathead" by the players, and his arguments with Durocher into the
1940s would become legendary.

During that week, the end had finally come for Walter Johnson in
Cleveland. The Big Train tendered his resignation, and was replaced as
manager by former Indians catcher Steve O'Neill—a favorite of the front
office—on Sunday, August 4. It began a big-league managerial run for
O'Neill that would include additional stops with the Tigers, Red Sox, and
Phillies through the 1954 season. One week later, Johnson would
announce that he was leaving baseball altogether, and was returning to
his 550-acre farm in Germantown, Maryland. "The Cleveland club just
wasn't as good as I thought it would be," he told a reporter in conclusion,
as he plowed his long-untouched fields. "Some players didn't live up to
the expectations I had for them. I wasn't able to get all I had hoped out
of the club. But that's baseball. Looking back over it, I don't think of a
single decision I made that I would change now." Johnson could also look
back over magnificent pitching career, one that logged more strikeouts
than anyone (3,509) to that time, and more wins than anyone to the present day (417) with the exception of Cy Young (511).

Nor were things so well for Cleveland's all-star outfielder Joe Vosmik. It was reported in early August that a 29-year-old woman by the
name of Minnie Barr of Norfolk, Nebraska, had sued him for $100,000.
Barr's suit alleged that Vosmik's breach of a promise to marry her caused
her "mental and physical anguish," "Which is ridiculous, and apparently
valued at the ridiculous sum," scoffed one newspaper about the frivolous
filing. Vosmik admitted that things had not gone well in the relationship,
but believed that "by-gones were by-gones" and thought that both he and

Barr had moved on with their lives. But Barr, looking for a little pocket change, decided to pursue the charge. Vosmik was currently leading the American League in hitting at .348.

On August 5, a strange situation occurred at Fenway Park that threatened Gehrig's consecutive games streak. He had suffered a lumbago attack (one of several he had experienced lately), and had to leave the game in the fourth inning as heavy rains started to fall in Boston. Both managers were later fined $100 by Harridge, who called what took place a "disgraceful exhibition" by the players as well. "Players Ben Chapman and Myril Hoag of the Yankees were guilty of indifferent basserunning," Harridge claimed, "and Bill Werber of the Red Sox guilty of misconduct in refusing to tag Chapman out at first base and his apparent deliberate bad throw to first base ... the actions of both teams [are] highly reprehensible and a gross imposition on the fans who paid their money with the expectation of witnessing a major league baseball game." The trouble began when the Yankees took the lead in the fifth inning, 8–2, and tried in every way possible to hurry the game along, so that the inning was completed and the game counted as an official contest; the Red Sox did the opposite, trying at every turn to bog the game down as the rains continued to fall.

Later that day the Red Sox's business manager, Eddie Collins, returned home from a scouting trip on the West Coast. He reported to Cronin that a player he saw in San Francisco named Joe DiMaggio might be better than most outfielders in the major leagues at the present time. The young player had been recently sidelined with a bad knee, but was personally sent a home remedy by Ty Cobb through the mail that had helped Cobb recover from a similar ailment back in 1919.

Conversely, things had not gone so well for Alabama Pitts on the ballfield, like DiMaggio, a legendary outfielder making his name in a lesser-known league. It was rumored that he would not be asked back to the Albany team for the 1936 season, but rather be sold to Harrisburg of the New York-Pennsylvania League. The 24-year-old Pitts, almost two months into professional baseball after being released from Sing Sing, was hitting only .217 despite playing an impressive center field. As his prospects for the year in baseball dwindled, the gifted athlete again began receiving offers from several professional football teams. According to Lawes, he had also received several job offers from the industrial world and even one for a performance routine in a vaudeville act. It was football that he wanted to pursue, however, and he received permission from the New York State Parole Board to sign with the Philadelphia Eagles— so long as he reported to similar boards in each NFL city that he visited

(Pitts would be taking advantage of a new rule agreed upon by NFL own-ers, whereby the rosters would be expanded from 22 to 24 players). And shortly thereafter, Evers would resign as the general manager of the Albany club with his team mired in last place.

The Cubs were happy to be back home to face the Pirates, as they had not seen the North Side since beating the Reds 11–7 back on July 28. There were more freebies in attendance than paid customers—4,500 school kids and 3,500 ladies joined the total throng of 14,000 for the afternoon's play. The Chicagoans still trailed the Giants by three games, as Terry's club had swept the Braves in a four-game series at the Polo Grounds and next whipped Brooklyn in the opener of another set. Hen-shaw took the mound against Birkofer, and the lefties squared off in a wonderful pitchers' duel. Birkofer allowed only four hits—all of them sin-gles, and two each to only Jurges and Demaree—but three errors, includ-ing one of his own, proved his undoing in a tough 2–1 loss to the Cubs. The Chicago defense, on the other hand, was solid, and Henshaw was able to scatter eight Pittsburgh hits in the victory. Like most managers in the National League, Grimm favored using southpaws against the big Pirate lefthanded bats of Vaughan, Suhr, Jensen, and the Waner broth-ers. So he fed them another one with French the following day, but Larry was outdueled by the crafty rookie Blanton in a 6–0 loss. Hartnett was still on the shelf, as Grimm did not expect his number-one catcher to be activated until the team would leave for an East-Coast swing through Brooklyn, Philadelphia, and back to New York beginning on August 13.

Down on the South Side, Louis continued his run at the heavyweight title by knocking out King Levinsky in the first round at Comiskey Park. By the time Levinsky had hit the canvas for the fourth and final time, the bout was only two minutes and twenty-one seconds old. The crowd of 39,195 was the largest to watch a fight in Chicago since Gene Tunney knocked out Dempsey in 1927 at Soldier Field. Levinsky took home $31,874.54 for his troubles, while Louis garnered $47,061.81. "Levinsky was more than badly beaten," reported Wilfred Smith, one of 28 writers who got a free train ride to Chicago from New York to cover the event. "He was humiliated. Only twice in those tortuous minutes when he steadily retreated, hoping to avoid ruthless pursuit, did the King throw his looping wild right. That right had brought Levinsky fame. But it failed him without effect." It was the fourth first-round knockout of Louis's young professional career, and his twentieth KO in his last twenty-four fights. In addition, none of his last seven opponents (Lazer, Biff Ben-ton, Roscoe Toles, Willie Davis, Gene Stanton, Carnera, and Levinsky) had gone more than six rounds with him. How did it feel to get hit by the "Brown Bomber," Levinsky was asked? "You simply get mum all over," he told the writers. Louis celebrated the victory by going out and purchasing six tailor-made suits, hand-stitched by a former bantamweight champion-turned-tailor, Joe Burman. The morning after the fight, Louis's managers were already setting up the paperwork for a September 24 bout with Max Baer. And on September 25, Louis would marry Miss Marva Trotter, a resident of the Englewood neighborhood of Chicago. Promoter Mike Jacobs was looking for a large venue in which to hold the title bout, and Chicago officials quickly pointed out that there were few bigger than Soldier Field.

After splitting the next two games with the Pirates, the Cubs entertained the Cardinals at Wrigley Field beginning on August 9 (the day before in New York, Gehrig had upped his consecutive-games streak to 1,600 while also hitting his 366 homer in a 9–6 loss to the A's). St. Louis was hot, having won six straight in the process of sweeping both Pittsburgh and Cincinnati at home. The Cubs' record stood at 66–41, two games back of New York and a game-and-a-half ahead of the Cardinals. After their early–July burst that saw them win eighteen out of nineteen, St. Louis had cooled in the past couple of weeks; but everyone in the league was wary of the Gas House Gang, for their ability to overcome great odds in the standings was proven with their climb over the Giants in the previous year's race. Their sparkplug Martin, however, was out with an elbow injury, and Collins was just returning to the lineup after suffering a bad cold. Opening things up was Warneke against Paul Dean, and the younger brother had his good stuff. The gathering on hand, which totaled 30,548, was the largest weekday crowd so far on the season at Wrigley; over half of these were ladies who got in free. In the first inning, Herman blooped a double over Durocher's head at short, ran to third on a hit by Klein, and scored on a sacrifice fly off the bat of O'Dea. That was all for the Cub offense, and Paul dominated onward. A Medwick homer in the sixth gave him the lead, 2–1, and it was all he needed in what turned out to be a 3–1 final. Herman's infield hit in the ninth was the only scratch Dean permitted for the final five innings, as the Cards "not only showed why they are champions, but why they must still be regarded as the real threat to the Giants," according to Irving Vaughan. The Cubs started out the day five percentage points ahead of the Cardinals, but finished it three behind.

Then it was Big Brother, as Dizzy went to the mound looking for win number nineteen—but he entered the game with seven losses, his same total against 30 victories in the magical 1934 season. "The results were disastrous," wrote Vaughan as he continued the story of the series.

"His [Dean's] best friends were Bill Jurges and Frank Demaree. Both elected to put on crazy throwing exhibitions in the third inning. That was ample for Dizzy's purposes." The Cardinals won again behind their ace, 4–2, as the Cub defense let French down who had pitched well for seven innings. Jurges, in addition to kicking a ground ball, misplayed a pop-up which drew the ire of the Southerners on the team—proof that the "internal Civil War" had not completely died down. In fact, when Bill Lee mentioned to Jurges in the dugout that "you had better get an iron hat before you are killed by a fly ball," Billy had to be pulled off a teammate once again.

Meanwhile in New York that day, George Selkirk was continuing to further his own name as Babe Ruth's replacement in right field for the Yankees. With two homers and a single, he drove in eight runs—one short of the American League single-game record, held by Jimmie Foxx—in an 18–7 drubbing of the A's.

Charlie Root prevented a sweep by beating Bill Walker on August 11, 3–2, which snapped the Cardinals' winning streak at eight. But the Cardinals had marched into a contender's park and won the series–the statement of their prowess had been made, and the Cubs tried to maintain confidence in themselves as legitimate contenders. The standings showed them as such; for despite losing the series, they were still only a few percentage points behind St. Louis, and still only two-and-a-half games from New York in the top spot. But Vaughan also pointed out that the Cardinals were a full four games ahead of their pace of a year ago.

Hartnett had announced before the Cardinals series that he would be available to pinch-hit only, but he did catch the final two innings of the last game, showing that his injury had healed. O'Dea was batting a fine .281 in 146 at-bats as his replacement, while Stephenson had racked up ten hits in his first 23 trips to the plate for a .435 mark. But what the Cubs sorely missed was Hartnett's experience behind the plate and his leadership with the pitching staff. Klein was helping to pick up the slack, as he was up to .292 with 19 home runs (still the only man on the team in double figures in that category), even though he had driven home only one of the last fourteen runners that had been in scoring position with him at the plate. Herman was batting a sizzling .319, and Galan and Hack also stayed hot, each above the .300 mark and both with more stolen bases than the entire Boston Braves club (although Berger, the only star remaining on the Boston team, tied a record on August 11 with four extra base hits in a game—a homer, two doubles, and a triple). Galan might have attributed the continued success to his new-found solitude; he was enjoying a single room while Bob Lewis shuffled the roster to find him a new roommate on the road. Galan made the request after his previous bunk-mate, Henshaw, repeatedly sleepwalked throughout the room and kept Augie awake—that, combined with the fact that Henshaw traveled with some of his personal collection of firearms.

It was off to Brooklyn, where the Cubs had won five out of six so far on the year. Greeting them there was their young batboy during trips to the East, Yosh Kawano. Little Yoshie would remain in the Big Apple until the White Sox came through, and then serve the White Sox as well. The Cubs' luck would not continue in Flatbush, as they dropped the next three out of five games at Ebbets Field. After losing a doubleheader on the first day, the Cubs came back behind Warneke to give him his thirteenth win, 11–3, as Demaree powered the offense with a bases-loaded triple. Even after the two losses the day before, Grimm's men had still beaten Stengel's troops twelve out of sixteen times on the year. Grimm was injured before the game; Herman hit a line drive off his right elbow as the skipper threw batting practice (the Cubs, unlike most of the teams, did not carry a reg-ular batting practice pitcher at the time). At first, Charlie thought he might have a broken arm, but tests came back negative. Whatever he offered in pre-game practice worked, as Warneke enjoyed an unusual bounty of runs to complement his work. Three solo homers decided the fourth contest, the drives by Jim Bucher and Tony Cuccinello out-doing the one by Hack in Root's 2–1 loss to George Earnshaw. Bucher's homer came with one out in the ninth, as Root left a curve ball up in the zone, and the batter took advantage of the mistake. Earnshaw had been recently released from the White Sox by manager Jimmy Dykes for repeated curfew violations while the team was on the road. Lee, in a rematch of the series opener—and with both hurlers working on three days rest—reversed the original decision on Johnny Babich and beat the Dodgers 7–1 to salvage one more victory on August 17. Hartnett had returned to the starting lineup, but struggled in an 0-for-5 day. Only 3,261 showed up to watch the finale, as the Dodgers returned to their usual bumbling ways in making three errors in the third inning, en route to five total, which opened the scoring for the Cubs. In a somewhat jealous tone, Stengel afterwards remarked that "the Cubs have the best defensive infield in baseball." Lee improved his record to 12–5, and it was his fifth win of the year over Brooklyn.

Across the city, the Cardinals took three out of five from the Giants in the Polo Grounds to close the gap, a series which included a double-header on the 14th that drew the largest weekday crowd in National League history with 50,868 looking on. After the day's play was complete on the 17th, the standings looked this way, as the Cubs hopped a quick train to Philadelphia for a doubleheader with the Phillies:

	W	L	Pct.	GB
New York	69	41	.627	—
St. Louis	66	42	.611	2.0
Chicago	69	46	.600	2.5
Pittsburgh	63	52	.547	8.5
Brooklyn	51	59	.463	18.0
Philadelphia	49	62	.441	20.5
Cincinnati	49	65	.429	22.0
Boston	31	80	.279	38.5

The Tigers were beginning to pull away from the pack in the American League, with a seven-game advantage over the Yankees. Earlier in the week, they had annihilated the Senators 18–2 behind Schoolboy Rowe, as Rowe had a remarkable 5-for-5 day at the plate in addition to shutting down the Washington bats.

The lefties split the twin bill for the Cubs in Philadelphia. Henshaw won the opener (with help from Warneke) 8–3, but French could not hold the Phils in the nightcap, and Warneke entered for the second time on the day in logging his thirteenth loss, 6–5.

Shoun made his major-league debut on the 19th, and Grimm thought he had found another quality lefthanded pitcher. Shoun went seven strong innings, but exited with a 1–0 deficit. In the top of the seventh, Herman started an apparent Chicago rally with his 45th double of the season, but was left stranded. It looked like the Cubs would go quietly in the eighth, as Jurges rolled an easy grounder to Mickey Haslin at short. Haslin threw wildly to first, however, and that allowed O'Dea to pinch-hit for Shoun. O'Dea promptly lined a double over the bag at first, a ball hit so sharply that Jurges had to stop at third. After Galan was intentionally walked to load the bases, Herman came up again, and with two strikes, lined a clutch single to center to score two runs and give the Cubs the lead. French faltered slightly in the Phillies' eighth, but Carleton came on to save a rousing 2–1 victory. Shoun had allowed thirteen baserunners (nine hits, four walks), but kept the Philly batters off-balance enough to prevent further scoring after a scratch in the first. The game was protested by Jimmie Wilson, as he claimed that a double play ball handled by Herman at second in the sixth inning was dropped, although the runner was ruled out by umpire George Barr. Chicago, now having played eight more games than St. Louis, trailed the second-place Cardinals by only half a contest. The Giants also had "games in hand" against the Cubs' total. "Grimm's athletes have played more games than the Giants, but the extra games of the former are shown on the red side of the percentage ledger," lamented Vaughan. "In other words, the Cubs have already lost games the Giants still have a chance to win. This is considerable of an edge [*sic*] for the New Yorkers."

Rain—something the Cubs saw so much of back in May—arrived in the City of Liberty the next day, so another doubleheader was slated for August 21. Starting things off, Root (11–7) had a four-run lead before he even took the hill, but that was only the beginning of a crazy day at the Baker Bowl. Later, Hartnett hit his tenth homer and Herman his fifth for a 10–4 lead in the fourth inning, an advantage that seemed insurmountable. "From then to the finish the Cubs were babes in the woods," the *Tribune* reported, "and blindfolded in the bargain." The Phillies scored eleven runs in their final five trips to the plate, which was shown as a 13–10 lead as the Cubs prepared to bat in the ninth. The Cubs pushed across a couple runs at that point, but fell short in a disheartening 13–12 loss. They vented their anger in the second game, however, as a thorough pasting of the Phils, 19–5, included a twelve-run sixth and six total errors by Philadelphia. By going 5-for-8 on the day, Klein—the former Triple Crown winner—finally reached the elusive .300 mark. Again, a pre-game mishap may have portended good things from the sticks on the day; this time Grimm steered clear of troubles, but batting practice catcher and Chicago schoolboy Rudy Laskowski was cracked on the side of the head by Galan's bat as he finished his round in the cage. Rudy was not seriously hurt, but the players were wondering whose body could be offered up next for a good day for the team at the plate.

It was back to New York, and Warneke (13–13) got the team ready to face the front-running Giants. The split of the doubleheader in Philadelphia dropped the Cubs a full four games behind Bill Terry's club, but Grimm's men still stood only a game behind the Cardinals for second.

Lost in the shuffle of the recent offensive success was Woody English. An All-Star in '33 and MVP finalist in '31, English was batting only .208 in 77 at-bats when the Cubs arrived at the Polo Grounds. Grimm had come to prefer the daily combination of Jurges at short and Hack at third, English's two main positions. He wasn't used to sitting on the bench. In 1930 and 1931, English had actually played in more games than the Cubs had completed—156 in each season (he was credited with two extra in each season, as individual statistics in rain-expunged games still counted). He had gotten accustomed to a new role on the team; full of pride, however, the veteran was always ready, and on August 22 his skipper came calling.

Warneke and the great lefthander Hubbell fought to a 3–3 tie through the tenth inning, when another torrent of rain fell and delayed the game for twenty minutes. When play resumed, the Cubs took their turns against reliever Allyn Stout in the eleventh with Demaree leading off. A walk was issued, but Stout then struck out Cavarretta and got Lindstrom to fly out to Joe Moore in left. With Jurges up, Stout then uncorked a wild pitch that sent Demaree to second. With first base open, Terry decided to walk Jurges with Warneke up behind him. O'Dea, batting from the left side, was sent up by Grimm to face the righty Stout. Terry countered with lefthander Al Smith, at which point Charlie turned to English. Just as if he had been playing every day, English aggressively jumped on the first pitch and drove a single over Bartell's head at short. Demaree scored, and when Moore fumbled the ball (who was perhaps miffed by the 0-for-17 slump he was currently in), Jurges tried as well but was cut down on the relay throw. Root retired the Giants in order in the eleventh for the save, and the Cubs crept a game closer. And Phil Wrigley, who brought his club good luck on his last trip through the East, was there again to cheer his boys on.

Wrigley's boys made it two in a row over the Harlemites, as Hack and Galan led a 16-hit Cub attack with four each against Clyde Castleman, while French picked up win number twelve in a 7–4 decision. For the season, the Cubs had now won more games against the feared Giants than they had lost (9–7), "who apparently are warming up to repeat their memorable nose dive of a year ago," noticed Vaughan. The Cardinals had just finished sweeping a doubleheader at Brooklyn, whereby only one game stood between them and New York with the Cubbies another lone contest behind. A sour note for the Cubs was that Hartnett was hurt again; he busted his ankle while sliding home in the fifth inning.

Also that day, Ford Frick announced that umpires Beans Reardon and Ziggy Sears were going to be fined undisclosed amounts for their arguments with the fans at Cincinnati back on July 17. He warned all league umpires against "haranguing or otherwise attempting to control the actions of baseball spectators." Soda bottles and other projectiles had been hurled at Sears, as a borderline call went against the Reds. He and Reardon went over to the stands to confront the fans they believed to be the perpetrators. While Frick understood the need for the umpires to defend themselves, he nonetheless continued that "the policing of the stands and crowds is strictly a matter for the home club, and upon failure of the home club to provide proper policing, it is within the province of the umpires to forfeit the game." The Cincinnati newspapers wanted to know if Reardon and Sears had been fined for poor work, since Reds manager Dressen was charged $50 for arguing; Frick indicated that they were not disciplined for that reason, and that "human judgment" on the umpires' part was part of the game, and needed to be respected.

When Carleton breezed through the first inning the next day, it appeared that the Cubs' pitching staff had the New York bats under wraps. But in the second frame the sleeping Giants were awoken, as twelve batters and four Chicago pitchers later, Grimm found himself trailing 8–0. The main aggressor had been Hank Leiber, who tied a major league record by hitting two home runs in the same inning, giving him a total of twenty on the year. Ott also nailed his twenty-eighth (which continued to lead the league) and Henshaw, Shoun, and Kowalik were needed to simply get the game to the third inning. Just as the Giants were completing their onslaught, Babe Ruth strolled down to the first row of box seats, "wearing an open neck shirt and a blue sport sweater," according to witnesses. The surrounding folks noticed him immediately, and roared a greeting. The Cubs eventually pecked away at the mountain in front of them, which included Herman's seventh homer of the season in the fifth, but not enough in time to keep Hubbell from his nineteenth victory, a 9–4 final (when Herman singled later in the game, he took over the league lead in hits from Medwick with a total of 174). Hubbell had entered in relief of Parmelee, who had walked five batters and hit Klein on the wrist by the time he was supplanted by the screwballer. "Carleton is to be stabled," Vaughan concluded in disgust, as he expected Grimm to remove the Texan from the rotation. "The new big four is to be made up of Charlie Root, Lon Warneke, Larry French, and Bill Lee." But Grimm had no such plans, as he expected Carleton to round into the form that helped the Cardinals down the stretch twelve months prior.

In Brooklyn, St. Louis kept pace with a 10–7 win as the Dodgers lost secondbaseman Cuccinello for the rest of the year with a broken hand. Frisch announced afterwards to the New York press that, regardless of the outcome of the current season, a "big shakeup" was going to occur within the St. Louis organization for the 1936 campaign. While not naming names, he accused several of the players of taking it easy until the previous couple of weeks, when the pennant race began to heat up. It was Rickey's *modus operandi* to trade players away at the peak of their careers— and that threat was imminent. Several players at their farm club in Houston were having outstanding seasons, and Frisch indicated that these players would get every opportunity to win a big-league job in the spring. Among these individuals were pitchers Bill McGee and Nelson Potter, as well as outfielder Lynn King—who was leading the Texas League in hits, stolen bases, and fielding percentage.

The wake-up call must have worked, for on August 25, the Dean brothers pitched the Cardinals into first place with a doubleheader sweep of the Dodgers while Bill Lee beat the Giants for his fourteenth win, 5–4. The Cubs had now beaten New York in seven of their last eight meetings, causing Terry to ponder the possibility of another championship slipping away. His Giants had simply become a mediocre team, playing exactly .500 ball over their last 46 games, but the Cubs had done no better, as they were 13–14 in their last 27 (all the while, the Cardinals had won four out of every five games since the beginning of July).

At Ebbets Field, the scene was eerily similar to the previous September, when Paul threw a no-hitter and Diz a three-hitter at the Dodgers in making their run at the Giants. The Cardinals' record now stood at 74–43, a half-game better than New York at 74–44. "Paul is learning faster than Dizzy learned," Ed Balinger of the *Pittsburgh Post-Gazette* warned the National League, "and if he gets proper control, he will be a greater pitcher than his brother." The Cubs had more wins than either club (75), but their 49 losses put them six behind St. Louis in that category. There was one thing that Terry held in his favor: while his mates couldn't beat the Dean brothers down the stretch in '34, they had downed the pair six times in nine tries so far in 1935.

Down at Comiskey Park in Chicago, Yankees centerfielder Combs collided with thirdbaseman Red Rolfe on a pop fly, and severely dislocated his shoulder. This incident, combined with the fractured skull he suffered in his horrific crash with the outfield wall in St. Louis in 1934, accelerated his decision to retire, which would come at the end of the season. The unsung cog in the "Murderers' Row" Yankees of the previous ten years, Combs—nicknamed "The Kentucky Colonel"—had led the American League in triples three times (1927, 1928, and 1930—with over 20 each year) and hits in the famed year of 1927 with 231.

And up from Comiskey on the lakefront, it was time for what was becoming a highly-anticipated annual event. For the second straight year, a collection of college football all-stars would take on the National Football League champion Chicago Bears at Soldier Field in front of an expected crowd of 85,000. The collegiate players were selected for the game from more than 737,000 votes submitted to 105 newspapers across the country in the preceding weeks, while seven million more votes poured in to select the college coaches for the contest. Among the college players that the pro coaches would be scouting at the game was a strong center from the University of Michigan named Gerald Ford, who would be matched up across from the Bears' powerful defensive tackle, George Musso. Ford, a Grand Rapids native, was listed at 6'1", 202 pounds, in the game program. A glee club from a local YMCA, as well as several brass bands, added to the festive atmosphere at the stadium.

While some would argue that the drizzling rains balanced the playing field, the college boys certainly gave the Bears all they could handle. With five minutes left in the fourth quarter, the collegians drove to the Bears' five-yard line but were thwarted and the pros hung on for a 5–0 victory. Earlier in the game, the University of Alabama's Don Hutson took off on a reverse run that appeared to have him headed for the goal line, but he was tripped up shy of the end zone by the back of his ankles in a desperate Chicago tackle, preventing the score. Hutson would have many more opportunities to haunt the Bears, however; he would go on to a fabulous pro career with Chicago's arch-enemy, the Green Bay Packers, and he would be considered the greatest receiver ever to play the game before the arrival of Jerry Rice in the 1980s.

With his Braves in town, McKechnie, who was promoted to general manager when the ownership shuffle of the Braves took place, left the team for a period of two weeks. During that time, McKechnie transferred field power to Hank Gowdy while he went on various scouting trips around the East. The Cubs presented Grimm with a desk clock for his birthday on the 28th, and he could not tell them for sure if he was 36 or 37 years old. The Cubs took two out of three from the hapless Braves, and the series was finished up by Lee's fifteenth win on August 29 which also saw the return of Hartnett to the lineup and his twelfth homer. As the standings showed, the Cubs still had more wins than the Cardinals or Giants, but more losses as well:

	W	L	Pct.	GB
St. Louis	76	45	.628	—
New York	75	47	.614	1.5
Chicago	77	50	.606	2.0
Pittsburgh	72	55	.566	7.0
Brooklyn	56	68	.451	21.5
Philadelphia	53	70	.430	24.0
Cincinnati	54	72	.428	24.5
Boston	33	89	.270	43.5

Two days later, Vern Kennedy pitched the first no-hitter in the history of Comiskey Park, striking out Vosmik to end the game as the White Sox beat the Indians 5–0. Kennedy, who lettered ten times in sports at Central Missouri Teachers' College in Warrensburg, also provided the offense as he cleared the bases with a three-run triple. Things weren't all that good for the South Siders though, as they were only treading water at 62–60 and stood an imposing 17½ games behind the indomitable Tigers.

And even though the Cubs were just two games back, they felt as if they were running in place, too. After a July that saw them go 26–8, they only managed a break-even mark of 15–15 for August. Overcoming the Cardinals or the Giants separately would be daunting enough, but both squads were looming as they gazed above. Even the Pirates were edging closer, as Pie Traynor's men had won their last ten in a row. The Labor Day weekend had arrived, the home stretch of the baseball season, when guts are checked with the durability of sore arms, wounded knees, and waning energy. Only the strong would survive, and it helped to have been through the battle before—Jay Dean of St. Louis, a veteran of such battles, was ready for war. "This country may have needed a good five-cent cigar," Dizzy told J. Roy Stockton of the *St. Louis Post-Dispatch* at breakfast one morning. "But what the Cardinals need is more Deans."

What the Cardinals *didn't* need was more home games—for amazingly, all of the remaining 30 games on their schedule would be played at Sportsman's Park. The Cubs would have about as many at Wrigley Field, save five games at the end of the schedule in St. Louis. That being the case, writers across the land were handing Frisch's men the pennant a month early.

An Amazing Run

After the Cubs and Reds split a doubleheader back at Wrigley Field on Labor Day (September 2), WGN announcer Bob Elson proclaimed that, in the second game, "The winning pitcher was Schott." A woman from Evanston who wasn't much of a baseball fan frantically called the station.

"Why was he shot?" she wanted to know.

In the Reds' locker room, word had come down from the baseball czar that veteran outfielder Chick Hafey, who had been fined $1,500 by the Cincinnati ballclub for leaving the team weeks ago to tend to his illnesses in California, would not have to pay the sum. Hafey's vision had been blurred from severe sinus problems, and he had suffered an injury to his throwing shoulder that never seemed to heal. Landis ruled that the Reds were not correct in administering the punishment, and granted Hafey's request to be put on the voluntarily disabled list. The other declaration coming from the commissioner's office was a change in the umpires' uniforms to start the month. "They turned up in their orthodox blue uniforms after a summer in their suits of convict gray," the *Tribune* noticed.

And it was also noticed by everyone up and down the block that Galan had topped his chicken-eating mark; Klein offered to pick up the bill at the Blue Star Restaurant on Southport if Augie could top his four-fowl performance in Pittsburgh, and a small crowd peeked through the establishment's window in amazement as he consumed five-and-a-half birds—in addition to a plate of potatoes and a salad. The Blue Star was one of a handful of Chicago restaurants that had recently earned the distinction of displaying a placard in the front window that read, "*Recommended by Duncan Hines*." Hines, a former printing press operator, had left his former work to find his true calling as a gifted restaurant critic.

Thankfully the Cubs had an open date for digestion, and then welcomed the Phillies to town on September 4. On his way to the ballpark that day, Grimm noticed a rotund young boy walking in the neighborhood. The two struck up a friendly conversation as they made their way around Wrigleyville, and Charlie was impressed with the boy's vast interest in baseball. His name was Paul Dominick, a fifteen-year-old likeness to Gabby Hartnett—or so Grimm had thought. Looking to ease the stress of the pennant race, Paul was immediately given a uniform and instructed to sit on the dugout bench during games as the team's mascot. Upon entering the clubhouse, Jurges (with no cue from Grimm) saw the lad and squawked, "Hey look—it's Hartnett!" All of the others agreed, and he was a must-have for all games thereafter—especially because the Cubs beat Philadelphia that day, 8–2. Galan smacked two home runs, one of which was a grand slam, and there was poultry for everybody.

They made quick work of the Phillies, beating them again 3–2 as Demaree had three hits, his average soaring to .322; again 3–2 the following day, for Warneke's seventeenth win as Galan tripled with two out in the eighth to tie the game and homered in the tenth to win it; and they completed the sweep behind Lee on September 7, a 4–0 shutout and his sixteenth triumph. Thinking that his rightfielder needed a rest, Grimm sat Klein down in the finale as the Hoosier had gone hitless in his previous eighteen trips to the plate. The frustrated Phils once again attacked Umpire Barr in the second inning, after Jimmie Wilson was called out on strikes. The catcher-manager then covered the plate with dirt, and the other players began throwing things out of the dugout in Barr's direction. "The Phils were just about ready to toss out the bat boy when Mr. Barr dashed over and ordered the firing to cease," described Vaughan as he watched from the press box. Barr tossed out a few of the rabblerousers for good measure, and when he returned to home plate to resume his normal duties, the verbal barrage started again as a few more contestants were asked to leave the premises.

Chicagoans were in a better mood—before the game fans honored their youthful firstbaseman with "Phil Cavarretta Day" at the ballpark. The hometown boy, at the time batting .278 with 66 RBIs, was presented with a new automobile from Mayor Kelly, compliments of the Chicago Italian-American community. He also got a new guitar from his fellow alumni at Lane Tech, which he also accepted graciously. Over 3,000 students, faculty, and supporters from Lane roared at every move their honored son made during the day. All four ballgames in the series were witnessed by Bud Tinning, who had been sent to Columbus of the American Association by the Cardinals. Tinning had been hit on the elbow by a line drive and was out for the season. With nothing better to do, he traveled to Chicago to watch his old friends play. Tinning, who was dealt to St. Louis after three seasons with the Cubs, would never pitch in the major leagues again.

Cavarretta would have ample room to test out his new vehicle. Later than week, Kelly announced that he was taking 2,000 unemployed Chicago men off of public aid and paying them salaries to participate in a major repair effort on the city streets—a job that wound up fixing nearly a thousand miles worth of municipal thoroughfare.

The four-game sweep of Philadelphia sailed the Cubs past the Giants into second place, but the Cardinals maintained a one-and-a-half game lead in completing their own four-game sweep over the miserable Braves, who were on their way to Wrigley. In one of the contests, star rookie centerfielder Terry Moore had six hits for St. Louis.

The Boston entry in the National League was almost a complete mystery. The addition of Ruth was supposed to supplement an otherwise strong unit, which had finished in fourth place with a 78–73 record in 1934. It may have been the abrupt exit of the Bambino that hastened the demise, for in essence, the same fine club took the field in '35. More likely, it was the complete collapse of the pitching staff, which had been an asset in the previous season. The free-fall could be simply seen in the records of their four main starters:

	1934	*1935*
		(through September 8)
Fred Frankhouse	17–9	8–12
Ed Brandt	16–14	5–14
Huck Betts	17–10	1–9
Ben Cantwell	5–11	4–21
Total	55–44	18–56

While the win-loss records were certainly altered by lower run support in the current season, Boston pitchers allowed over 130 more hits in '35 than in '34. But to their credit, they were battling in the absence of any semblance of support—hitting, administrative, or otherwise (Berger was the one regular player with impressive stats, batting .301 with 30 home runs and 108 RBIs when the team arrived in Chicago; his 30 round-trippers had recently overtaken the league lead from Ott, and was second to Greenberg's 34 in all of baseball. The Braves' next closest starter was firstbaseman Buck Jordan with a .275 mark and *four* homers).

Carleton, who had been banished from the starting rotation by Grimm, was summoned for the first game of the doubleheader. This decision was made due to Tex's success against McKechnie's club, and he did not disappoint. He and his mates beat up on Brandt for a 5–1 score.

Frankhouse, along with Braves' shortstop Bill Urbanski, visited a paralyzed young man at Alexian Brothers Hospital in Chicago the night before. Frankhouse made it a point in various cities to make visits to local police stations to offer his appreciation, and on this trip, he learned the fate of the stricken youngster as he talked with the policemen at the Sheffield Avenue station. The young man was the son of a Chicago police officer, Bernard McGovern, and had become disabled from an accident while playing a game at DePaul University. Inspired by the time spent at the hospital, Frankhouse reverted to his effective form of 1934. He limited the Cubs to five hits, but the home team made each one count in another win behind French, 2–1, for six in a row. Three of the five Cub hits off Frankhouse came in the very first inning (Herman, Lindstrom, and Demaree), and was all the offense French needed. Meanwhile, St. Louis had lost two of three to the Phillies, splitting a twin bill as Dizzy Dean won his 25th in the opener. But his team stranded 16 runners in the nightcap to lose 4–2, and Collins lost to Curt Davis in the finale. The Cardinals were now fending off the Cubs by only one game.

Grimm's troops couldn't get any closer on September 10, as a 4–0 shutout by Root was mutually excluded by another victory for the Cardinals by Hallahan, 4–2 over the Phillies in Sportsman's Park. In Chicago, it was the 22nd beating of the year applied to Cantwell, who seemed to be marching towards the single-season record of 29 set by Vic Willis in 1905. And despite the "pennant fever" that was supposed to be engulfing Chicago, only 4,500 bothered to show up and watch the game. It turned into utter destruction in the last meeting, as Hack logged four hits and Hartnett three to lead a 15–3 dismantling of Boston. The visitors had a semblance of a chance until the eighth, at which time the Cubs showed them the door with an eight-run outburst. It was Lee's 17th win, as another paltry showing of 5,225 fans appeared.

After the sweep, the Cubs finished their schedule against the Braves for the year with an overpowering nineteen wins versus three losses, including eleven victories in a row.

Now less than two weeks away was the Louis-Baer fight, and Joe was asked about his World Series prediction. "They're just about in," he said of the Tigers for the American League nomination. "I think the Cubs are the team they'll have to lick in the World Series." Baer, meanwhile, had another prediction for the coming weeks—that he would win in two. "I don't expect to see him on his feet after the second round," the former champ said. "And if he is, he'll be doing some awfully funny things standing up. Why, he can't use his right without winding up like a baseball pitcher. If he winds up like that against me, he'll never complete the pitch. I am seriously considering taking a punch at him at the weighing-in scales, just to show him who will be the boss on the night of the 24th.

"Louis, at 21, is facing such a situation as I experienced at the same age. He's meeting a better man. When I was the same age I met Ernie Schaaf in New York and received a lesson that, in my experience, I didn't expect."

Louis was growing a bit edgy; he pummeled a sparring partner named Sal Ruggerello in front of 1,500 onlookers as he felt the helper was getting a little too aggressive.

The Dodgers came to town to face Warneke, and the Brooklynites could do nothing to slow the Chicago team down. Big Lon won 13–3, "and all of the 13 runs were earned," noticed Vaughan, "because the hapless Casey Stengel troops refrained from indulging in any of the comical maneuvers for which they are nationally famous." Again the offensive hero was Galan, who produced four hits in five at-bats, including his eleventh home run that challenged Hartnett (12) for second place on the team behind Klein (20). But Dean was equal to the task again, and Diz beat his archrival Hubbell and the fading Giants for his 26th win in St. Louis, 5–2. Frisch went to the well once too often, calling upon Dean in relief the next day in the tenth inning. The Giants lashed out for three runs against him in posting a 13–10 win, as Dean suffered his ninth defeat in the three-hour, forty-minute game. And although the Cubs won their tenth straight in a 4–1 whipping of the Dodgers, the Cardinals (87–50) held onto to first place—where they had been since August 25—over Chicago (89–52) by four percentage points, .635 to .631. It was Friday the 13th, and some had sensed that the Cardinals' luck had finally run out.

Paul Dean was supposed to start the next day, but had fainted while attending a boxing match in St. Louis the previous night and was shelved. In his stead went Hallahan, and the fortunes of the old lefty were going the way of his team as well. He and Collins held the Giants in check until the eleventh, when a single by Joe Moore plated Castleman for a 5–4 New York lead. The G-men finished things off with a double play in the bottom half, and all of a sudden, first place was for the taking by the Cubs with a win over Brooklyn at Wrigley.

Grimm handed the ball to the old veteran Charlie Root. It didn't matter too much who strode to the hill for either side, however, as the

Friendly Confines turned into a launching pad. Those warm southerly winds continued to blow from the south and straight out to left, and the baseball was ripped to all corners of the park. Herman slapped two doubles for an impressive season total of 51, while Lindstrom added two of his own along with a triple. Freddie had been installed in centerfield and Demaree moved over to right, as Klein had been in the throes of a hitting slump amidst the success of the rest of the team. The club refused to be beaten as the combination of Root, Henshaw, and Kowalik held on for a breathtaking 18–14 endurance, their eleventh in a row.

The Giants looked to be more of a threat to the Cubs than the Dodgers had been, and Cardinal followers took some relief in that thought.

The newsboys, waving copies of their wares, were joyfully hollering on the corner that the Cubs were in first place with two weeks to go. The papers reported the standings on September 15:

	W	L	Pct.	GB
Chicago	90	52	.633	—
St. Louis	87	51	.630	1.0
New York	83	52	.614	3.5
Pittsburgh	79	63	.556	11.0
Brooklyn	61	75	.448	26.0
Cincinnati	61	80	.432	28.5
Philadelphia	58	79	.423	29.5
Boston	34	101	.251	52.5

The Giants beat the Cards again on the 15th, 7–3, as over 42,000 stretched Sportsman's Park to its limit to see Dizzy Dean once again go against Hubbell. It was Dean's second loss in the series, and the third time that the overworked pitcher had thrown in the last four days. He was pounded for twelve hits in the first five innings, as his club slipped another game behind the unstoppable Cubs, who won their twelfth straight behind Hartnett's first-inning homer which just reached the screen in right field. It was Gabby's thirteenth blast on the year, and his first since August 29 at Boston. The game in St. Louis was typical of a Giant-Cardinal pennant drive contest, "jammed with color and curse words, flying spikes, and flying fists," according to wire reports. In a display that would make modern-day bleacher bums "proud," Mel Ott was doused with debris and derogatories as he chased down a crucial flyball in the eighth inning off the bat of Gelbert. Just as he made the catch a soda bottle nailed Ott in the back, but he managed to hang onto the ball. After throwing the ball back to the infield, Ott turned and raced toward the seats in pursuit of the attacker. Amid police officers and angry fans, he was out of sight for several minutes, and the rest of the Giant dugout rushed out to his aid. When the New York club took the field in the ninth in pursuit of the final three outs, Ott was flanked on each side by St. Louis policemen at his right field position. Fortunately, none of the three men had a ball hit their way, and Hubbell finished off the Cards in quick order. Terry had summoned his ace lefthander before his turn in the rotation, for he knew he needed his best against Dean; as a result, the Cubs would not have to face Hubbell in their upcoming series at Wrigley Field. As he was not due to take the mound in Chicago, Hubbell got permission from Terry to fly to his hometown of Oklahoma City and greet his new 8½-pound son born the day before.

As they left town, the Dodgers were in their usual spot at this point of the season—battling just to get in the first division. They had a number of quality young players, however, and this gave them hope for the future. One of them was centerfielder Len Koenecke. He had all of the "tools"—running speed, a good throwing arm, a potent bat—but also had a temper problem, which led to his release from the team after the Dodgers lost their next game, 1–0, to the Cardinals and Paul Dean on September 16 in St. Louis. After receiving news of his release after the game, Koenecke went to Detroit and chartered a private plane, which was to fly him to Buffalo. Minutes into the flight, he began nudging pilot William Mulqueeney and co-pilot Irwin Davis on the shoulder, apparently for no reason. Mulqueeney later reported that he asked Koenecke to sit back and settle down, which he did, but the nudging began again moments later. The pilot reported that Koenecke had been drinking, and although quiet at the beginning of the flight, he appeared to be "very stressed."

Due to the disturbances that Koenecke was causing, Mulqueeney then asked Davis to subdue the ex–Dodger, an attempt that was unsuccessful. "Then, I had to come to a decision," Mulqueeney later told the *New York Times*. "It was either a case of the three of us crashing or doing something to Koenecke." The scrap escalated, as the two men in charge struggled to maintain control of the aircraft. "I watched my chance," Mulqueeney continued with his account, "grabbed the fire extinguisher, and walloped him [Koenecke] over the head. With the passenger quiet, I took a look around, saw the open field with possibilities of a fair landing and came down."

That was near Long Branch Race Track in the vicinity of Toronto, and when the plane touched down, Koenecke was found dead of a brain hemorrhage from the blow delivered by Mulqueeney. Koenecke had gotten to Detroit from Chicago via another flight, during which he was also disruptive and "offered to fight several other passengers," according to stewardess Eleanor Woodward. The next day, the Dodgers emerged from their dugout at Sportsman's Park in St. Louis with black bands on their left arms in Koenecke's memory. He was buried three days later at Repose Cemetery outside of Adams, Wisconsin, near his hometown of Baraboo.

Paul Dean's triumph did lift the Redbirds momentarily, but the joy was short-lived as Warneke (19–13), described by Vaughan as a "Giant tamer of consequence," won his seventh straight start back in Chicago by manhandling New York 8–3, making it thirteen consecutive triumphs. Herman got hits number 200 and 201, including his 52nd double, while Galan added two two-baggers himself and Hartnett a pair of RBI singles. Cavarretta topped off the Cubs' scoring in the fifth inning with his seventh home run of the year. And Demaree was the defensive star, robbing Ott of a round-tripper with a one-handed catch in the fourth. Herman, whose .324 average was good for eighth in the league, was modestly challenging the major league record for doubles of 67, set by Earl Webb of the Red Sox in 1931. Ahead of St. Louis by two games with ten to play, the Cubs could wrap up the pennant by winning half their games and the Cardinals and Giants having to play no worse than .700 ball.

In the days before cell phones and all-day bleacher parties, Cubs tickets had suddenly become a hot item in the city. Bob Lewis received many requests for press passes, some authentic and some phony. One of the latter variety was attempted by a man posing as a Chicago fire marshall, who asked to be allowed into the park. Lewis called his bluff when the would-be-chief threatened to have him thrown in jail if he was not admitted, in accordance with the fire code; when Lewis implied the same fate for the imposter, he vanished quickly down Addison Street.

Over in Pittsburgh, an incredibly small showing of less than 500 fans entered the gates of Forbes Field on September 16, as Gus Suhr set a National League record by playing in his 619th consecutive game in the Pirates' 5–3 win over the Braves. It was also agreed on this day that the American League representative would host the first two games of the World Series, beginning on October 2, as a large convention being held in St. Louis over that date encouraged Cardinal officials to make the concession; they believed they would not be able to accommodate the large crowd expected for both events (obviously, not too much thought was given to home field advantage in this era).

Apparently nothing could derail the Cubs, and next in line for fun was French (16–10) as the train rolled along to victory number fourteen in as many tries, 5–3, as Herman and Demaree charted two more hits each to their bustling totals. No longer were the pitching outfits of the

Cardinals or Giants claiming exclusivity of domination in the National League; for with the exception of Carleton's 5–1 win over the Braves in the first game of the doubleheader on September 9, the Cubs' "New Big Four" of Warneke, French, Lee, and Root had accounted for all of the victories during the streak. In St. Louis, Jesse Haines' 200th career win was only half the story as the Cardinals split a doubleheader with the Dodgers, 4–2 and 8–7, to slip another half-game further away from the Cubs. The second game only went seven innings, as darkness fell upon Sportsman's Park, and the joke was on Diz, as Brooklyn pushed three runs across the plate on him in the top half of that inning for the deciding margin. And after the Cubs demolished the Giants 15–3 behind Root (15–8) and twenty hits in the third game of their series, Terry threw up his arms in a dejected New York locker room and announced that he was through playing for his "quitting outfit." This frustration was perhaps due to a throw by Bartell towards home plate late in the game that flew into stands, leading Grimm to call it afterwards "the wildest throw I ever saw." The toss whistled over the head of catcher Gus Mancuso, and caused several spectators in the seventh row to scatter when it landed. While it wasn't true that Terry was finished as a player, the New York papers once again began their wailing and gnashing of teeth from another apparent Harlem collapse, now two painful years in a row. Terry also had complaints about the Cubs' ballpark—in particular, the white t-shirts that glistened in the centerfield bleachers that impaired his batting eye. "I swear, I can't see the ball," he told Harold Burr of the *New York Post*, even though Terry had been visiting the field at Addison and Clark for the previous twelve years. "I'm not afraid of the Cubs; I'm afraid of their park." By 1953, people sitting in the lower centerfield seats at Wrigley would become a thing of the past.

With Phil Wrigley looking on and sipping cold lemonade in the front row, his Cubs scored the knockout punch on the men of Coogan's Bluff with an amazing sixteenth in a row the following day, September 19, Lee (19–6) beating Hubbell 6–1. The winning streak was the longest in the National League since 1924, as the Cub righthander held the Terrymen scoreless for eight innings when only a scratch hit off the bat of Cuccinello avoided a shutout. Seven more hits had come from Herman in the past two days, including his 53rd and 54th doubles. Hartnett's average was up to .351, which trailed only Vaughan (.387) and Medwick (.357) in all of baseball. His personal guest at the Giants' series was golf pro Tommy Armour, who had just signed a deal to remain the top man at the Medinah Club for the next five years. Over 123,000 other fans joined Armour at Wrigley Field for the critical four-game set with the

Giants, which was one-fifth of the total attendance to that point at the park for the year.

It was the eighth win in a row for Grimm's troops over New York in Chicago, and eleventh in the last twelve contests overall, leaving the Giants seven-and-a-half games behind. And combined with the last two trips to Chicago made by the "eastern" clubs (the Giants, Braves, Dodgers, and Phillies), the Cubs had won 31 out of 34 games. It was at this point that Terry predicted that the Cubs would beat out the Cardinals for the pennant.

Rumors had started that Hubbell, seeming to lose his magical touch from the Giants' 1933 championship run, was being shopped around to several teams, in particular Pittsburgh. While the Cubs' dismantling of the Giants proved to the Cardinals that their awesome streak was comprised of wins against quality opponents as well as weak ones, no more ground was gained as the Redbirds won their last two against the Dodgers to stay two-and-a-half games back.

A sort of "break" lay ahead for the Cubs, as they would play only two games in the next five days before the winner-take-all, five-gave battle in St. Louis starting on September 25 to finish the season:

> Friday, September 20—off day
> Saturday, September 21– home vs. Pittsburgh
> Sunday, September 22—home vs. Pittsburgh
> Monday, September 23—off day
> Tuesday, September 24—off day

While the rest was welcome, there was fear that the hiccup would end the hot streak—at precisely the wrong time. With the Cardinals having ten games to play as opposed to the Cubs' seven, the St. Louisans would have a chance to make up some ground in half-game chunks before Chicago got to town. Grimm held a light practice session on the 20th before the Pirates arrived at Wrigley, and he also planned to wait well into Tuesday night before leaving for St. Louis. This was because, in addition to allowing the players a bit more time with their families in Chicago, Grimm wanted to avoid a conflict with a large national meeting of the American Legion in St. Louis, which was scheduled to depart the city on Tuesday afternoon.

While the Cubs were beginning their two-game set with the Pirates, the Tigers had clinched the American League pennant with a doubleheader sweep of Hornsby's Browns in Detroit. The pennant hopes of the Yankees—the lone true threat to the Tigers—were essentially dashed back in mid–August, when shortstop Frankie Crosetti tore cartilage in his left knee by pulling too hard on a knot in his shoelaces. The crowd of 31,000 at Navin Field in Detroit was relatively nonchalant, business-like, and expectant of the outcome; "a few hats were tossed on the field," said one witness, but it was an otherwise subdued event. When the crowd departed, Navin ordered fifty workmen to install 2,000 feet of new sod around the infield. Much of the original grass had been damaged earlier in the summer by the presence of a theatre company, which had performed in the park while the Tigers were out of town. Back inside the offices, nearly 100,000 applications per day started being received for World Series tickets and were handled by forty extra girls that had been quickly hired to help with the influx. Still uncertain of the outcome in the Senior Circuit, officials from both the Cubs and Cardinals had World Series tickets ordered from the printer, but had not yet put them on sale. Unfortunately, the office workers at Wrigley gave out mixed messages, as they erroneously approved the orders of tickets that came by phone; after a couple of hours, however, the practice was stopped.

The same day in Detroit, it was announced that the Ford Motor Company, who pioneered the sponsorship of World Series radio broadcasts the previous year, would once again be the benefactor of the games at a price of $100,000. The Columbia Broadcasting System, the National Broadcasting System, and the Mutual Broadcasting System were all approved to handle the chores. While World Series games had been heard on the radio since 1923, it was 1934 before the games couldn't be aired free of charge by any station or network that wanted to secure the job. With most of the money going to the players, however, some writers such as Dan Daniel predicted a backlash from the owners. "The magnates believe that the players have been getting too much World Series dough," he revealed in his *New York World-Telegram* column, "and at the joint meeting in December some owners are sure to holler for the whole air kitty."

As the Cubs finished their practice on the open date, September 20, the reporters caught up with Grimm just coming out of the shower in the locker room. He slipped into a pair of shorts, and began taking questions about his amazing club. "Back on September four," he recounted, "I called a clubhouse meeting and I says, 'We're home for the last long stand, and we either do or we don't; but we are going to be loose, win or lose.' I kept emphasizing that we got to be loose, and that if there is any tightening up, or pressing, or choking, our goose is cooked." Extra evidence of their comfort was seen in the solid defense that the team had played during the streak; in the past 16 games, the Cubs had made a total of twenty errors, five of them in one game. It was at this point that the press first labeled the charging club as the "Grimm Reapers," and when word of this title reached St. Louis, the Cardinal faithful began to fear the loss of their crown. But confidence remained high among the players, especially with the most confident one of all. "What I'm worrying about is how I'm going to pitch to Hank Greenberg of the Tigers," Dizzy Dean said while striding past reporters, taking another World Series appearance for granted. "The Cubs? We'll, you can bet that I'll take two of the five games with them m'self."

Several of the Cubs—including Lindstrom, Galan, Klein, Hartnett, Carleton, Lee, and Jurges—enjoyed the rest of the day by taking in the horse races at Hawthorne Park. They all found the afternoon relaxing, but only Lee found it profitable. After they lost their money on wages, they turned their attention to trying to find a girlfriend for Galan, a confirmed bachelor. "I am strictly a stag," Galan asserted in self-defense. "I like the gals all right, but never had a durable romance."

Klein then wanted to know if any young lady ever took an interest in the fine money Galan was making as a ballplayer.

"Let one try it," Augie added, this time in self-defense of his bankroll. "I might go for dinner and a bucket of beer, but I'll salt the rest."

Despite being the "loose leader," Grimm stayed after his men, knowing that they could not afford to look past the two games with the Pirates. The Cardinal war would come soon enough, and would be all the tougher if they went South with a couple of losses under their belts. It would be Henshaw, the young lefty and Chicago native, in the first one against Pittsburgh. The Cubs had beaten Pie Traynor's club 13 times in 20 tries for the year, and Henshaw owned six of those victories. While no one wanted to jinx things by looking ahead, people around the North Side were feeling good about the Cubs. "They're at their peak," the *Tribune* readers were calmed by Vaughan. "There are no injuries; the remaining schedule is so arranged that the pitchers are assured of proper rest, and the Cardinals undoubtedly are weary." Only Demaree, with a busted thumb that resulted from a vigorous slide into second, was slightly hurt; indeed, with another two days off looming before the start of the big series in Sportsman's Park, Grimm knew that he had just about every weapon in his arsenal at his disposal to use against the Pirates. Even in a worst-case scenario, in which the Cubs would lose two to the Pirates and the Cardinals win all five from the Reds and Pirates, the Cubs would only be one game behind. But everyone knew the heroics of which the St. Louis players were capable, so the Chicagoans stayed on guard.

It took a while for the Cub bats to separate from the Pirates, as former bruin Guy Bush kept pace with Henshaw for a 0–0 score into the fifth inning. Before the game started, Henshaw had been worried that he might be rusty, as he had only thrown one-and-a-third innings since September 1. In the fifth the Cubs scored twice, added two more the following inning on Galan's twelfth homer, and appeared to be on cruise control. In the eighth, Lavagetto scored on a single by Padden to get Pittsburgh on the board. Then, three straight hits by Jensen, Bud Hafey, and Lloyd Waner brought Warneke in from the bullpen. With the tying and go-ahead runs on first and second, he coolly forced Young at third on a bunt, got Lavagetto to roll into a force at second, and got Red Lucas to ground out to Herman as he closed things out for a 4–3 close one—the Cubs' seventeenth in a row. Three more hits for Herman, including his 55th double, had the locals thinking "MVP" for Billy. Massive crowds had returned to Wrigley literally overnight, as a packed house of 38,624 cheered on the home team. And parking lot owners outside Wrigley Field, sensing the large gathering and a possible World Series taking place, took advantage by jacking up their prices to the then-outrageous sum of one dollar per car.

As spectators strolled out of the park to their high-priced parking spaces, they awaited the results from down Route 66.

The pressure was mounting in St. Louis. Having fallen behind 6–3 by the eighth inning, the Cardinals stormed back to tie as the pilot light for the Gas House Gang was lit once again. But in the Cincinnati ninth, Lew Riggs slammed a two-out, two-run triple that regained the lead. The deflated Redbirds scored once in their half, but fell 9–7, and the Cub lead climbed to three-and-a-half games.

In a turn of events, however, it was the Reds who played as if under scrutiny the next day, September 22. They made seven errors in the first game of a doubleheader as St. Louis rolled, 14–4. Hallahan started the contest, but was replaced in the second inning after falling behind 3–0. In came rookie Mike Ryba, and the youngster pitched two-hit ball over the final seven innings. Dizzy Dean held the Cincys to three hits in the nightcap for a 3–1 win and a sweep for the day, hoping that the Pirates could steal one from the Cubs for a most profitable afternoon. It was Dizzy's 28th win of the year, as he and brother Paul (who had nineteen) were almost identical to their magical total of a year ago. Their forty-seven victories constituted more than half of the team's total (93).

By beating the Pirates in the final regular season game at Wrigley Field on the year, the Cubs could keep the Cardinal charge at a half-game for the day. Taking the mound against the Bucs was the Pirates' old colleague, Larry French, who had been such a valuable addition to the Chicago staff since the season's beginning. After Galan scored in the first to stake him to a 1–0 lead, French mixed his pitches effectively to stymie the Pittsburgh bats. By the time the Pirate ninth rolled around, he had scattered nine hits and held a 2–0 lead. He then retired the heart of the order with ease, and the win—his sixteenth again ten losses—was wildly celebrated by the faithful at the ballpark. Earlier, more than a thousand people were left wandering around outside the yard—"with money in their pockets, but nowhere to spend it"—as Cub officials were forced to close the sold-out ticket windows well before game time. French, in leading the Cubs to their eighteenth straight, had disposed of Traynor's men in less than two hours and frustrated them to the point of leaving twelve Pirates out on the bases.

As soon as the overflow crowd had completely left the park, the Wieboldt Company entered with its cranes and began work to install temporary bleachers in the outfield in preparation of the World Series. The massive equipment actually appeared at the location the evening before, an ominous prelude to passers-by that post-season baseball was once again coming the North Side. The portable bleachers, at a cost of $29,000, would be placed behind both the left and right field walls. They would extend well onto Waveland and Sheffield avenues, covering a distance of over 800 feet and providing accommodations for 12,000 extra spectators.

With a three-game cushion, the Cubs could relax for two days while the Pirates headed south to buffer them from the Cardinals until Grimm and the troops arrived. The skipper once again planned light workouts for each of the two free days.

The Cardinals played like a beaten team, the Pirates blasting five St. Louis pitchers for a 12–0 whipping as Frisch's club sank further into despair. Perhaps the city residents knew something bad was in store, for just over 6,700 fans showed up to watch. High in a corner of the upper deck, a young man played "Taps" on a bugle, signaling his belief of the end to the St. Louis pennant hopes before the Cubs even got to town. But Hallahan brought the deficit back to an even three, as he sent the Pirates packing on three hits with a convincing 11–2 decision, his four-teenth win and the first time he had won in nine starts following his impressive stretch through July. The Cards needed to win at least four out of five to catch the Cubs.

The Giants were out of the race, so National League fans in New York turned their attention to the Baer-Louis fight to take place in Yan-kee Stadium the night of September 24. The fight, considered by experts to be the biggest non-title bout to date, would begin at 10:00 P.M., was scheduled for 15 rounds and would be seen by an anticipated 90,000 or more. "Neither has even been knocked off his feet as a professional fighter," Ward admired about the two men. "Fans expect to see one of the most savagely-fought heavyweight bouts in years." Baer (26) was a bit older than his opponent (21), and outweighed Louis 210 to 198. People were jamming into the city from all over to see the fight; one report had 1,400 travelers on six New York Central inbound trains during the day.

The actual attendance turned out to only be 84,831, as scalpers let go of $5.75 seats for a single dollar by the time ten o'clock rolled around ("This is the cheapest crowd I ever saw," commented one of them). Those who witnessed the match were privy to more quick work by Louis. He knocked Baer down twice in the third round, and continued the assault until Max went down for good in the fourth. Baer collapsed to his knees, and stayed in that position until the referee counted to ten. It could have been halted at either flooring in the third, but Baer got up on a nine-count the first time and was saved by the bell on the second knockdown (Dempsey, incidentally, had been in Baer's corner during the fight—but he was not introduced to the crowd, and was hardly recognized by the spectators around him). For his twelve minutes of work, Louis was paid over $217,000. It was the start of a grand honeymoon for Louis, as he and Marva were married a few hours before Joe went to the stadium. Soon after, the champion Braddock was asked if he would give Louis a shot at the title. He responded, "Absolutely," feeling that Baer was unnecessarily scared in fighting Louis. "As soon as he saw a little blood, he became panic-stricken," Braddock said. "He didn't offer any opposition." Baer wouldn't offer any more opposition to anybody, as a matter of fact—the ex-champion decided to retire.

A three-game lead was apparently enough to start making further plans, as the Cubs announced that World Series tickets would go on sale on October 1. Fans would need to buy seats for all three games at Wrigley; one would need $19.80 for a box seat to the three games, or could choose to pay $16.80 to sit in the grandstand for all three. No single game tickets would be issued, except for $1.10 bleacher seats to be sold the day of each game.

Grimm smiled as he strutted into Sportsman's Park, the place where he worked as a soda vendor while growing up on the north side of St. Louis. He vowed not to repeat his mistake of 1932, whereby he felt he had let the club "relax" after clinching and was subsequently swept by Ruth and the Yankees in the World Series. "Even if we breeze in [to the pennant] Thursday afternoon, we'll play the other three games with the Cardinals just like the championship depended on each of them," he assured the folks back home. "The only regular who is going to get any let-up in his routine is Gabby Hartnett. The big boy's fingers are all bunged and his lame ankle continues to bother him. So the minute we are over the top, out comes Gabby.

"There are several reasons we won't let down aside from the tuning up business," Grimm continued. "Naturally, we want to run our winning streak as high as we can. We can't tie the Giants' 1916 record of 26 straight this season, but 23 straight would look pretty good in the record books. We also have a chance to run up a total of 102 victories for the season, a total no Cub team has reached since 1910," he pointed out to the *Tribune*.

In the event that the Cubs and Cardinals finished the season tied, Frick announced that a two-game playoff would begin at Wrigley Field on September 30, and then head to Sportsman's Park the following day. If a third and final playoff game was necessary, a coin flip would decide the home park. To cover the series for the fans back in Chicago, Bob Elson announced on WGN that the station would broadcast all of the games from St. Louis. They would need to obtain special permission from the Cardinals to relay the final game of the season, as the St. Louis club had rules forbidding the broadcasting of any games on Sunday, even by the visiting team.

After having beaten what most considered insurmountable odds the previous season, the Dean boys were counted on to carry the Cards past the Cubs. It was Frisch's plan to throw the brothers every other day, which was fine with both, for each would have pitched *every day* if their arms had allowed. Paul had established himself with his no-hitter at Brooklyn last September and his two wins in the World Series against the Tigers; now it was another opportunity to prove his mettle to the St. Louis faithful on a hot, overcast day in the Midwest. But the Cubs had their own sources of support; for along with the usual contingent of fans from Chicago, a large number of Cubbie followers from Indiana, Wisconsin, Iowa, and downstate Illinois made the trip as well.

Business-like as always, Paul traipsed to the mound as the crowd roared in support. After striking out Galan and Herman to start the game, he allowed a double to Lindstrom that flared over Martin's glove at third. Unshaken, Paul came back to fan Hartnett for his third strikeout of the inning. He resumed his effective start in the second by retiring Demaree, before Cavarretta made his way to the plate. Grimm was now getting concerned that the pressure of the pennant race would ultimately affect Cavy, but the teenager coolly peered out at Paul and waited for a good one. He got his pitch, and rocketed a ball on top of the pavilion in right field for a 1–0 Cub lead, almost exactly a year to the day when he hit his first big-league homer as a 17-year-old.

As good as Paul was, Warneke was even better. He retired 22 of the first 23 hitters he faced, the lone safety an infield single by Lynn King in the fourth, who had just been brought up from the Cardinals' minor league team at Houston. Paul resumed sitting the Cubs down with ease as well, and the 20,000 observers felt that the Cardinal bats would awaken in time. In the eighth, the Cubs touched second base for the first time since Cavy's homer, as Warneke dinked an infield single towards Durocher and stopped at third on Herman's 56th double. The men were left stranded, however, and momentum appeared to shift back to Frisch's club. At that point Warneke permitted the second St. Louis hit, a double off the bat of Collins on a play in which Galan failed to make a shoe-string catch. A groundout by Bill DeLancey to Herman moved Collins to third, as the Cards were 90 feet away from tying the game. This seemed almost a certainty when Durocher, playfully nicknamed "Captain Slug" by Frisch in jest of his usually-light hitting, drove a screamer that hooked around Galan in left. Undaunted by his misplay of Collins' ball, Augie turned the opposite direction in a sprint, crashed into the concrete wall, and rose with the ball in his glove to end the inning with the 1–0 Cub lead intact. In the ninth, Gelbert, Spud Davis (batting for Dean), and Martin went quietly in order. Nineteen in a row.

Grimm led the frenzied stampede into the clubhouse where he yelled repeatedly, "They can't stop us!!!" And about his hurler, Cholly said, "it was the best pitched game I've ever seen when something was at stake." Warneke had finished off the Cardinals with just 88 pitches and no walks, in a game played in an hour and 35 minutes, and the Cubs clinched a tie for the National League pennant. He allowed only eight balls to reach the outfield in getting his twentieth win and seventh straight—a personal streak that including the taming of every club except Pittsburgh in the preceding weeks. "Amazingly steady, even spectacular, support saved him," wrote Vaughan about the iron-clad Cub defense that was behind Arkansas Lon; he was referring in particular to Herman, who had a hand in fourteen chances. In addition to Galan's dramatic, game-saving catch, the other seven assisting Warneke had flopped on the Missouri dirt all day long, repelling attacks at every angle.

In addition to holding all Cardinal hopes in his right hand for game two, Diz had been in a bad mood anyway, because he lost $25 in a bet he had placed on Baer for the Louis fight. It was reported that Dean had gotten an inside tip on the fight from Jack Dempsey. "It's hard to beat a team playing perfect baseball," Dizzy said of the Cubs, "But I'm going out tomorrow and beat 'em anyway. I'm going to pitch more than a perfect game."

"It's amazing how well the Cubs have been playing," added his manager, Frisch. "They're a good, young, hustling outfit and only a super-human effort by the Cardinals will beat them. I'm hopeful my team, which plays best in a tight spot, will do it."

As Warneke notched his twentieth win in the opener, the Cubs were going for another pair of twenties the next day—their twentieth win in a row and the entry of Bill Lee into the individual twenty-win club. Lee, once the property of the Cardinals, looked to avenge his sale to Chicago by the St. Louis club two years earlier. Lee brought in an even 1–1 record for the season against St. Louis; Diz, enjoying an unusually-good season against Chicago, stood at 5–1 for the year against the northern men. But a steady rainfall postponed the dramatics, and the teams prepared to do battle in a decisive doubleheader the next day, September 27. Phil Wrigley hopped a train home to Chicago at noon upon the announcement of the cancellation, but promised to return quickly to partake in the awaiting celebration.

Only 10,694 came to see the standoff, for the weather was threatening once again. Those present had to see if their beloved Cardinals could stay alive in the pennant race. The second game of the doubleheader was of no consequence if they dropped the first, so Dizzy was run out to the mound once again. As he always did, Dean slid his feet out to the mound with his head down in concentration while the home folks roared. Geared up from the adrenaline, he retired Lindstrom on a double-play ball after Herman had singled. In the bottom half, the Cardinals parlayed three Cub errors—by Herman, Hack, and Lee—into two runs. This was the impetus Dean needed, it was figured, and the Cards were on their way back. But after Lee led off the third by flying to right, Galan opened a barrage by doubling to the wall in right field. Herman then lined a single to left, and when Medwick fumbled the ball in the grass muddied by the recent rain, Galan came across the plate with the Cubs' first run while Herman took second. Lindstrom then promptly drove him home with another hit, and the game was tied. The Cubs took the lead in the fourth, when with Hack on second with two outs, Lee bounced a ball high past the mound on which Dean got his bare hand, but it squeezed through the middle, over the second base bag, and into center field for the score.

The day grew cooler and darker, and like the Confederate charge on Little Round Top at Gettysburg, wave after wave of Cub attacks tried to chip away at the St. Louis hopes. They touched Dean for single runs in the seventh, eighth, and ninth, which accounted for a 6–2 lead as the Cards got ready to take their final, futile swings. Dean had gone the whole way, enduring fifteen Chicago hits; Frisch hoped that his unit would ultimately raise a counter-assault. But the Cubs, who later described the great

Dean that day as a "tired ball pitcher," had done the requisite damage. Smirking in Dean-like confidence as he readied himself on the hill, Lee turned down the St. Louis bats in one-two-three order in the ninth as the crowd moaned in disbelief.

The Cubs, who, back on the Fourth of July were over ten games off the pace, were now the National League champions.

Waiting in the front row behind the Cubs' dugout was Mrs. Grimm, who immediately got a big kiss on the cheek from her man after the final out was made (in two weeks, the couple would celebrate their 13th wedding anniversary). The Cubs had a brief between-game celebration in the clubhouse, as Dizzy came in to congratulate them and wish them luck (and, of course, give them advice) against the Tigers. But Diz wasn't as kind to his own teammates; as usual, he complained that he and Paul had to shoulder the load of the pitching staff, a unit that had "less depth than a trout stream," he was quoted as saying in the St. Louis papers. The exhausted Dean had finished the year with 324 innings pitched, and just as in the Cardinals' championship season the year before, had ended the season twenty pounds lighter from its beginning.

There were numerous heroes for Chicago, most notably Lee, Lindstrom, Galan, and Hack, the latter three combining for ten of the hits. It was another rapid game—an hour and thirty-nine minutes—as both managers cleared their benches for the second contest. Grimm had made it clear that he wanted the winning streak to continue, and when the club had emerged from the locker room, he was seen exhorting his mates down the right field line to do just that. And after spotting the Cardinals a 3–0 lead in the sixth, Root and the boys roared back to win the nightcap, 5–3, for their twenty-first win in a row. Herman had amassed a total of five hits on the day (two in the first game, and three in second), which vaulted him over Medwick once again for the league lead with 222. Medwick, who was 1-for-8 for the afternoon, stood at 219. He and the rest of the Cardinals retreated to their dressing room with their tails dragging, even though the loyal St. Louis fans stood and cheered as they left the premises.

Having returned to St. Louis—and planning to stay—was owner Phil Wrigley, who vowed to remain with his club until they broke the record of 27 consecutive wins. When informed that it wasn't possible in the remaining schedule, he replied, "Well, they can win four straight in the World Series, and that would be 27." It was now time for a full-fledged celebration in the clubhouse, and smiles and hand-slaps were all around. "At last, I have amounted to something!" Lindstrom shrieked, as he grabbed the head of a laughing Lee around his arm and held him under the showers. "After being a bum for three years, I've helped my old hometown to win a pennant. And we'll smack those Tigers down, too. Don't forget it!"

After the second game, Hartnett, Lee, Warneke, and Root were excused, and they boarded a train back for Chicago. Hartnett's ankle and hand were still causing him misery, so Grimm gave him and the three pitchers the assignment of scouting the Tigers, who were currently playing the White Sox at Comiskey Park (poor weather in Chicago had postponed the Sox-Tigers contest on this day, so Cochrane came down to see the Cards-Cubs contest—and may have been on the same train back to Chicago with the four enemy troops). Back north, Cochrane superstitiously selected the Edgewater Beach Hotel in Chicago for the Tigers' lodging during the series, as it was the inn for victories by AL teams with the A's in the 1929 World Series and the Yankees in the 1932 classic over the Cubs (it was during the 1929 series that Cochrane set the record for most chances by a catcher, 61). As evidenced by Cochrane's motives, few walks of life involve more superstition than being a ballplayer.

The angry Medwick let out his frustration the next day, and the winning streak finally ended with a 7–5 loss tagged to Kowalik. French had started and held a 5–5 tie into extra innings as the Cubs scored three in the ninth to knot it up. Medwick, who had four hits on the day, got his last rap when he homered in the eleventh win it. But Herman kept ahead of the overall hit list with three more. Still struggling was Klein, who ran a hitless string to twenty straight at-bats through the fifth inning. But at that point, he walloped a pitch from Jim Winford for his twenty-first homer, a most welcome sight for Grimm who was worried that the slumping Klein might be becoming a non-factor in the World Series.

In the season finale, Carleton was handed the ball in the park where he celebrated a Cardinals championship a year earlier. Once again he was headed to the postseason, and he and the Cubs ran into the rookie pitcher Bill McGee. Ironically, Carleton would help prevent his former teammate Medwick from overtaking Herman for the league hit title; Ducky had one and Herman two, giving Herman the final edge, 227 to 224 (it may well have been "payback" for Tex, as he and Medwick had fist-fought on several occasions, most notably inside the batting cage before a game in 1934). One of Billy's knocks was yet another double, leaving him with an outstanding total of 57 for the year. The youngster McGee made quite an impression on the Cardinals, Cubs, and all observers, as he held the other Chicagoans to one other hit and one walk over nine innings for a 2–1 St. Louis win. Despite being just another victim along the Cubs' road of torment during September, the Cardinals were still the only team against which Chicago had a losing record (8–14) for the 1935 season. Nonetheless, the Cubs had won 100 games for the first time in 25 years.

The victors arrived back in Chicago on a special train at the Dearborn Street Station around midnight on September 29. Once on the train, they had wanted to immediately get to the process of dividing up the World Series shares, but decided to wait until the next day at home so that Hartnett and the three absent pitchers could take part in the discussions. The next afternoon, the team would board another train for Detroit in advance of opening the series on Wednesday, October 2. Back in 1932, they completely cut Hornsby out of the series money, because he had been relieved of his managerial duties in August of that year when Grimm took over. As the team got together to divvy up the extra cash, Woody English, the team captain, presided. Grimm stayed out of the proceedings, for he felt he shouldn't have input in the matter.

Over in the American League, Buddy Myer of the Washington Senators needed four hits on the last day of the season to win the batting title over Vosmik in the slightest of margins, .349 to .348. Vosmik, thinking that his lead over Myer going into the day was safe, sat out the first game of a doubleheader against the Browns. After getting word of the tremendous day that Myer was enjoying, he nervously entered himself in the second contest, and went 1-for-4 to finish one point behind Myer. Also on the last day, Pittsburgh's Pep Young became the first non-pitcher since 1893 to achieve the "Platinum Sombrero"—officially known as striking out five times in one game. And the Tigers didn't do so well in tuning up for the World Series, as the White Sox tied an American League one-inning record with ten singles in the second as they pummeled Eldon Auker, 14–2. Auker, the side-armer who threw that way because it was thought that the Jayhawk grew up in low-ceilinged Kansas tornado shelters, would still finish with the league's best winning percentage at .720 (18–7).

Nobody could catch Vaughan for the National League batting title, as his .385 mark topped all of baseball. Berger's 34 homers and 130 RBIs for the sickly Braves led the circuit, while Foxx and Greenberg tied to lead all of baseball with 36 home runs each. Foxx couldn't approach Greenberg's RBI total, however, as the Detroit slugger accumulated 170, which matched Klein's 1930 amount and still places both men for the eighth-most in history. Galan capped an awesome rookie campaign by leading the NL in stolen bases (22) and runs scored (133), and, amazingly, did not ground into a single double play in 733 plate appearances (although ironically, he did hit into one triple play earlier in the season). From the mound, Dizzy Dean led in wins (28), complete games (29), and strikeouts (182), while French tied for honors in shutouts (4) and Lee's

20–6 record was good for the best winning percentage in baseball (.769). The Cubs also dominated the team offensive categories, setting the pace in NL batting average (.288), runs scored (847), on-base percentage (.347), doubles (303), and walks (464), while the pitching staff allowed the fewest hits (1,417) and had the most complete games (81).

The Boston Braves' 115 losses were the most ever in the National League for a 154-game schedule, easily surpassing the mark of 109 set by the 1928 Phillies. It would remain the overall record until the expansion New York Mets dropped 120 contests in 1962. As part of the Braves' figure, Cantwell wound up with 25 of the losses, the last pitcher in baseball to lose that many; strangely enough, he had only recently led the majors with a .667 winning percentage (20–10) in 1933. In November, the Braves would be temporarily taken over by the National League until the club could straighten out its books, which were in disarray; a month later, the league approved the nomination of Bob Quinn as the team's owner and president, who had previously been the general manager of the Dodgers.

It had been three years since Babe Ruth and the Yankees had humiliated the Cubs in four straight in the 1932 postseason. Jolly Cholly's army was now back, and looking for revenge on the American League. They would face a Detroit team also looking for respect, never having won a World Series and being humbled at the hands of the Dean brothers twelve months earlier.

Hold That Tiger

After wading through the lines of early campers—and hundreds of handshakes—to pick up their complimentary series tickets at the Wrigley Field box office, the Cubs hurried to the station and left Chicago on the 4:10 Pennsylvania train bound for Detroit on Monday, September 30. The special train had a total of 75 travelers on board, the non–Cubs being a few passengers who had no idea the team would be joining them when they purchased their fares weeks or months earlier. Not on any of the cars was young Paul Dominick, the lucky charm of the winning streak, but he bid the Cubs farewell at Union Station as each player rubbed his head for good fortune.

Upon arriving in Detroit, Grimm had only one line for the reporters when he got off the train. "I think we can take the hides off those Tigers," he told the writers, in very much the same spot and manner in which Dean had spoken a year earlier.

After relaxing for the rest of the evening, Grimm planned a workout for the team on Tuesday at Navin Field, the time of which depended upon when Cochrane would decide to do the same with his club. The team had also decided to split the World Series pot 26½ ways, with the half share going to the newly-arrived pitcher Shoun and another $250 to outfielder Johnny Gill, who had been with the team for only a couple days. In addition to the players that had been on the club all season, full shares were voted for traveling secretary Bob Lewis, coaches Red Corriden and Roy Johnson, and trainer Andy Lotshaw. Clubhouse boy Joe Bernardi would enjoy a $1,000 bonus, and batboy Gilly Hasbrook a cool $500. A full winner's share was expected to be around $5,000, as compared to the 1908 figure of $1,317 for the winning Cubs team that year.

The Cubs and Tigers had met 27 years earlier in that 1908 Series, with Chicago getting its last world championship in five games under player-manager Frank Chance. The 1908 season had been the middle of a three-year pennant run for the Tigers, under the leadership of manager Hughie Jennings and the hostile play of Ty Cobb. Being the only American League titles the team would garner until 1934, they could never quite get over the top. Chance's Cubs swept them in four straight in 1907, and Fred Clarke's Pirates outlasted them in seven contests in 1909. Cochrane, who had been sold off from the A's by Connie Mack for $100,000 in 1934, had become the darling of the Motor City; despite losing the World Series to the Cardinals that year, he was showered with gifts from appreciative city fans. Navin, after many years of struggling, felt he finally had a championship team in place behind the veteran Cochrane. "Mr. Navin was like all the owners then," said Gehringer. "He was in it to make a living. He was hard to deal with. I remember one year during the Depression he had to borrow money from the bank to take us to spring training." But good times had returned, and attendance in Detroit had nearly tripled between 1933 and 1935, with 920,000 coming out to the ballpark to watch the pennant-winning Tigers.

The Cubs would be making their ninth appearance in the World Series in 1935. There were eight players on the '35 Cubs that participated in that 1932 tilt against the Yankees, including Jurges (who batted .364 in that series), Hartnett (.312), Demaree (.286), Herman (.222), English (.176), Hack (no average), along with pitchers Warneke and Root (who lost one game apiece). The rookie Demaree had taken the place of regular centerfielder Johnny Moore, and hit the only Cubs home run in the series.

Among other laurels, the 32-year-old Cochrane could be described as a "winner," as this was his fifth pennant as a player in the past seven years. He was the reigning American League Most Valuable Player (he beat out Gehrig and his Triple Crown in '34), and the catcher-manager had a wealth of weapons at his disposal. After a terrible start to the season that saw them fall into last place, the Tigers righted themselves and let their immense talent take over. Along with himself and Greenberg, Cochrane's primary offensive force was Gehringer, who topped the 200-hit mark, drove in 108 runs, and hit .330. Cochrane batted .319 with 33 doubles, while outfielders Pete Fox (.321, 38 doubles, 15 home runs) and Leon "Goose" Goslin (34 doubles, .292) were also part of a potent lineup. Goslin had recently gotten a shipment of new bats, and he grinned wantonly for the reporters as he showed one off. "This one's for Warneke," he announced, waving the stick strongly in both hands. The only injury present on the club was that of thirdbaseman Marv Owen, who re-injured a bad thumb in the season-closing series at Comiskey. Owen was in the middle of the big controversy in the final game of the '34 series with Cardinals, as Medwick slid hard into him at third base while tripling. The fans, already annoyed by their team's 7–0 deficit in the sixth inning, showered Medwick with debris as he took the field for the bottom half. Medwick was then ordered from the game by Landis for Medwick's own safety—a safe call for Landis himself as well, for the game was essentially out of reach for the Tigers at that point. History will never know what his decision would have been if the score had been closer.

Off the mound for Detroit, the curve-ball artist Bridges (21–10) and the towering Rowe (19–13) ran roughshod over the American League during the year. Bridges led the league in strikeouts with 163, while Rowe topped all pitchers with six shutouts and batted .312 in 108 at-bats. They joined Auker for a powerful threesome, which Grimm knew would be tough to beat in a seven-game series. Warneke was Charlie's choice for the opener. "It's still Lon for the pitching job," the skipper said, when asked about his thoughts for Game One. "And nothing short of a kidnapping will make me change. The rest of the lineup will be made up of the same fellows who carried the load during the last three weeks of the race. Just let us win that first battle, and we'll be hard to catch." Hartnett was the only injured Cub when they arrived, and he added that the couple days of rest had aided his sore ankle and hand. But as the Cubs finished up their practice on Tuesday the 1st, Grimm—who despite being in the big leagues since 1919 was getting his first looks at Navin Field—wanted to take a few extra swings in the cage; his last batted ball glanced off the thumb of Shoun, who was throwing the batting practice. Even though it hit him on glove hand, the shot broke Shoun's thumb. The practice, which had been a interrupted a few times by a drizzling rain, was then called off permanently. As the Cubs gathered their things to head to the clubhouse, they continued to gaze in amazement at the proximity of the left field stands. Navin had ordered the installation of temporary seating in that location, bringing the distance of a home run to that part of the park down to only 300 feet, two inches. While righthanded hitters Hartnett, Herman, Jurges and others were happy to see the addition, the pitchers were not.

Normally a dollar for the grandstand and 50 cents for the bleachers, ticket prices at Navin Field for the series would rise to sums of $5.50 and $3.50. Scalpers outside the hotels then started pushing the rate upwards of $60. Meanwhile, back in Chicago, a crowd of nearly 10,000 had formed around Wrigley Field, as they waited sleepy-eyed but anxious for the opening of the ticket windows in the morning. Makeshift tents had been set up all around the park, and card games were going on in many of them to help pass the time. "If I only had a radio and a glass of beer, things would be perfect!" said one of the hopefuls as he threw down a pair of queens. Sixty officers had been dispatched by the Chicago Police Department to keep a lookout, but no disturbances were reported. The cops did estimate that over half of the standees were women, passing the time by "knitting, some trying to read by the dim glow of the street lights, and others fast asleep in steamer chairs." Hot coffee was provided by a kind gentleman who had brought along a gasoline stove. "Plenty of bottles were spotted," reported another policeman, "but few contained milk." As the crowd grew larger and larger, however, a few cops and Cubs employees allegedly fell into some impropriety. It was reported by the *Tribune* the next day that six officers and two Cub workers had helped scalpers obtain tickets, as many other fans waiting in line all night never got seats. The club had hired spotters to notice suspicious behavior in the ticket lines, and they noticed a few individuals being escorted to the front of the line by the police. These individuals were later identified as scalpers and arrested. Phil Wrigley admitted that a mail system would have prevented such occurrences, but was impossible with the short time frame involved. Captain George O'Connor of the Chicago Police dispatched new officers to the scene, and "order" was soon restored. Coincidentally, the Illinois General Assembly had just passed a law, having taken effect July 5, "Prohibiting the sale of baseball, theatre, and other amusement tickets for a price more than the price printed on the face of the ticket ... the price of the ticket shall correspond with the price shown at the box office or at the office of original distribution." For the games scheduled at Wrigley Field during the series, the department planned on 464 policemen to be on duty at the park.

Jolly Cholly made no bones about his expectations to win. "Manager Grimm says that his best forecast on the series is the Cubs in five games," Burns revealed. "He would not be shocked if it went six. He does not expect it to go seven."

As the first game got underway at 1:30 local time, the Cubs' dugout was flanked by Phil Wrigley on one end and Mr. and Mrs. Kenesaw Landis on the other, the latter wearing fresh orchids presented to her beforehand. The umpires were George Moriarity, Bill McGowan, Ernest Quigley, and Dolly Stark, who scrambled out to take their positions. Moriarity, who himself had been a player and major league manager with the Tigers in the late 1920s, would be behind the plate for the opener. He was well remembered by the people in Detroit, and interested persons sought his autograph as if he was an active player. It was the second

World Series assignment for Stark, the third for McGowan, the fifth for Moriarity, and the sixth for Quigley. Quigley had been the athletic director for 14 years at St. Mary's College in Kansas, while Stark was in the middle of a tenure as baseball coach at Dartmouth.

"Tiger Fever" was everywhere around town; Superintendent Frank Cody of the Detroit Public Schools had even instructed building principals in the city to allow the system's 250,000 students to listen to the games over the radio in their classrooms. And Henry Edwards, who was in charge of the press arrangements in Detroit for the series, told some colleagues that there were at least 60 more newsmen covering this championship than a year ago.

It was an all–Arkansas matchup on the mound, as Rowe and Warneke prepared to begin the fight. Cochrane admitted he made a mistake in the '34 series by not pitching Rowe in the first game against Dizzy Dean; instead, he went with Alvin "General" Crowder. Privately, Cochrane felt that Dean would have beaten any of his pitchers, and when word of this leaked, he had given the Cardinals an extra psychological edge. He vowed to not take the same route again, and this time he opened with his best.

Rowe, with his 6'4" frame, took long steps to the mound, and was impervious to anything but his duty. In the '34 series, he had been subjected to the usual taunts by the Cardinals, particularly Durocher and infielder Pat Crawford who yelled, "How'm I doin', Edna???" It was in reference to Rowe's finacee, Edna Skinner, who was in the first row behind the Tiger dugout. Edna, now Mrs. Rowe, was back home in El Dorado, Arkansas, caring for the couple's new baby. With no "mouthy Deans present," as the Tigers called the pair, Rowe was the man in charge—and he intended to prove it to the crowd of over 47,000. He coldly stared down Galan as Augie entered the box, ready to get the 1935 World Series underway.

But Galan, the 23-year-old who had risen to the occasion so many times in his first season as a starter, was undaunted. After taking the first pitch for a strike and fouling off the second, he drove the ball back at Rowe with authority. The white apple sailed off of Billy Rogell's glove at short, and lingered in the outfield grass between him, Gehringer, and centerfielder Jo Jo White long enough for Galan to pull in at second with a double. With the very first batter, Detroit fans got a glimpse of the man who, with his speed, had brought an extra dimension to the normally-plodding Cubs' offensive package. Next was Herman, and Rowe righted himself to fire a strong inside fastball that Billy squibbed down the first base line. Rowe went down to calmly retrieve the ball, but upon throwing to first, it slipped from his grasp and nailed Herman in the back, who a second later collided with Greenberg. Galan, who had been moving to third since contact, didn't stop running and came home with the series' first run. Lindstrom then sacrificed Herman to second, and Hartnett promptly lined a single to right for a 2–0 lead.

For Warneke, it may just as well have been an Arkansas pickup game behind the barn back in his home of Mount Ida. "Lon just stood out there and pitched and fielded and chawed his tobacco," Burns described the ease with which he began to dispose of the Detroit hitters.

Starting what Arch Ward would later call "one of the finest pitched games in World Series history," Warneke burned through White, Cochrane, and Gehringer easily in the first. Fox got the first Tiger hit with two out in the second with a single to left, but was stranded. At this point, Moriarity took off his mask and walked over to the Cubs' dugout, warning Grimm and his charges to not verbally harass Greenberg any further; they were on him because he was constantly rubbing his arm, apparently the result of his collision with the much-smaller Herman in the first inning.

In the fourth, it looked as if Warneke had finally become rattled; he walked Greenberg and Goslin on nine pitches. But more ground-ball outs followed, as Warneke's vaunted curve ball evaded the barrels of the Tigers' bats. While the fans expected a surge in the sixth with the sluggers up once again (Gehringer, Greenberg, and Goslin), Warneke recorded two groundouts and a pop fly to Hack without much trouble.

He stayed in the groove to the ninth, when leading off the Chicago half, Demaree caught hold of a shoulder-high, 2–2 fastball from Rowe and drove it over the screen in left field, giving the Cubs another insurance run and a 3–0 lead. It was only his third homer of the year, but his second career dinger in World Series play. The Schoolboy came back to get Cavarretta and Jurges to strike out, giving him a total of eight on the afternoon. When Fox got his second hit in the ninth inning with one out, it appeared that Detroit might mount a rally, but Rogell tapped out to Cavy and Owen rolled an easy one to Jurges to finish things off, and the Cubs jumped out ahead in the series.

Rowe had pitched a fine game himself, but it would have been difficult for anyone to have beaten Warneke on this day. To further illustrate his domination, he tied the World Series record for assists by a pitcher with nine (including four in a row in the third and fourth innings)—testimony that the Tigers failed to get good wood on him all game long, as harmless tappers squeaked toward Lon's waiting glove at the mound. "If I had thrown Cochrane out in the fifth, I would've broken a record, wouldn't I?" he realized afterwards, citing a play in which he tagged the Detroit catcher instead of throwing to Cavarretta. "But what's the difference? I was out there to win. Records didn't mean nothin' to me. I won one if I never win another. Boy—that's fun. When I passed those two guys in the fourth inning I just said to myself, 'Calm yourself and settle down to do your work.' That's just what I did."

"Lonnie was in trouble only that once," said his catcher Hartnett about the dangerous fourth frame. "Aside from that, he seemed able to put the ball right where he wanted it."

"He had nice stuff and good control," admitted Cochrane. "Anybody that can keep a ball over the plate with a little stuff on it is plenty tough."

In addition to the nine of his own, nine more groundouts were completed by the four men behind Warneke. Despite a slow start to the season, he had hit his stride at the right time—he had not lost as a starting pitcher since August 8 against Paul Dean. And once again it was a flawless display by the Cubs' infield, suddenly being mentioned by sportswriters as among the greatest defenses of all time. The Tigers were sensing October gloom once again, as they now had been held scoreless in 21 consecutive World Series innings dating back past their Game Seven collapse against the Cardinals in 1934.

"It's terrible that Lynwood lost his game," mourned Edna Rowe back in El Dorado, as Lynwood, Jr., slept through the contest as it was broadcasted on the radio. "But I'm not discouraged."

The Cubs, meanwhile, were exuberant in the locker room. While Grimm and the boys knew it was only one game, they were on the right road. "Helluva shot, Frankie!" he yelled over to Demaree, who returned a grin. "Great third-basing, Stanislaus [said to Hack]! Nice going, everybody. You guys are all gennel-muns."

Across the world that same day, Mussolini's troops invaded Ethiopia, as bombs from his Italian airplanes fell on Addis Ababa and British warships stood on guard in the Suez Canal in preparation for world war. Initial reports had counted 1,700 civilians killed in the Ethiopian capital from the air attacks.

The box score from Game One:

Chicago	AB	R	H	RBI
Galan, lf	4	1	1	0
Herman, 2b	3	1	0	0
Lindstrom, cf	3	0	1	0
Hartnett, c	4	0	2	1
Demaree, rf	4	1	2	1
Cavarretta, 1b	3	0	0	0
Hack, 3b	4	0	0	0
Jurges, ss	4	0	1	0
Warneke, p	3	0	0	0

Detroit	AB	R	H	RBI
White, cf	4	0	1	0
Cochrane, c	4	0	0	0
Gehringer, 2b	3	0	0	0
Greenberg, 1b	3	0	0	0
Goslin, lf	3	0	0	0
Fox, rf	4	0	2	0
Rogell, ss	4	0	0	0
Owen, 3b	3	0	0	0
Rowe, p	3	0	1	0

E—Rowe, Goslin, Greenberg

```
Chicago  2 0 0  0 0 0  0 0 1   3-7-0
Detroit  0 0 0  0 0 0  0 0 0   0-4-3
```

A few hours after the first game was completed, a steady, drizzling rain hit the Detroit area and lasted into the overnight hours. It stopped in time for the second contest, but left the field in a slow, soggy state. As unhittable as Warneke's curve ball was in Game One, the Cubs would be facing perhaps an equal "hammer" in Game Two. Bridges, who, statistically had out-pitched Rowe in many ways over the past two seasons, looked to even things up with his own deadly breaking ball. But Grimm was confident in his response.

"Root, with his side arm delivery, is the kind of fellow who should bother those Tigers," he said, also noting the experience that the 36-year-old slinger possessed. Root was looking to atone for his losses in the opener of the 1929 World Series to Howard Ehmke and the Philadelphia A's, as well as the third game of the 1932 series to George Pipgras and the Yankees.

Very cool temperatures in the low forties greeted the players as they took the field; Grimm would later say that it was coldest game he had ever witnessed. While the crowd was nearly as large as the first game with 46,742 in attendance, scalpers had much difficulty getting rid of some tickets as the first pitch approached. One even gave away an admission "for a cup of coffee and a hot dog," according to a witness. Snow had been seen falling in the downtown Detroit area earlier that morning, but there was no accumulation. To help keep themselves warm, a throng of sportswriters had caught up with former Cubs pitcher Pat Malone in the overnight hours, who was wandering the entertainment district and invited the scribes to help him spend the $250 he had in his pocket.

In small breaks of sun in the overcast sky, one could get a little warmth if seated in the lower boxes of the stadium. The Tigers and their followers were growing increasingly edgy, and they knew today was the time to strike. Bridges had the misfortune of getting wet as he took his warmup tosses in the bullpen, but not due to rain; a hose from the sprinkler system had busted loose, and its random fire wound up in the direction of the Tigers' pitcher. He wiped himself off and took the mound as the game got underway eight minutes late (which was actually an improvement on the 18-minute tardiness of Game One). After retiring the Cubs in the first, Bridges' friends opened up with fierce salvos on Root in the bottom half. First was White, who led off with a single. He scored when Cochrane doubled, who was subsequently plated by a Gehringer hit for a quick 2–0 advantage. Before Gehringer knocked his single, he drove a ball long out of the park onto Trumbull Street (in the days before the stadium was double-decked), but it was blown foul by a gust of wind at the last moment. Next was Greenberg, perhaps the most frustrated of Navin's employees. The inviting screen in left field had been erected specifically for his bat, but the big slugger had failed to get the ball out of the infield on Warneke in Game One. The oral insults continued to flow from the Cubs dugout, despite more warning's from Moriarity and his crew. Continued control of the feared hitter was expected, with a strong wind blowing straight in from left and the cold conditions not favorable to hitting. But Greenberg saw his way clear to a vulnerable toss from Root, took a mighty hack, and lofted a long one high into the portable bleachers beyond left field. The stadium rocked with appreciation as he trailed his beneficiary Gehringer to the plate, and Bridges was staked to a 4–0 lead. Henshaw was ordered from the bullpen by Grimm, and Root left the field with yet another opportunity for a Series win strewn in his wake. Grimm also had French ready, but did not want to waste him on a game that was getting out of hand very quickly. Little Roy got three outs in succession as the Cubs tried to climb out of the hole.

The Chicago bats were held without a whimper by Bridges in the second and third as well, but in the fourth, the Cubbies were starting to dig in at the plate. Lindstrom, right on top of a fastball, fouled one back towards the press area. Chatting with the reporters there was Babe Ruth, and he stuck out his right hand at the last moment to catch the ball (earlier in the day at his hotel, Ruth had to retreat back into the elevator, for he was besieged by autograph seekers when the door opened. The next time he went out the back way, stopping for "a handful of cigars" at the hotel commissary and then dashing out into the street). Lindstrom was quickly retired, but Hartnett followed with the first Chicago hit, a line-drive single to center field. He was left stranded when Demaree flied to White.

Babe Ruth greets the two managers, Charlie Grimm and Mickey Cochrane, at the 1935 World Series. (Chicago Historical Society)

In the Tigers' half of the fourth, Henshaw lost control as he hit Owen, allowed an infield hit to Bridges, and walked White to load the bases. After Owen scored on a wild pitch, Cochrane walked to fill the bases once again. Then Gehringer, perhaps the greatest hitting secondbaseman of all time, cracked a single to score two and make it 7–0 as a grumbling Grimm replaced Henshaw with Kowalik. The Cubs finally got on the board in the fifth when a single by Jurges scored Cavarretta, but it was all they could muster. Detroit would add their eighth run in the seventh inning, and Greenberg tried to score another from first on a single, but was gunned down on a perfect throw relay throw by Herman. Greenberg was hurt after crashing into Hartnett at the plate, and it was feared he had broken his wrist. He would be taken to a local hospital for an X-Ray. The Cubs failed to mount any more significant offense, and the Tigers ran away with an 8–3 win to even the series.

Bridges finished his work by allowing six Cub hits, four walks, and striking out two, averaging four pitches to every batter he faced. He was not overpowering, but spread the Chicago baserunners around so as not to produce a major threat. The Tiger clubhouse, contrasted with that of the Cubs from the previous afternoon, was relatively quiet in an aura of assuredness after the game. "I'm glad I won," Bridges said simply. "I felt confident I would when I started." While Greenberg's wrist was not broken, it was diagnosed as a severe sprain and his status for Game Three at Chicago the next day was in question.

Grimm, meanwhile, was philosophical about the loss. "That's the way to get beat," he said. "Get the hell kicked out of you, and have it over with."

The box score from Game Two:

Chicago	AB	R	H	RBI
Galan, lf	4	0	0	0
Herman, 2b	4	0	1	2
Lindstrom, cf	3	0	0	0
Hartnett, c	4	0	1	0
Demaree, rf	4	0	1	0
Cavarretta, 1b	4	1	0	0
Hack, 3b	3	0	1	0
Jurges, ss	3	1	1	1
Root, p	0	0	0	0
Henshaw, p	1	0	0	0
Kowalik, p	2	1	1	0
Klein, ph	1	0	0	0

E—Kowalik

Detroit	AB	R	H	RBI
White, cf	3	2	1	0
Cochrane, c	2	1	1	1
Gehringer, 2b	3	2	2	3
Greenberg, 1b	3	1	1	2
Goslin, lf	3	0	0	0
Fox, rf	4	0	1	1
Rogell, ss	4	0	2	0
Owen, 3b	2	1	0	0
Bridges, p	4	1	1	0

E—Greenberg 2

Chicago	000	010	200	3–6–1
Detroit	400	300	100	8–9–2

There was no day for rest, as the Cubs had to get on a five o'clock train to head to Chicago for the third contest on Friday, October 4. The Tigers would arrive in town an hour earlier than the Cubs, and Cochrane had them head straight to their waiting accommodations at the Edgewater. A crowd of 50,000 was expected at Wrigley, and the temporary bleachers installed in the outfield were anticipated to be filled. The 12,000 tickets for that area of the park would go on sale at 7:00 A.M., and folks lined up well before the hour to get their passes. The "stop and go lights" were turned off on Lake Shore Drive between Belmont Avenue and Irving Park Road, as officers instead manned the intersections in the swarm of cars that was expected. There was not a vacant hotel room to be found in the city. The Edgewater was filled with Detroit fans; the Congress Hotel, where the Cubs would all stay together, had been sold out for weeks; the Sherman, Morrison, and Drake establishments had been booked for a while, too, mostly with customers from Michigan and southern Illinois.

While on the train ride across Indiana, Greenberg noticed that his hand not only failed to improve, but rather had increased in its swelling. He told Cochrane that he would wait all the way up until game time for a decision to play or not, and Mickey scrambled to make a contingency plan.

Pitching for Detroit was Auker, and the Kansan was no stranger to World Series play. Just one year earlier, he had helped restore Tiger hopes with an impressive 10–4 victory over Carleton at St. Louis in Game Four. Unlike many of his teammates, Auker was impervious to superstition as he was the only player in the major leagues at the time who dared to wear uniform number 13. Grimm handed the ball to Bill Lee, and he also dismissed the notion that Root was incapable of winning the big games.

"Root had as much stuff as he's ever had," the manager said of his pitcher's performance in Game Two. "What ruined him was a couple of badly-pitched balls, due probably to being overcautious. He let Cochrane have an inside pitch and Mickey doubled to right. He pitched an inside ball to Greenberg and that's the one that went into the left field bleachers for a home run. That's what happens to a good pitcher if he happens to be a bit shy on control."

The weather was not as cool for Game Three; the winds settled over the lake and made for a relatively pleasant October afternoon on the North Shore. The actual attendance fell short of expectations at 45,532, as ticket poachers once again struggled, for some reason, to release their wares come game time. Evidence of this was provided by a fan named Michael Hammerman, who, according to the *Tribune,* had purchased two box seats for 25 cents each just before the Cubs took the field. Not far away from Hammerman's reservation was Mayor Kelly, and the chief removed his overcoat in declaration of a fine day. Earlier in the week, Kelly had ordered the draping of a banner over the entrance to City Hall that read, "CUBS, CHICAGO IS PROUD OF YOU." Seated next to him was Postmaster General James Farley, the mayor's guest of honor. Phil Wrigley, who was known to thumb his nose at tradition from time to time, ignored protocol and raised the 1935 National League pennant flag to the top of the pole in centerfield before the game (typically, pennant-winning clubs would wait until the following season to note the title). But Wrigley loved his Cubs, and expected great things from them; he fully anticipated an early Cub championship in '36, as he announced that the team would clinch in plenty of time to process World Series tickets by mail only for the following year. But for now it was Lee, winner of twenty games on

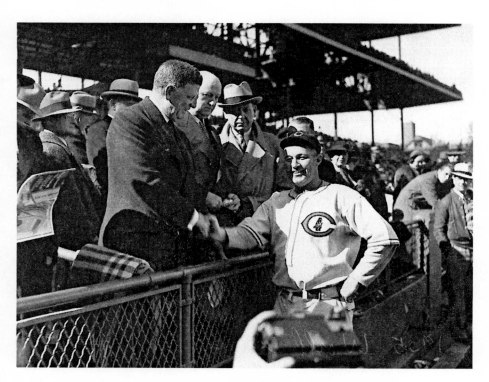

Gabby Hartnett shakes hands with Chicago Mayor Ed Kelly before Game Three of the World Series on October 4, 1935 at Wrigley Field. To Mayor Kelly's left is Postmaster General of the United States, James Farley. (Chicago Historical Society)

the season, taking the hill as he and his teammates in shining white uniforms exited the dugout and spread out over the field to the loud cheers of the home crowd. The infield at Wrigley Field stood bold with new grass sod, laid while the Cubs were finishing the regular season in St. Louis. Off in the distance behind Lindstrom, who stood in center, it could be seen that roughly 3,000 bleachers seats went unclaimed as the game began.

Greenberg was not ready to go, so Cochrane shifted Owen over to first base as Herman "Flea" Clifton got the call at third.

At the beginning of the season, Galan and Demaree both had seemed destined for the bench in a revamped outfield that included veterans Klein, Lindstrom, and Cuyler. As it turned out, both of the youngsters had played key roles in the Cubs' rise, as Cuyler was released and Klein saw more of the bench with his late-season slump. Demaree was inserted into the fifth spot in the lineup once again by Grimm, and with the game scoreless in the bottom of the second, he came to the plate. After falling behind on two strikes, Demaree slammed another long one, deep into the center field stands, and the Cubs jumped out to 1–0 lead. It was Demaree's fourth hit of the series, the most on the Cubs team and second only to Gehringer's five when the day's play was done. He then gave the bat to Farley, who in turn passed it along to his son. The edge was increased to 2–0 in the same inning, as Hack singled, stole second, waltzed into third on Clifton's error, and scored when Lee grounded out to Gehringer at second. Demaree came to the rescue in the fourth with his glove, when Cochrane lifted a bleeder down the right field line with Demaree playing deep. He charged in, and at the last moment slid feet-first while scooping his hands underneath the ball for a clean catch. In Cub fifth it was the other young flychaser's turn at the plate, as Galan smacked a clutch single to score Jurges for a 3–0 lead on Auker. The Tigers got on the board in their half of the sixth, when Goslin raced all the way home when Fox whistled a line-drive triple past Cavarretta's glove at first that wound up in the right field corner. But any further threat was squelched when Hartnett picked Fox off third with a snap throw. Fox wasn't too upset about the decision by Quigley, but third base coach Del Baker was— and was ejected for arguing. Hartnett had been making big plays all day long, as he had twice already lunged into the stands to take pop-ups away from spectators. Lee then struck out Rogell on three pitches, and the Cub lead stood at 3–1 entering their half of the sixth.

In that inning, Cavarretta was on first with one out when he attempted to steal second. Moriarity called him out, but Grimm, who was in the third base coaching box, disagreed and charged the umpire, claiming that Gehringer never tagged him. Moriarity quickly ejected Grimm from the game, and several Cub players rushed from the dugout to keep him from further penalty. Red Corriden and Roy Johnson then took over the reins of the ballclub.

Lee took the 3–1 lead into the eighth, when his skills started to evade him. With the Tigers batting, the Cubs' dugout continued to give it to Moriarity, who promptly ejected English and Stainback, the leaders of the chiding. When play resumed, White walked and was driven to third on a double by Gehringer that zoomed past Demaree to the wall. Next was Goslin, and he hit a line smash that struck the first base bag, bounded over the head of Cavarretta (who was not having the luckiest day of his life), and into right field to score the tying runs. Warneke then entered to relieve Lee, and hits followed by Fox and Rogell to give the Tigers a 5–3 lead.

Bloody but unbowed, the Cub bats rallied in the ninth. They had recorded three straight hitless innings off Elon Hogsett and Rowe, who had replaced Auker (before the game, the large, heavy-hitting Rowe had asked Cochrane if he could replace Greenberg at first base, but Mickey declined). Cavarretta flew out to White at the wall to start the inning off of Rowe, but Hack followed with a single. Then Klein, banished to the bench, was brought in to pinch-hit for Jurges. He punched a single through short, Hack stopping at second as the crowd murmured with hope. Then O'Dea, who was batting for Warneke, singled sharply to right to score Hack and send Klein to third. Galan finished the climb by scoring Klein on a sacrifice fly, and the game headed into extra innings. But because English had been ejected, the club no longer had a bona fide shortstop to take the place of Jurges. Hack was inserted, even though he had never played the position in his professional career. To complete the platoon, Lindstrom was brought in to play third, Demaree moved from right field over to center, and Klein took over in right. French and Rowe each sat the enemy down effectively in the tenth, as the game moved on.

The defensive maneuvers by Chicago prevailed in that inning, but failed them in the eleventh. With one out, a single by Rogell got past Hack at short, a ball that Jurges would surely have reached. After Owen forced Rogell on a poor bunt, Clifton sent a roller down to Lindstrom at third. But Freddie, not having played the hot corner in some time, could not grasp the ball and runners were safe at first and second. Although frustrated by these events, French stayed composed long enough to fan Rowe for the second out. Then White, with the count 2-and-2, laced one of the biggest hits of the series with a single to center, plating Owen for a 6–5 Detroit lead.

Sensing victory, Rowe was at his best in the bottom half. He got

Hack to ground out to Clifton; Klein, after fouling off six pitches, struck out on a pitch that would have been ball four; then Stephenson, batting for the first time in weeks, was called upon to pinch hit for French. Rowe blazed a fast one by him for strike three, a pitch Stephenson observed without swinging. The Tigers were in command of the series with a 2–1 lead in games.

It was announced after the game the Landis would initiate an investigation into the play (and the following events) that forced Grimm, English, and Stainback from the field. He first received Moriarity's report on the events, and then waited to get the side of the Cub players. While the Cubs were disappointed in their own play, as well as the decision of Moriarity, they didn't believe that the umpire was showing favoritism towards his former team, the Tigers. "A squawk about an umpire in a losing game never is a graceful thing," Grimm pointed out, as he sat back in his locker chair and gave a deep sigh. "The Tigers won a great game, and we've got to come back tomorrow whether we like Moriarity or not.

"I cannot keep from saying, however, that in all my baseball I never have heard an umpire abuse members of a ball team with the language Moriarity used to Herman, to Jurges, to English, and to me, and then to the entire bench."

Cochrane, over in the visitors' clubhouse, agreed that it was a hard-fought contest. "What a battle it was," he reflected, while pondering his own 0-for-5 day at the plate. "It was a big game for us to win. It was the toughest World Series game I've ever played in."

"Y'know," Rogell yelled from across the room, "that was just another of those real Tiger games—that's all."

The box score from Game Three:

Detroit	AB	R	H	RBI
White, cf	5	1	2	1
Cochrane, c	5	0	0	0
Gehringer, 2b	5	1	2	0
Goslin, lf	5	2	3	2
Fox, rf	5	1	2	1
Rogell, ss	5	0	3	1
Owen, 1b	5	1	0	0
Clifton, 3b	4	0	0	0
Auker, p	2	0	0	0
Walker, ph	1	0	0	0
Hogsett, p	0	0	0	0
Rowe, p	2	0	0	0

E—Clifton, Cochrane

Chicago	AB	R	H	RBI
Galan, lf	4	0	2	2
Herman, 2b	5	0	1	0
Lindstrom, cf-3b	5	0	2	0
Hartnett, c	4	0	0	0
Demaree, rf-cf	4	1	1	1
Cavarretta, 1b	5	0	0	0
Hack, 3b-ss	5	2	2	0
Jurges, ss	1	1	0	0
Klein, rf	2	1	1	0
Lee, p	1	0	0	1
Warneke, p	0	0	0	0
O'Dea, ph	1	0	1	1
French, p	0	0	0	0
Stephenson, ph	1	0	0	0

E—Herman, Cavarretta, Lindstrom

Detroit	0 0 0	0 0 1	0 4 0	0 1	6-12-2
Chicago	0 2 0	0 1 0	0 0 2	0 0	5-10-3

After being an "also-ran" through the last two Septembers and Octobers, Carleton was getting a chance to start another World Series game. While the Dean family had picked up all four wins in the '34 version, Tex had dropped that fourth game to Auker at Sportsman's Park. In that contest, he was removed by Frisch in the third inning after the Tigers had touched him for three runs. The Cardinals came back to tie, but the Detroit bats picked on the rest of the St. Louis staff en route to the 10–4 decision (Carleton also came in relief of Dizzy Dean in Game Five, pitching a scoreless inning as the Tigers won again, 3–1, their last victory in the series as Paul and Dizzy won the final two). Carleton had become a somewhat-forgotten man in Grimm's pitching plans down the stretch, as he had won only once in the Cubs' 21-game winning streak towards the pennant. His opponent would be Crowder, Cochrane's surprise choice in the '34 opener but a hero of the 1933 American League pennant drive by the Washington Senators, a year in which he led the AL in wins with 24. Like Dizzy Dean, Crowder had really begun to hone his pitching skills while in the army, and thus he was saddled with the nickname upon entering professional ball. He was plenty ready, as he had gone to bed at 7:30 the previous night in preparation for his important duty. It was the most pivotal of games, and the two veteran pitchers—both wearing the number "16" on their backs—went to work.

Perhaps now more intrigued after the Cubs fell behind in the series, the crowd swelled to 49,350 for the fourth contest. More policemen were employed on the scene, and extras were posted on the rooftops of buildings on Sheffield and Waveland to prevent free-seekers from those vantage points (Police Commissioner James Allman ordered officers to arrest anyone found up on the buildings, citing the city code that listed more than 40 persons in such a place as dangerous to the stability of a roof). Deciding that he did not want to influence the outcome of the series in any way, Landis announced he would deal with the Cubs-umpires feud after the championship was decided. Cochrane went with the same successful lineup as the day before, with Greenberg still on the shelf but available if needed. All of the locals that took their seats were privy to an early treat, as the husky catcher Hartnett belted a homer to the opposite field in right to give Carleton a 1–0 head start. The pitch was "outside and shoulder-league, right where I like 'em," Gabby said afterwards. Carleton teetered on the brink of disaster in the first few innings, permitting a total of eight baserunners in the second and third. But only one would score, as Gehringer stroked another hit, a double off the glove of the hard-charging Lindstrom in center to send Crowder across home.

It was in the sixth that the Cub defense—which had rescued them time and time again during the regular season—failed them once again in the series. Strangely enough, consecutive miscues were committed by two of the most sure-handed men. Carleton had already recorded two outs in the inning when Clifton catapulted a long fly to Galan in left. Augie sprinted back towards the wall, but turned and centered himself in plenty of time to make a two-handed catch. He thought he had done just that, but the ball fell free as the surprised Clifton pulled into second. Next was Crowder, who bounced a three-hopper to Jurges at short, a play that Billy had made a thousand times in his life. But he reached down lazily, and the ball took a funny hop with the "english" that the far end of Crowder's bat provided. Jurges did not get his glove down in time, and the ball went through his legs into left field as Clifton came around third with the go-ahead tally, 2–1. After a walk to White, Galan made extra-sure of his catch of a pop fly off the bat of Cochrane to end the inning, but the damage had been done.

Time quickly escaped the bruins after that, as Crowder rolled through their next three chances. Root, who replaced Carleton after a pinch-hitter disqualified Tex in the seventh, kept the Cubs within one run (the pinch-hitter was Klein, and he grounded out after sending a long, crooked ball out of the park, not ten feet to the right of the foul pole). In the last stanza, the crowd rose to its feet when Demaree's one-out single was followed by one off the bat of Cavarretta, signaling a possible rally for

Chicago. But the veteran Crowder, not about to let another chance at a postseason win slip away, bore down to go after the final two outs. It took only one more pitch, as Hack lined a hard grounder to Rogell at short who picked it cleanly, flipped to Gehringer, and the "Mechanical Man" did his usual flawless duty in turning the double play to end the game. News of Alvin's victory brought great joy to Mrs. Crowder, who had been bed-ridden in a hospital in Winston-Salem, North Carolina, for the past six months with a serious but undisclosed illness. "I've just prayed that boy would win one game—one game in a World Series," the grateful wife said of her husband. "For three years, that's all I've been living for."

The Tigers were now one win away from their first world championship, and the Cubs one defeat shy of seeing their dramatic September pennant run being achieved in vain.

The box score from Game Four:

Detroit	AB	R	H	RBI
White, cf	3	0	1	0
Cochrane, c	4	0	1	0
Gehringer, 2b	4	0	2	1
Goslin, lf	3	0	1	0
Fox, rf	5	0	1	0
Rogell, ss	3	0	0	0
Owen, 1b	4	0	0	0
Clifton, 3b	4	1	0	0
Crowder, p	3	1	1	0

Chicago	AB	R	H	RBI
Galan, lf	4	0	0	0
Herman, 2b	4	0	1	0
Lindstrom, cf	4	0	0	0
Hartnett, c	4	1	1	1
Demaree, rf	4	0	1	0
Cavarretta, 1b	4	0	2	0
Hack, 3b	4	0	0	0
Jurges, ss	1	0	0	0
Carleton, p	1	0	0	0
Root, p	0	0	0	0
Klein, ph	1	0	0	0

E—Galan, Jurges

Detroit	0 0 1	0 0 1	0 0 0	2–7–0
Chicago	0 1 0	0 0 0	0 0 0	1–5–2

Backed into a corner, Grimm knew that he had to go with his hottest pitcher. That person was Warneke, coming back on just a day's rest after his relief appearance for Lee in Game Three, and four days removed from his brilliance in Game One. In a similar manner, Cochrane ran Rowe out to the mound once again, hoping that his top gun could find enough strength to end the series in Chicago. As chance would have it, Moriarity was back behind the plate for Game Five, and the Cubs shuddered at this prospect in the potentially-decisive contest.

It was October 6, and readers of the Sunday morning paper were not only greeted with World Series updates, but also news from the Atlantic Ocean. It was announced that the salvage ship *Orphir*, on patrol in the North Atlantic, came across a 600-foot piece of wreckage that was believed to be the *Lusitania*, a liner sunk by German U-boats at the outset of World War One which claimed 1,195 lives, 123 of whom were Americans. At 312 feet below the surface, diver James Jarratt encountered the tip of the massive boat, a grim discovery at a time when the world was fearing global war once again.

The house at Addison and Clark was packed, as 49,237 waited to see if the Cubs could stave off elimination. The sold-that-day bleachers were full to the brim, while the ticket windows in that part of the park closed just a few moments before the game got underway.

The Cubs surprised the Schoolboy with three hits in their first two chances, but they did not result in any score. Up came Herman, baseball's hit king on the season to lead off the Chicago third. He drove a ball deep into the right-center gap, and after a half-second hesitation around second, turned on the jets to race into third with a triple, "the fastest bit of baserunning in the series," according to Ward. Following him to the plate was Klein, in the starting lineup only because of a minor injury to Lindstrom. The Indy native, his confidence rejuvenated by quality pinch-hitting of late, took advantage of a mistake made by Rowe. The big righthander left a straight fastball waist-high, and Klein deposited it behind the back row of the right field bleachers, striking a brick wall behind the seats for a 2–0 lead. The fans behind the Cubs' dugout were delirious as Herman greeted him at home plate. Meanwhile, Warneke looked strong once again as he did not permit a Tiger baserunner to reach third base through the first six innings, and had allowed only three hits and no walks. But half of that work had been done in excruciating pain; for it was unknown to all in the park except Warneke that he had pulled a muscle in his pitching shoulder back in the third inning, first felt when he unleashed a nasty curve ball to Rowe.

Having to leave the game at the start of the seventh and still holding a 2–0 lead, Warneke gave way to Lee. Originally, Louisiana Bill was to be saved for Game Six in Detroit, but seeing as there was no tomorrow in defeat, Grimm commanded him to the mound as Warneke informed the skipper that he could not pitch any further. A shaky start for Lee had the Cub fans yelping in fear, as he walked Goslin on four pitches while Root hurried to loosen up in the bullpen. On one of the pitches, Moriarity initially called a strike but then changed it to a ball, which caused a few of the Cubs to hurl their warmup jackets out of the dugout. Moriarity issued a warning to the bench, after which Hartnett was nearly ejected from the game as he turned around from his catcher's position and uttered a few not-so-carefully-selected words. Clifton next bounced into a double play, and the Jurges-Herman-Cavarretta trio struck once again.

In the bottom half of the seventh the Cubs could have added an insurance run, but a perfect throw from Fox allowed Cochrane to block the plate as Jurges was called out. Although he had clearly not reached the plate, Billy used the opportunity to give to Moriarity further grief and Grimm and three other Cubs had to drag him away from the scene.

The eighth went smoothly, and the Tigers strung together enough hits for only a single run in the ninth as the Cubs headed back to Detroit with the win, 3–1. It was the second loss of the series for Rowe, and while still only one victory away from the title, Tiger followers began to imagine another Fall Classic collapse to a National League opponent. Gehringer, like Greenberg, had hurt his wrist, but it was a mild sprain; and Owen was still nursing his bruised thumb on his throwing hand, which he said was affecting his hitting as well. It was a large thumb indeed, as it helped hold seven baseballs that Owen could fit into one of his hands.

Warneke told the press that he had gotten eleven hours of sleep before the game, and 14 hours before his opening game shutout. Grimm jokingly then suggested that he try for twenty, in the hopes that he might pitch once again before the series was done. In a more serious tone, the wise-minded Grimm stated "Lon Warneke's arm is worth more to me than all the World Series that will ever be played." Given the circumstances and his competitive nature, it was difficult for Lon to give up on his manager. "I didn't tell Charlie I was through because I wanted to win," Warneke said to reporters as he lay on his stomach on a trainer's table, receiving treatment on his shoulder from a heat lamp while he enjoyed a mouthful of chewing tobacco with his head tilted sideways. "But eventually I had to for the good of the club. I knew I had nothing left in the arm today." As Woody English turned up the volume on the clubhouse radio that was reviewing the big moments of the game, Warneke turned his head back in that direction and smiled. Despite

Grimm's tongue-in-cheek suggestion for some extra repose, Vaughan wasn't optimistic about another Warneke appearance in 1935. "Whether he can come back if the series goes into the seventh game is doubtful," he opined in his *Tribune* column that he clicked out after the game. In agreement, trainer Lotshaw looked sympathetically at the shoulder, and then glanced at the media men and shook his head.

Also in the locker room, French found Grimm and asked enthusiastically for the assignment to pitch Game Six. It had already been granted to him.

The box score from Game Five:

Detroit	AB	R	H	RBI
White, cf	4	0	0	0
Cochrane, c	4	0	2	0
Gehringer, 2b	4	1	1	0
Goslin, lf	3	0	1	0
Fox, rf	4	0	2	1
Rogell, ss	4	0	0	0
Owen, 1b	3	0	0	0
Walker, ph	1	0	0	0
Clifton, 3b	3	0	0	0
Rowe, p	3	0	1	0

E—Owen

Chicago	AB	R	H	RBI
Galan, lf	4	1	0	0
Herman, 2b	4	1	2	1
Klein, rf	4	1	2	2
Hartnett, c	4	0	1	0
Demaree, cf	4	0	1	0
Cavarretta, 1b	4	0	0	0
Hack, 3b	2	0	0	0
Jurges, ss	3	0	1	0
Warneke, p	2	0	1	0
Lee, p	0	0	0	0

```
Detroit    0 0 0   0 0 0   0 0 1   1-7-1
Chicago    0 0 2   0 0 0   1 0*    3-8-0
```

Both teams left Chicago on separate, special trains, each departing Union Station at around five o'clock (the series games had been starting at 1:30 P.M., unlike the customary three o'clock games during the regular season. This allowed the teams some extra time for travel at night with no off-days scheduled during the series). The Cubs left town with their president Phil Wrigley aboard, but the Tigers almost left town without their equipment. The Commonwealth Transfer Company, in charge of taking the bats, balls, gloves, and other necessities to the train station, delivered an empty truck when it arrived at the depot. At about the same time, an American Railway Express driver just happened to drop by Wrigley Field and randomly ask if there was anything that needed to be hauled. When informed of the special cargo that needed to be delivered, the good samaritan hurried the items to the grateful Detroit club, still waiting at the terminal. To pass their time on the ride, the Tiger players enjoyed a deluge of congratulatory telegrams sent to them by well-wishers back in Michigan.

As the Cubs rode along, Warneke joined Klein for supper. The hurler frequently circled his right arm in a futile attempt to loosen it. The team knew it was headed for a battle, but took some solace in the knowledge that the Cardinals pulled the same trick a year earlier: beating the Tigers twice in their own park to win the title. But you can't win two before you win one, so they focused on the business at hand behind the lefthander, French, who carried the hopes of the North Side with him into Navin Field. Last October, when Medwick was pelted with fruit, bottles, and other assorted missiles, it was the culmination of total frustration for the Detroit faithful; for even though there were still three innings left to play in the '34 series, all hope had been lost. The final score in Game Seven that year was 11–0, while Paul Dean beat Rowe and the Tigers the previous day 4–3. Before the day was finished, the Tiger fans knew that they were going to be bridesmaids once again, dashing a hope that began with their team being odds-on favorites to beat the Cardinals when the series had started. So to say that the Motown fans were "hungry" on October 7, 1935, would be a severe understatement—they were famished for a baseball championship, a tantalizing dream that even the great Ty Cobb could not deliver to the city.

While his opponent for the day (Bridges) had significant World Series experience under his belt, it would be the first start in the postseason for French. Under managers George Gibson and Jewel Ens, he had been part of Pirate teams that finished second in '29, '32, and '33, but never part of a group that got to hoist the National League flag until this autumn. As the big moment approached, all signals were "go" for French. "He is well rested, in peak physical form and eager to accept the assignment," reported Burns before game time.

Klein was given the nod to start once again in right, as Demaree copied his shift to center from the previous game to take the place of

Lindstrom, who was revealed to have a broken finger from a collision earlier in the series.

A change in the Tiger lineup involved Gerald "Gee" Walker, previously used only as a pinch-hitter in the series, who took over in center
field for White. Clifton remained at third and Owen at first, as Greenberg was still not physically in a position to help the club. With White
out, Clifton—despite being 0-for-11 to this point in the series—was elevated to the lead-off spot, while Walker was placed in the six hole.
Cochrane maintained the highest confidence in Goslin, for while the
Goose had a reputation of being weak against lefthanded pitchers,
Cochrane refused to drop him from the cleanup spot in the batting order
when French was announced as the pitcher for the day.

It would be the home team that struck first, as part of the 48,420
fans looked on (the attendance figure at this contest pushed the Tigers
over one million for the year, a new club record). After the Cubs went
scoreless in the first, singles by Cochrane and Gehringer were followed
by a two-out double off the bat of Fox, his fourth extra-base hit of the
series that scored the Tiger catcher. The Cubs came back to tie in the
third, as after a single by Jurges, French failed to get a sacrifice bunt down
but Galan came through with a single, sending Billy to third. Herman
then lined a single to right, scoring Jurges but with Galan being thrown
out at third on a laser throw from Fox. Galan leapt up and hollered that
he had been pushed off the bag by Clifton; it was now *his* turn to give
Moriarity an earful, as the maligned umpire had rotated down to third
base for the sixth contest. Of course, Augie's complaints did nothing to
change matters, and when he took his place in the treacherous left pasture in Detroit, he was besieged with taunts—but at least no fruit or bottles this year, unlike in Medwick's previous plight.

Detroit reclaimed the lead in the fourth as Bridges, batting with men
on first and third, bounced a ball to Hack that Stan tried to turn into an
inning-ending double play. Bridges was too swift down the line, however, and his hustle scored Walker to jump his club back ahead, 2–1.

Unshaken by the attack—or else feeling a growing sense of urgency—
the Cubs came right back in the fifth. After Jurges lofted a lazy fly ball
to Fox to open the inning, French lined a clean single in Fox's direction
as well. Next was Herman, and the man upon whom Grimm depended
for quiet leadership all year came through once again. He turned on a
low-and-in fastball, and watched it ride out of the park on a "rope" as
Chicago pulled back ahead, 3–2, on the secondbaseman's eighth homer
of the year. They had a chance to augment the lead in the sixth, but Hack,
who had doubled with two outs, got caught between second and third on

a ground ball to Clifton. Demonstrating great agility, Stan was able to avoid Flea's tag, but was called out by Moriarity for running out of the baseline. Because it was Moriarity on the decision, Hack raised a minor protest, but he was clearly out. Grimm either agreed or was tired of dealing with the umpire—he turned quietly and strutted back to the Cubs' dugout.

It was in the bottom of that inning that the Tigers evened things again, much to the Cubs' discouragement. French was one out away from escaping, but he then allowed a double by Rogell to the left field corner and a sharp single in the same direction by Owen, his first hit of the series. For a moment, it looked as if Galan would have a chance to throw Rogell out at the plate, but he lost his grip on the ball as he set himself to fire it in. Bridges then struck out, as the teams entered the final three fateful innings all even, 3–3.

Herman logged his third hit and Cochrane his second in the seventh inning, but each was left stranded by his club. Both teams were held scoreless in the eighth as well, and the Cubs could feel the pressure beginning to mount. The Tigers could afford a game-ending mishap and live to play another day; the Grimm Reapers could not. Hack stepped to the plate to open the final frame, knowing that he somehow needed to get on base—that was his only job in this situation.

Anyone who has played the game is familiar with the "give"—that is, the moment that the ball hits the bat in just the right part of the wood, and the contact is barely felt. It is almost a natural surrender of the ball, resigned to its fate of a long travel afterwards. Hack got precisely this feeling, precisely at the right time. After taking a pitched ball, he drove a fat one from Bridges long over Walker's head in center, caroming around the flag pole and landing the Cub at third with nobody out. His teammates had three chances to nudge him ninety feet, and it could happen in any number of ways.

The first chance belonged to Jurges, who was 1-for-3 on the day. Bridges opened him up with a knee-buckling curve, a called strike. With nobody out and the go-ahead run on third, Jurges waited patiently for a pitch he could drive. That being the case, he let the next pitch go by and he was fooled by a curve ball that he didn't expect, and the count was 0-and-2. Now he had to adjust and put the ball in play. He expected a fast one out of the zone, but Bridges went right back to his bender again, and Billy swung through it to post the first out. French was the next man due, and most expected Grimm to tap the bench for a new swinger, but he didn't. French walked to the plate and like Jurges, watched the first two pitches go by for strikes, both curveballs and the fourth and fifth such pitches in a row. French then saw a sixth straight breaking ball, and he dinked one lightly back to Bridges at the mound. Hack had no chance to score, so he scampered back to safety at the bag as the pitcher fired to Owen for the second out. The final opportunity belonged to Galan, and he also watched the first two pitches go across for strikes, curve balls number seven and eight in a row. Grinding the bat in his hands, anxious for the next, Galan swung early and popped a harmless fly to Goslin in left, ending the inning with Hack left in his tracks on the third base line.

French was determined to show that Grimm made no mistake by leaving him in the game, seeking to bring the contest into extra innings. After running the count full on Clifton to open the Detroit ninth, he fanned the part-timer as Clifton remained hitless in sixteen at-bats in the series. Then came Cochrane, and the fans rose to their feet to inspire their hero. He was their darling, and was expected at this very moment to put an end to the Chicago men. He was caught off guard by a French change-up, but managed to bounce the ball back through the middle with some authority. Herman, straining for all he was worth, extended his left arm across his body while airborne, and knocked the ball down in diving to his right. But Cochrane, still one of the fastest catchers in the game, streaked across first before Herman could even make a throw. As Gehringer got in the batter's box, the outfielders took a few steps back; they wanted everything hit out to them to be kept in front of their bodies to keep Cochrane from scoring. The infield retreated a couple of steps as well, a strategy that paid dividends as Cavarretta was able to knock down Gehringer's screaming liner that was destined for the right field corner. He made the play on Gehringer, even though Cochrane was able to move to second base. There he was—30 yards, a left turn, and another 30 away from the plate—hoping to bring Detroit its first championship as Goslin came to the plate.

It was fitting that ice water-veined Goslin was up in this situation, he the veteran of five World Series, including the last three (he was with the Senators in their battle with the Giants in the 1933 championship). And Goslin was certainly capable in clutch situations, as he had won Game Two of the '34 World Series with a hit in the bottom of the twelfth inning. He stood in the batter's box one week shy of his 35th birthday, as French believed the Goose would be easy bait once again (in four previous trips to the plate on the day, Goslin had failed to get the ball out of the infield). Aggressively, French went hard and inside, and Goslin weakly fouled one off. Sensing a vulnerability on the inner half of the plate, French went back there again on the next pitch. But Goose was ready, and his quick-trigger cut slashed the ball into right field for a hit. Klein came charging, as a cataclysmic event was looming at the plate for one team or the other. Cochrane sprinted around third with all he had, and the bouncing throw handcuffed Hartnett as Mickey scored while the ball skipped away. It was Goslin's 129th—and last—at-bat in World Series play, the special one for which he had waited his whole career. The Tigers had won, 4–3, and were the 1935 World Champions.

"I never saw a greater World Series game," stated Landis, as he picked up his hat and left his box seat, watching Tiger fans crazed with joy storm the field.

The box score from Game Six:

Chicago	AB	R	H	RBI
Galan, lf	5	0	1	0
Herman, 2b	4	1	3	3
Klein, rf	4	0	1	0
Hartnett, c	4	0	2	0
Demaree, rf	4	0	0	0
Cavarretta, 1b	4	0	1	0
Hack, 3b	4	0	2	0
Jurges, ss	4	1	1	0
French, p	4	1	1	0

Detroit	AB	R	H	RBI
Clifton, 3b	5	0	0	0
Cochrane, c	5	2	3	0
Gehringer, 2b	5	0	2	0
Goslin, lf	5	0	1	1
Fox, rf	4	0	2	1
Walker, cf	2	1	1	0
Rogell, ss	4	1	2	0
Owen, 1b	3	0	1	1
Bridges, p	4	0	0	1

E—Fox

Chicago	0 0 1	0 2 0	0 0 0	3–12–0
Detroit	1 0 0	1 0 1	0 0 1	4–12–1

After marching over the field, Tiger followers spilled onto the streets, causing a ruckus "that for exuberance was an Armistice Day, a Mardi Gras, and an American Legion convention all rolled into one," according to a report. When he tried to return to his hotel room, the hero Goslin couldn't even open the door of his taxi cab as grateful fans pressed themselves against it. After a few minutes of smiles and waves, Goslin ordered the cab to drive off from the jubilant mob and drop him off at a more anonymous location. Back at Navin Field, Goslin previously had to use an alternative exit too, as anticipatory fans had surrounded the usual portal for the players. It was obvious that the win was a great tonic for the city. "I believe we helped bring Detroit out of the Depression," Auker would say later in life.

What did Cochrane think of Bridges? "A hundred and fifty pounds of courage," he stated proudly among the shouts of victory in the locker room. Then, he seemed to echo Grimm's description of Warneke from Game One. "It was the finest exhibition of pitching I ever saw in a World Series game. In the ninth inning, after Hack had tripled, Bridges threw nine of the best curves I ever looked at to get the next three men." The Tigers had won the series in spite of missing their basher Greenberg for most of it, as Marv Owen and Flea Clifton went a combined 1-for-36.

After scoring the winning run, Cochrane, amidst all the successes of his glorious career, called it "my greatest day in baseball."

The debates began immediately all over Chicago. Why didn't Grimm pinch-hit for French in the ninth? Hadn't he three able hitters (O'Dea, English, and Stephenson) available on the bench? Hadn't French labored eight innings, and allowed ten Tiger hits? And wasn't Hack carrying the most important run of the year on third base? Of course, the preponderance of the people stood in that corner; on the other hand, a few pointed out in defense of Grimm that there was nobody out at the time Jurges came up, so probability foretold that either he or French could have successfully plated Hack, with Galan also waiting in the hole—but of course, none of them brought Stan home.

"We did our best, so what the hell?" Grimm reasoned with reporters in the locker room. "We still are National League champions, and that's more than anyone expected. We are not world champions, but nobody can say that we were badly beaten. It just wasn't in the books for us to win, so forget it and have a good time during the winter."

While the parks were not filled every time, the combined ticket and radio revenue from the 1935 World Series totaled $1,073,794, the third most in history. The 1925 and 1926 series had generated more money, and without the $100,000 radio boost that the '35 event enjoyed. As a result, the Cubs wound up getting $4,554 per man, while the Tigers gathered $6,544 for each share on the winning side, slightly more than the Cardinals had received in 1934.

The Cubs returned home, and began unloading their gear at the clubhouse at Wrigley Field. Grimm quickly departed on another train for

Missouri, where he had some personal business to address, in addition to spending some time at his farm there to "unlax." Phil Wrigley eagerly anticipated his return, for the manager promised to talk trades to make the team stronger for 1936. The other Cubs, meanwhile, all had different plans as the offseason was now upon them. Warneke planned on going directly to Arkansas to go "a-fishin' and a-huntin'"; Stainback and Root were going to drive to California, after the latter made a stop at home in Middletown, Ohio. Root also wished to spend some time in Honolulu, "sunning on Waikiki Beach and learning the ukulele." Demaree and French were headed out West, too, with Larry wishing to pursue a film career on the side. Close behind them would be Hack, who would be spending the coming months in Sacramento while looking for a house to buy. Galan would be down the road in Berkeley, visiting his parents but staying out of the family laundry business. English was headed to Florida and Jurges to Hot Springs, Arkansas, while Klein went back to the Southport area of Indianapolis "to dig in for the winter." Passing him by would be Herman, taking some time off down in his home in New Albany, Indiana.

Cochrane, whose parents and brother came all the way from Bridgewater, Massachusetts, to see his glory in the series, was getting ready to go on a camping trip with former baseball great Tris Speaker and a few other friends to Cody, Wyoming. Some fans in Detroit had put Cochrane's name on the ballot for the upcoming city council election, despite lacking his consent. Landis, with his decision on the Moriarity situation presumably made already, was heading to Mackinac Island for ten days before returning with his verdict.

Five weeks after seeing his beloved Tigers win their first title, Frank Navin died of a heart attack while riding his horse on November 13, 1935. His shares were subsequently purchased by Walter Briggs, who had already owned half of the club. Briggs immediately commenced an intensive rehabilitation of Navin field, a dream that the deceased owner had held for a long time.

It was the site upon which one of the Cubs' last hopes for a world championship was broken. On these grounds, Hack would visit his own infamous spot on the field years later.

"I wanted to see if I was still on third," he said of his memories of being stranded by his teammates in the top of the ninth.

Epilogue

The 1935 Cubs remain the last team in franchise history to win 100 games in a season, a season in which they outscored their opponents by a total of 250 runs. But despite finding success, the team only drew just over 692,000 fans in '35, with the nation still reeling from the effects of the Great Depression (even though this figure was second-most in the National League). Things would soon improve, however—the Cubs' attendance would inch up to almost exactly 700,000 the next year, but then swell to 895,000 in 1937 as people once again had a relative degree of spending money.

After returning from his trip to Mackinac Island, Landis announced on October 24 that he was fining everyone in the "Moriarity Incident," including Moriarity himself, Grimm, Stainback, and English, the same amount—$200. A few days earlier, Hartnett was honored with the 1935 National League Most Valuable Player award and Greenberg was a unanimous choice in the AL, with Dizzy Dean and Wes Ferrell the runners-up. Sadly, Dean's batterymate with the Cardinals, catcher Bill Delancey, would suffer a cruel fate. In 1936 he was stricken with tuberculosis, which put him out of baseball for four years. He made a brief comeback for twelve games with St. Louis in 1940, but could not fully regain his strength. Delancey died of the illness on his 35th birthday—November 28, 1946—cutting short the life, and less importantly the career, of potentially one of the greatest catchers of all time.

In 1936, the first class would be inducted into the newly-dedicated National Baseball Hall of Fame at Cooperstown, New York, wrongfully thought by some at the time to be another short-term gimmick to pull the game out of the Depression; rather, it turned out to be a permanent shrine for the ages. The original group included Ruth, Mathewson, Cobb,

Walter Johnson, and Honus Wagner. The year would also see the Cubs fall from their National League perch, as they finished with an 87–67 record, five games behind the Giants and tied with the Cardinals for second place. Reasons for the drop included injuries and slumps that ailed Cavarretta (which caused Grimm to have to play 35 games at first base), and a basic lack of power hitting. Klein was sent back to the Phillies (along with Kowalik) for Curt Davis and outfielder Ethan Allen on May 21, leaving a large home-run gap in the batting order. Klein would set a National League record later in the season with four home runs in a game against the Pirates on July 9 at Forbes Field in Pittsburgh. The final homer would be the difference-maker, as it sent the Phillies to a 9–6 win in ten innings. Meanwhile, it would be Mel Ott who would dominate the overall power scene, leading the National League in home runs in 1936, 1937, and 1938.

The Reds would pay dearly for their misdiagnosis of Johnny Mize's injury—much more than the $55,000 they got back from the Cardinals—as "Big Jawn" hit the major league scene in St. Louis as a rookie in 1936 with a .329 average and 19 home runs. Notwithstanding the oversight, there were some things of which the Cincinnati club could be proud. Thanks to the Reds and MacPhail, night baseball appeared to secure a beachhead in the National League as another set of such games was approved for 1936 (it was once again voted down in the American League for the 1936 season, however). A total of 130,337 fans had attended the seven night games in Cincinnati, as club and league officials were pleased with the response.

And as he indicated, Bill Terry's last season as a player was indeed 1936, and he continued to manage the Giants through 1941. "Memphis Bill," one of the finest firstbasemen of the era, wound up with 2,193 hits and a .341 career batting mark.

In addition to Klein, also missing from the Cubs in 1936 was Lindstrom (who finished his career playing 26 games for Brooklyn that year and batting .264, a swan song cut short by a leg injury), but Grimm had generally kept true to his intent in keeping the '35 pennant-winning club intact—despite Phil Wrigley's wish for more trades. Nonetheless, the cohesiveness that was once enjoyed on the club appeared to unravel, as egos began to grow and collide. The "dog days" of the summer were said to be the beginning of Grimm's demise as manager, spotlighted in August by a run-in with Jurges, Herman, and Galan about their alleged lackadaisical effort in the field.

After spending more than $1 million, Briggs was able to bring the capacity at Navin Field to almost 55,000, and the stadium in Detroit became the first in the majors to be enclosed and completely double-decked. The construction was a local sign that the economy was starting to rebound, and by mid–1937, gross production of U.S. factories had reached the same level at the time of the market crash in 1929. When government spending gradually reduced, however, it caused what was termed the "Roosevelt Recession."

Also entering an age of better stability was heavyweight boxing, as Louis beat Braddock in 1937 for the heavyweight title, beginning his reign of twelve years with the belt.

As in the government, there had also been quite a bit of wheeling-and-dealing that went on between baseball clubs in the winter months before the 1936 season. Most notably, Jimmie Foxx followed Cochrane in being the next A's star to be sold off by Connie Mack to relieve Depression-incurred debts. Foxx, along with pitcher Johnny Marcum, was sent to the Red Sox for $150,000. Al Simmons, who had already spent three seasons with the White Sox after his glory years with the A's, was sold to the Tigers for $75,000. He would take over in center field for Jo Jo White, looking to make the champions even stronger. But passing them up were the Yankees, winning the AL flag by nineteen-and-a-half games over Detroit and starting a run of four straight World Series titles for the Bronx men. A major factor in the Yanks' success in '36 was the arrival of the 21-year-old DiMaggio, who played the outfield with skills unlike what anyone had ever seen before. They beat the Giants in six games in the 1936 World Series, and McCarthy returned from his illness to cement a true dynasty.

Warneke, French, Lee, and Carleton tied for the league lead in shutouts in 1936 with four each, along with Al Smith of the pennant-winning Giants, Blanton of the Pirates, and Walters of the Phillies. In a game that season on August 10, Carleton had to be dragged off the field at Sportsman's Park in St. Louis, when his long-standing feud with Dizzy Dean had finally boiled over. They had been chirping at each over from the dugouts for several innings, and Carleton had had enough. He charged over towards the Cardinals' bench as Dean came out and met him halfway, after which the benches cleared and the two men had to be restrained (it was the very day, in fact, that the Cardinals would overtake first place in the National League—albeit temporarily). Shortly after the season was over, Warneke was dealt to the Cardinals for Rip Collins and Roy Parmelee, giving him a chance for more banjo-picking; he was named a charter member of Pepper Martin's "Musical Mudcats," with Martin, Warneke, Bill McGee, Bob Weiland, and Frenchy Bordagaray all tooting away at homemade instruments. During the year, Warneke struck out future managing great Walter Alston in the only major league at-bat Alston would ever take.

Herman's 57 doubles in 1935—a feat he would repeat in 1936—remains the Cubs' all-time mark. He would also go on to lead the National League in fielding for secondbasemen in two of the next three years. In addition, Herman appeared in ten consecutive All-Star Games from 1934 to 1943, batting a sparkling .433 in those contests (in 1934 he was the only player ever to enter and re-enter the All-Star Game, with permission to do so given by American League manager Cronin). The streak may have been longer if not for his service in the United States Navy the following two years, in which he saw the end of World War II. He left the Cubs in mid–1941 to become part of Durocher's rebuilding of the Dodgers in Brooklyn, as "The Lip" hand-picked Herman, Medwick, Camilli, and others to turn the Bums into contenders—nearly overnight. Brooklyn raced to the pennant in '41 (their first in over twenty years) and nearly knocked off the powerful Yankees in the World Series. Herman displayed amazing consistency over the course of his career, hitting over .300 and scoring over 100 runs eight times each. He would enter the Hall of Fame in 1975.

Jurges, Herman's long-time double play partner, had arrived in New York two seasons earlier than Billy, joining the Giants in 1939. He had been traded along with Demaree and O'Dea for Bartell, Leiber, and Mancuso in December 1938. Jurges earned his first All-Star appearance with the Cubs in 1937, during which he enjoyed his finest offensive season with a .298 average and ten triples. After seven years in Harlem, he returned to the Cubs for one final season in 1946. Unfortunately, beanballs to the head would affect Jurges' career. He had been hit by pitches often, but when he and Medwick were getting pitches in the "noodle" a bit too regularly, some players around the league in the early 1940s took a lesson and began putting a padded liner inside of their caps for at least some protection.

The Jurges trade signaled the start of a decline for the promising Demaree, who had previously gone on to be the starting centerfielder for the National League in the 1936 and 1937 All-Star games (Galan would join him on the 1936 All-Star roster, and become the first Cub to hit a homer in the mid-summer classic).

Cuyler played 1936 and 1937 with Cincinnati, and then finished his playing career in 1938 as a part-time outfielder with the Dodgers. He would wind up his career just shy of 2,300 hits, with a career average of .321, 157 triples, 328 stolen bases, and ultimately, an election to the Hall of Fame in 1968. Klein would follow him to Cooperstown in 1980.

The career of Woody English would slowly dissipate, with one notable exception: while playing for the Dodgers in 1937, he hit the well-known "Abe Stark Clothier" sign on the wall at Ebbets Field and won a free suit.

In 1942, Hack would set a record of 54 consecutive games at third base without an error. He would retire a year later, when disagreements with new manager Jimmie Wilson couldn't be resolved. When Grimm regained control of the club in 1944, he encouraged Hack to come back. He did, and the encore allowed Stan to become the 82nd player to reach 2,000 hits on August 30, 1945. When he retired for the final time in 1947, only Cap Anson had more hits as a Cub than Hack's 2,193.

Some claimed that Cavarretta's early entry into the major leagues stunted his development as a ballplayer, but his impact on the team upon his arrival cannot be underestimated. When he knocked his 14th career homer midway through the 1936 season, only Ott had more round-trippers as a teenager than him. After setting an All-Star Game record in 1944 by reaching base five straight times, Cavy took home an MVP and batting title in 1945 with a .355 mark despite the fact he only hit six home runs, as he led the Cubs to their last pennant (and yet another defeat at the hands of the Tigers in the World Series). Cavarretta would get a shot at managing the Cubs in 1951, replacing former Gashouser Frankie Frisch. Cavarretta would win less than half of his games as the skipper; he was fired by Phil Wrigley before the start of the 1954 season when Cavy predicted that the Cubs would finish no better than fifth place. At this point Hack got a crack at the job, but after three more years Stan couldn't finish any higher than sixth himself.

Two years after his full-time debut with the Cubs, Galan would become the first major leaguer to homer from both sides of the plate in the same game on June 25, 1937. Three years later, he suffered a broken kneecap that took away much of his blazing speed. At the end of 1940 he became another reclamation project for Durocher in Brooklyn, and by 1941 was enjoying the pennant that Leo had delivered to the Dodgers. Galan would play on successfully for eight more seasons, and finish a seventeen-year major league career in 1949, splitting the season with the Giants and A's. He then returned to his home area of northern California to play and coach for the Oakland Oaks of the Pacific Coast League.

Moving on to Brooklyn as well, Carleton would fire a no-hitter at the Reds on May 30, 1940, as a member of the Dodgers; Warneke would get his no-no against the Reds on August 30 the following year while hurling for St. Louis. The Cubs paid $75,000 to re-acquire Warneke from the Cardinals in 1942, but would lose him for much of the next couple years as a result of military service. After serving his country, Warneke would wind up his career in 1945 with 193 career victories, 31 shutouts, and over 1,100 strikeouts. Not content being separated from the game, he rejoined the major leagues four years later as an umpire, a job he performed until 1956. Later, the multi-talented Warneke was elected a county judge back in Arkansas.

The game could not shake Charlie Root either, as he pitched in the majors until he was 42 years old (1941), and followed that up with seven more years "barnstorming" and playing in the minor leagues. Root has pitched in more games (605) and innings (3,138) than anyone in Cubs history, and his 201 wins also remains a franchise mark.

Lee was dealt to the Phillies on August 5, 1943, in exchange for catcher Mickey Livingston. Before he left town, however, Lee tied a Cub record in 1938 by tossing four straight shutouts, also accomplished by Mordecai "Three Finger" Brown and Ed Reulbach. He returned to the North Siders in 1947, losing twice in 14 appearances. Late in his career, Lee complained of poor eyesight and tried wearing glasses when he pitched. They helped for a while, but couldn't hide a more serious problem. Later in life, Lee would lose his sight altogether.

French was also picked up by Durocher near the end of the 1941 season, where Leo's Dodgers were charging towards the pennant (he could definitely be labeled a "workhorse" for his longitudinal efforts, as only Hubbell pitched more innings in the decade of the 1930s than French's 2,481). French bolted out to a 15–4 record the following year in 1942, but his love for the Navy was too great. He enlisted a second time in 1943, disposing of his other dream of Hollywood stardom. It was a career he would maintain until retiring as an officer in 1969.

Long forgotten on the bullpen bench, Hugh Casey would not resurface in the major leagues for four more years, when he finally appeared—not surprisingly—in a Brooklyn uniform in 1939. After that one season as a starter, Durocher moved him almost exclusively to the bullpen where he flourished for a time, leading the National League in saves in 1942 and 1947 (being credited in hindsight, as saves were not originally logged in this era). Tragically, he committed suicide at the age of 37, the result of despondency over the breakup of his marriage. Clay Bryant, on the other hand, would emerge as a prominent starter in the Cubs' pennant run in 1938 after three nondescript seasons in relief. Bryant would win 19 games on the year and lead the league in strikeouts with 135 before the Cubs lost to the Yankees in the World Series. A competent hitter as well, Bryant would end his career in 1940 with a .266 lifetime batting mark.

Alabama Pitts wound up back in his home area of Charlotte to continue playing professional ball, and later went on to Gastonia. He then returned home to Valdese, North Carolina, looking to settle for the remainder of his life. His local fame was still immense, as he worked for a textile mill and played baseball for its team at night and on weekends. Many minor league teams were still folding from the fallout of the Depression, and dispensed stars of the various defunct teams found their way to such towns. A rage still burned inside of Pitts, and it was released in June, 1941. At a dancehall after a Saturday night game, he got into a fight with a man wielding a knife. Pitts was stabbed repeatedly, but refused to let bystanders take him to the hospital. As a result, Pitts died of his wounds on June 5, 1941, one day shy of the sixth anniversary of his release from Sing Sing Prison.

And Ruth, wearing down more than ever, would make only one more official appearance in a baseball capacity, that as a coach with the Dodgers for half of the 1938 season. He would pass away on August 16, 1948, partly caused by the tumultuous frolicking that he enjoyed earlier in his life.

Hartnett and Dean, the two front-runners for MVP in '35, would become significant teammates just three years later. On September 28, 1938, Hartnett hit his famous "Homer in the Gloamin'," a twilight dinger off Pittsburgh's Mace Brown as the sun went down at Wrigley Field, giving the Cubs a win and first place over the Pirates. "A lot of people have told me they didn't know the ball was in the bleachers," Hartnett revealed about the ball hit in half-darkness. "Well, I did—maybe I was the only one in the park who did. I knew it the moment I hit it." The day before, Dean had gutted out his noted comeback victory with an arm so sore "I thought it'd fall off any minute," Dean said.

"You could see the man was suffering out there," Cavarretta explained. "And here we all were young, healthy, and strong. You'd say, 'My God, let's go out and win it for Diz.'" It was the culmination of a September nearly as amazing as the one in 1935—for the Cubs had won 21 of their last 25 during the month.

Dean had been sent to the Cubs in 1938 for Stainback, Shoun, Curt Davis, and $185,000, as the Cardinals believed his arm was dead. The price tag was thought by some in the Cubs' front office to be too high, fearing that it would escalate the price of obtaining star players in the future. While he brought the Cubs another pennant as a rookie manager (and still player) in 1938, Hartnett soon found that the leadership role was not as easy as he thought. He had taken over for Grimm, who was let go by Wrigley on July 20 with the Cubs in third place, and Jolly Cholly found his new calling in the Cubs' radio booth (the previous July, Hartnett had taken over for Grimm as well, covering an 11-game stretch in 1937 when Grimm was out of action with a sickness—which, upon his return on July 27, had still confined him to a seat cushion in the dugout for most of the following weeks). After being obliterated by the Yankees in four straight in the 1938 World Series, Hartnett utilized virtually the entire train trip back to Chicago from New York to berate the players. He became less and less able to relate to them, but it could not tarnish a brilliant career. After starting with Cubs in 1922, he remained a bruin until playing one final season with the New York Giants in 1941. Retiring thereafter, he left the game with more putouts (7,292) and chances (8,546) than any player in National League history. Hartnett held the single-season (37) and career (236) record for homers by a catcher until those marks were broken by Roy Campanella in 1953 and 1957, respectively (Yogi Berra also caught him on the career list in 1956). The first catcher to attain 200 home runs and 1,000 RBIs in a career, Hartnett would gain a Hall of Fame birth in 1955. And his understudy, O'Dea, carved out a nice career for himself as a pinch hitter, leading the National League in such appearances while with the Giants in 1941. His three pinch hits in the Cardinals' 1944 World Series win over the Browns tied the record, and his Game-Two hit in the 11th inning won that contest for the Redbirds.

When Grimm was brought back to manage the Cubs a third time in 1960, he joined Bucky Harris of the Washington Senators as the only men to manage a team in three different stints (Danny Murtaugh and Billy Martin have done it since, for a total of four). But 17 games into the season he fell ill, and turned the reins over to Lou Boudreau. Grimm and Boudreau were actually "traded" for each other, in effect, as the latter had been broadcasting Cubs games on WGN radio, and now the former would assume that role once again. Amazingly though, Grimm was not finished on the field—he returned for a fourth time as part of Phil Wrigley's infamous "College of Coaches," an ill-fated experiment of having multiple coaches in lieu of a manager in the early 1960s.

The jolly man continued on as an instructor with the Cubs into the 1970s, enjoying a mostly-retired life in the Phoenix area. When Charlie Grimm died on November 15, 1983, his family had his ashes scattered over Wrigley Field, abiding by his final wish.

Appendix A

Final 1935 Standings

NATIONAL LEAGUE

	W	L	Pct.	GB
Chicago	100	54	.649	—
St. Louis	96	58	.623	4.0
New York	91	62	.594	8.5
Pittsburgh	86	67	.562	13.5
Brooklyn	70	83	.457	29.5
Cincinnati	68	85	.444	31.5
Philadelphia	64	89	.418	35.5
Boston	38	115	.248	61.5

AMERICAN LEAGUE

	W	L	Pct.	GB
Detroit	93	58	.615	—
New York	89	60	.597	3.0
Cleveland	82	71	.535	12.0
Boston	78	75	.509	16.0
Chicago	74	78	.486	19.5
Washington	67	86	.437	27.0
St. Louis	65	87	.427	28.5
Philadelphia	58	91	.389	34.0

Appendix B

1935 Chicago Cubs Final Batting Statistics

	G	AB	R	H	2B	3B	HR	RBI	SB	AVG
Stephenson	16	26	2	10	1	1	0	2	0	.385
Hartnett	116	413	67	142	32	6	13	91	1	.344
Herman	154	666	113	227	57	6	7	83	6	.341
Gill	3	3	2	1	1	0	0	1	0	.333
Demaree	107	385	60	125	19	4	2	66	6	.325
Galan	154	646	133	203	41	11	12	79	22	.314
Hack	124	427	75	133	23	9	4	64	14	.311
Klein	119	434	71	127	14	4	21	73	4	.293
Cavarretta	146	589	85	162	28	12	8	82	4	.275
Lindstrom	90	342	49	94	22	4	3	62	1	.275
Cuyler	45	157	22	42	5	1	4	18	3	.268
O'Dea	76	202	30	52	13	2	6	38	0	.257
Stainback	47	94	16	24	4	0	3	11	1	.255
Jurges	146	519	69	125	33	1	1	59	3	.241
English	34	84	11	17	2	0	2	8	1	.202
Grimm	2	8	0	0	0	0	0	0	0	.000
								Team—		.288

Appendix C

1935 Chicago Cubs Final Pitching Statistics

	W–L	G	GS	CG	IP	H	BB	SO	Sho	ERA
Shoun	1–0	5	1	0	13	14	5	5	0	2.77
Lee	20–6	39	32	18	252	241	84	100	3	2.96
French	17–10	42	30	16	246	279	44	90	4	2.96
Warneke	20–13	42	30	20	262	257	50	120	1	3.06
Root	15–8	38	18	11	201	193	47	94	1	3.09
Henshaw	13–5	31	18	7	143	135	68	53	3	3.27
Casey	0–0	13	0	0	26	29	14	10	0	3.81
Carleton	11–8	31	22	8	171	169	60	84	0	3.89
Kowalik	2–2	20	2	1	55	60	19	20	0	4.42
Bryant	1–2	9	1	0	23	34	7	13	0	5.09
Joiner	0–0	2	0	0	3	6	2	0	0	6.00
									Team—	3.26

Appendix D

1935 Chicago Cubs World Series Statistics

BATTING

	G	AB	R	H	2B	3B	HR	RBI	AVG
O'Dea	1	1	0	1	0	0	0	1	1.000
Kowalik	1	2	1	1	0	0	0	0	.500
Herman	6	24	3	8	2	1	1	6	.333
Klein	5	12	2	4	0	0	1	2	.333
Hartnett	6	24	1	7	0	0	1	2	.292
Demaree	6	24	2	6	1	0	2	2	.250
Jurges	6	16	3	4	0	0	0	1	.250
French	2	4	1	1	0	0	0	0	.250
Hack	6	22	2	5	1	1	0	0	.227
Lindstrom	4	15	0	3	1	0	0	0	.200
Warneke	3	5	0	1	0	0	0	0	.200
Galan	6	25	2	4	1	0	0	2	.160
Cavarretta	6	24	1	3	0	0	0	0	.125
Lee	2	1	0	0	0	0	0	0	.000
Henshaw	1	1	0	0	0	0	0	0	.000
Stephenson	1	1	0	0	0	0	0	0	.000
Carleton	1	1	0	0	0	0	0	0	.000
Root	2	0	0	0	0	0	0	0	—
								Team—	.238

PITCHING

	W–L	G	GS	CG	IP	H	BB	SO	Sho	ERA
Warneke	2–0	3	2	1	16.2	9	4	5	1	0.54
Carleton	0–1	1	1	0	7	6	7	4	0	1.29
Kowalik	0–0	1	0	0	4.1	3	1	1	0	2.10
French	0–2	2	1	1	10.2	15	2	8	0	3.38

	W–L	G	GS	CG	IP	H	BB	SO	Sho	ERA
Lee	0–0	2	1	0	10.1	11	5	5	0	3.48
Henshaw	0–0	1	0	0	3.2	2	5	2	0	7.36
Root	0–1	2	1	0	2	5	1	2	0	18.00
									Team—	2.96

Appendix E

1935 Detroit Tigers World Series Statistics

BATTING

	G	AB	R	H	2B	3B	HR	RBI	AVG
Fox	6	26	1	10	3	1	0	4	.385
Gehringer	6	24	4	9	3	0	0	4	.375
Crowder	1	3	1	1	0	0	0	0	.333
Cochrane	6	24	3	7	1	0	0	1	.292
Rogell	6	24	1	7	2	0	0	1	.292
Goslin	6	22	2	6	1	0	0	3	.273
White	5	19	3	5	0	0	0	1	.263
Rowe	3	8	0	2	1	0	0	0	.250
Walker	3	4	1	1	0	0	0	0	.250
Greenberg	2	6	1	1	0	0	1	2	.167
Bridges	2	8	1	1	0	0	0	1	.125
Owen	6	20	2	1	0	0	0	1	.050
Clifton	4	16	1	0	0	0	0	0	.000
Auker	1	2	0	0	0	0	0	0	.000
Hogsett	1	0	0	0	0	0	0	0	—
								Team—	.248

PITCHING

	W–L	G	GS	CG	IP	H	BB	SO	Sho	ERA
Hogsett	0–0	1	0	0	1	0	1	0	0	0.00
Crowder	1–0	1	1	1	9	5	3	5	0	1.00
Bridges	2–0	2	2	2	18	18	4	9	0	2.50
Rowe	1–2	3	2	2	21	19	1	14	0	2.57
Auker	0–0	1	1	0	6	6	2	1	0	3.00
									Team—	2.29

Appendix F

Personal Data on the 1935 Chicago Cubs

	Born	*Died*
Bryant, Clay	11-16-11/Madison Heights, VA	4-9-99/Fort Lauderdale, FL
Carleton, Tex	8-19-06/Comanche, TX	1-11-77/Fort Worth, TX
Casey, Hugh	10-14-13/Atlanta, GA	7-3-51/Atlanta, GA
Cavarretta, Phil	7-19-16/Chicago, IL	
Cuyler, Kiki	8-30-98/Harrisville, MI	2-11-50/Ann Arbor, MI
Demaree, Frank	6-10-10/Winters, CA	8-30-58/Los Angeles, CA
English, Woody	3-2-07/Fredonia, OH	9-26-97/Newark, OH
French, Larry	11-1-07/Visalia, CA	2-9-87/San Diego, CA
Galan, Augie	5-25-12/Berkeley, CA	12-28-93/Fairfield, CA
Gill, Johnny	3-27-05/Nashville, TN	12-26-84/Nashville, TN
Grimm, Charlie	8-28-98/St. Louis, MO	11-15-83/Scottsdale, AZ
Hack, Stan	12-6-09/Sacramento, CA	12-15-79/Dixon, IL
Hartnett, Gabby	12-20-00/Woonsocket, RI	12-20-72/Park Ridge, IL
Henshaw, Roy	6-29-11/Chicago, IL	6-8-93/La Grange, IL
Herman, Billy	12-7-09/New Albany, IN	9-5-92/West Palm Beach, FL
Joiner, Roy	10-30-06/Red Bluff, CA	12-26-89/Red Bluff, CA
Jurges, Billy	5-9-08/Bronx, NY	3-3-97/Clearwater, FL
Klein, Chuck	10-7-04/Indianapolis, IN	3-28-58/Indianapolis, IN
Kowalik, Fabian	4-22-08/Falls City, TX	8-14-54/Karnes City, TX
Lee, Bill	10-21-09/Plaquemine, LA	6-15-77/Plaquemine, LA
Lindstrom, Freddie	11-21-05/Chicago, IL	10-4-81/Chicago, IL
O'Dea, Ken	3-16-13/Lima, NY	12-17-85/Lima, NY
Root, Charlie	3-17-99/Middletown, OH	11-5-70/Hollister, CA
Shoun, Clyde	3-20-12/Mountain City, TN	3-20-68/Mountain Home, TN
Stainback, Tuck	8-4-11/Los Angeles, CA	11-29-92/Camarillo, CA
Stephenson, Walter	3-27-11/Saluda, NC	7-4-93/Shreveport, LA
Warneke, Lon	3-28-09/Mount Ida, AR	6-23-76/Hot Springs, AR

Bibliography

Alexander, C. (1995). *John McGraw*. Lincoln: University of Nebraska Press.
Castle, G. & J. Rygelski (1999). *The I-55 Series: Cubs vs. Cardinals*. Champaign, IL: Sports Publishing.
Cava, P. (2002). *Tales from the Cubs Dugout*. Champaign, IL: Sports Publishing.
Golenbock, P. (1996). *Wrigleyville*. New York: St. Martin's Press.
Holtzman, J. & G. Vass (1997). *The Cubs Encyclopedia*. Philadelphia: Temple University Press.

Excerpts taken from the following newspapers:

Brooklyn Eagle, Chicago Daily News, Chicago Tribune, Cincinnati Enquirer, Cincinnati Post, New York Daily News, New York Post, New York Times, New York World-Telegram, Philadelphia Enquirer, Pittsburgh Post-Gazette, the *Sporting News, St. Louis Post-Dispatch*, and the *St. Louis Star-Times*.

Index